Advance Praise For
The Crime Of Our Time

"Danny Schechter is the people's economist. The clairvoyance of his opus transcends mainstream statistics-gatherers because he examines the real world, reporting the American condition as told to him by the real people who live it everyday. *The Crime Of Our Time* combines Schechter's signature bold passion, keen analysis, and solid empathy for those caught in the cross-fires of the financially powerful and politically connected. Like Schechter's other works, *The Crime Of Our Time* is ahead of its time, and we could all learn from Schechter's astute, heartfelt, and exceedingly accurate observations and predictions."
— **Nomi Prins, former managing director at Bear Stearns and Goldman Sachs, author of** *It Takes a Pillage*

"Excellent investigative journalism like Danny Schechter's in *The Crime Of Our Time* actually protects capitalism against the cancer of white-collar crime by educating law enforcement, businesses, investors, anti-fraud professionals, and the public about schemes used by criminals who victimize our economic system for their own personal gain."
— **Sam Antar, convicted white-collar criminal**

"Danny ranges wide over the political and cultural landscape, pointing fingers, naming names and holding no sacred cows in his quest to determine what went wrong with our economy and who was responsible. His work is the antidote to to a biased, compromised and sclerotic mainstream media."
— **Aaron Krowne, editor of the** *Mortage Lender Implode-O-Meter* **(www.ml-implode.com)**

"Fully living up to his well-deserved reputation as the news dissector, Danny Schechter goes right for the jugular in this rich and informative analysis of the financial crisis and its roots. Not errors, accident, market uncertainties, and so on, but crime: major and serious crime. A harsh judgment, but it's not easy to dismiss the case that he constructs."

— Noam Chomsky

"Did the current economic crisis result simply from market forces, misjudgment and greed? Or was it a deliberate criminal manipulation of markets to extract wealth from the masses? In *The Crime Of Our Time*, Danny Schechter turns his polished investigative and reporting skills to exploring the theory that it was a crime. In veteran journalist prose, he establishes the crime's elements, identifies the players, and exposes the weapons that have turned free markets into vehicles for mass manipulation and control."

— Ellen Brown, author of *Web of Debt*

"Danny Schechter brings both the needed economics expertise and the media credentials to the important task of exposing and analyzing the elements of crime and corruption woven deep into the fabric of our economic system's current crisis. *Plunder* and *The Crime Of Our Time* are important contributions toward understanding an historic moment of change in the economy and society of the United States."

— Richard D. Wolff, professor of economics emeritus, University of Massachusetts, Amherst

"Regulations have always been the mechanism used by societies to prevent flagrant abuses of power, the enslavement of the working class and the rise of a parasitic power elite. The erosion of regulations, as Danny Schechter makes clear in his book, permits the powerful to legalize crime. Theft, fraud, deceptive advertising, predatory lending, debt sold to investors as assets become the currency of a false economy. And when this fictitious economy crashes those who engaged in these crimes, because they have hijacked the reigns of power, are able to loot the U.S. Treasury in the largest transference of wealth upwards in American history. There are many forms of terrorism. And this economic terrorism, as Schechter writes, is perhaps even more dangerous to the nation than the attacks of 9/11."

– **Chris Hedges, author of** *Empire of Illusion: The End of Literacy and the Triumph of Spectacle*

"With *The Crime Of Our Time*, Danny Schechter has made himself the clean-up hitter in the line-up of investigative journalists. He has continued his pioneering work on how the actual existing real world of capitalism works – not the fairy tale version that dominates solitical and media discourse. This book is truly revelatory and must reading for anyone trying to understand the financial currents that have run the economy into the ditch. With *The Crime Of Our Time*, Danny Schechter has smashed the ball 500 feet over the centerfield fence."

– **Robert W. McChesney, media historian and co-author of** *The Death and Life of American Journalism*

THE CRIME
OF OUR TIME

WHY WALL STREET IS NOT TOO BIG TO JAIL

DANNY SCHECHTER

**Director of *PLUNDER*
and *IN DEBT WE TRUST***

Published by:
The Disinformation Company Ltd.
111 East 14th Street, Suite 108
New York, NY 10003
Tel.: +1.212.691.1605 Fax: +1.212.691.1606
www.disinfo.com

Library of Congress Control Number: 2010930111

ISBN: 978-1934708-55-2

Cover Design: Greg Stadnyk

Text Design: Tony Sutton, ColdType.net

Distributed in the U.S. and Canada by:
Consortium Book Sales and Distribution
34 Thirteenth Avenue NE, Suite 101
Minneapolis MN 55413-1007
Tel.: +1.800.283.3572
www.cbsd.com

Distributed in the United Kingdom and Eire by:
Turnaround Publisher Services Ltd.
Unit 3, Olympia Trading Estate
Coburg Road, London, N22 6TZ
Tel.: +44.(0)20.8829.3000 Fax: +44.(0)20.8881.5088
www.turnaround-uk.com

Distributed in Australia by: Tower Books
Unit 2/17 Rodborough Road
Frenchs Forest NSW 2086
Tel.: +61.2.9975.5566 Fax: +61.2.9975.5599
Email: info@towerbooks.com.au

Attention colleges and universities, corporations and other organizations:
Quantity discounts are available on bulk purchases of this book for educational
training purposes, fundraising, or gift giving. Special books, booklets, or book
excerpts can also be created to fit your specific needs. For information contact
the Marketing Department of The Disinformation Company Ltd.

Managing Editor: Ralph Bernardo

10 9 8 7 6 5 4 3 2

Printed in the United States of America

For those who saw, anticipated, knew,
and were ignored:

Frederic Bastiat,
Fernando Pecora,
Nouriel Roubini,
and J. K. Galbraith

And, as always, Sarah Debs Schechter

ACKNOWLEDGEMENTS

My deep appreciation for their support goes out to my colleagues. In this case, Sharon Kayser who writes about finance, Tobi Kanter who first copy- and line-edited the manuscript with additional help from Cherie Welch.

My thanks also to Ray Nowsielski who produced with me *Plunder: The Crime Of Our Time*, the film on which this book is based.

Special thanks to ColdType.net's Tony Sutton, who has also put up with and facilitated my earlier projects, and to Disinformation's managing editor, Ralph Bernardo, for his editorial and design expertise.

Also, my gratitude to the Globalvision team, Rory O'Connor, Eric Forman, David Degraw, Cherie Welch, Ryan Bennett, Steven Grail, Jessica Hyndman, Iris Chung, Herb Brooks, Sean Inonye, Shane O'Neill, Frank Meagher, Jessica B. Lee, Will Lepczyk, Mikhael Page, Margeux LaCoste and Lexy Scheen who helped my quixotic struggle to turn an idea into a film without the funding I needed and support hoped for.

Hopefully, this book will inspire readers to see my film, *Plunder*, and encourage film viewers to get more background information on the issues I have addressed.

SELECTED PREVIOUS WORKS BY DANNY SCHECHTER

CONTENTS

PREFACE
Larry Beinhart

Dear Prosecutors,

Tell your secretary to hold your calls, close your office door, and take a private moment. Lean back in your chair. Close your eyes. Conjure up these names: Thomas Dewey, Rudolph Giuliani, Eliot Spitzer ...

... Hold it. Clear the image of Ashley Dupre in her bikini from the back of your eyelids ... OK ... now ...

Meditate on the headline: *Dewey Defeats Truman.*

He didn't, quite. But the crusading prosecutor had three terms as governor of New York and came within an eyelash of becoming president.

Rudolph Giuliani, the crusading prosecutor, went on to serve two terms as mayor of New York, became a serious presidential contender, and along the way became exceedingly rich.

Eliot Spitzer went from crusading prosecutor to attorney general of the state of New York to its governor. If he hadn't been "Client Number 9," a run at the presidency would have been in his future, too.

Someday, someday, someone is going to use that base – crusading prosecutor – to make it all the way to the White House. It could be you.

When you think of Tom Dewey, you think "Gangbusters!"

He took on big time racketeers. Waxey Gordon, Dutch Schultz, Louis "Lepke" Buchalter – the head of Murder Incorporated – and Lucky Luciano, the *capo di tutti capi*, head of all organized crime in the United States.

But he also prosecuted Richard Whitney.

Who, you may ask, was Richard Whitney? The Whitneys

arrived in North America in 1630. Richard went to Groton and Harvard, he became a broker, and then went on to become president of the New York Stock Exchange.

Alas, he had losses he could not cover. He turned to embezzlement. Thomas Dewey concted him and sent him to Sing Sing.

Dewey was also involved in the prosecution of Stephen Paine, a partner in, and son of the founder of, Paine Webber. Stephen had helped finance and facilitate the looting of six investment trusts.

Rudy Giuliani picked up where Dewey left off.

Giuliani headed up the biggest racketeer trial in history, using RICO laws to go after the heads of all Five Families at once.

But the prosecutions that made his reputation were against financiers.

Ivan Boesky was, by title, an arbitrageur, someone who makes money on the difference in the prices of the same item in different markets. In actuality, he was more like a hedge fund operator who invested large sums of money betting on the market. In particular, on the big swings that came with mergers and takeovers. He learned, early on, that it was easy to bet wrong and if the bet was big enough, he could be ruined by it, and nearly was. Boesky decided that he would rather bet only when he was certain. That would only be profitable if his certainty came before other people became certain. The only way to do that was to cultivate individuals who could give him inside information. Which Ivan did, and by the time he was charged, he had made $200 million dollars. That was back in the eighties, when a couple of hundred million was big money.

Boesky accepted a plea bargain. For three and a half years in prison and $100 million fine, he talked.

Boesky's testimony led to a RICO Act indictment of Michael

Milken, the Junk Bond King. Milken also cut a deal. It cost him $900 million in fines and settlements.

Eliot Spitzer started out in the New York DA's office.

He went after the Gambino Family, and got them with anti-trust violations.

It was as New York's attorney general that he went after white-collar and corporate crime. In fact, the cases he went after go to the heart of the fiscal crisis we're currently in.

The big investment banks all have analysis departments. They are supposed to provide accurate and factual reports on the companies that the banks are trying to get other people to buy, sell, and invest in. Frequently, they were not. They were stretched, spun, even downright fraudulent. Spitzer went after Goldman Sachs, JPMorgan Chase, Lehman Brothers, Deutsche Bank, Merrill Lynch, Credit Suisse First Boston, Morgan Stanley, Salomon Smith Barney, and UBS Warburg. Together they were fined $1.435 billion and forced to change their practices.

Spitzer went after predatory lending in housing. The attorneys general of several other states followed his lead. The Bush administration stepped in, successfully, to stop them.

He went after AIG for fraud. They settled for $1.4 billion and the removal of their chairman. In May 2008, the *Wall Street Journal* ran an op-ed that said "A careful and lengthy look at the evidence available so far suggests ... that the AIG case, like so many others that Mr. Spitzer brought, was an example of prosecutorial excess." In September 2008, AIG collapsed, requiring an $85-billion bailout.

So, dear prosecutor, where will you look to make your reputation?

Sadly, the days of the great gangsters, with their gats and their molls, their fedoras and one way rides, are largely over with. Dewey and Giuliani did their jobs.

Do not despair.

The greatest rip-off of all time just took place before your eyes.

Trillions of dollars. Gone. Disappeared. Leaving nothing behind but debts. And a bunch of billionaires.

The general mass of us, the people, are outraged, baffled and helpless. Nobody was at fault! There's no one to blame! The whole edifice of modern capitalism started tumbling down, the government rushed in to shore it up, at our expense, and there's no one at fault?

People are losing their jobs, their pensions, their savings, their homes.

But nobody's going to prison? Nobody has to answer for anything?

For your own sake, for glory and fame, Wall Street, the big banks, the hedge funds and insurance companies, are there, waiting for you. For our sake, to give us some satisfaction, to put some fear of the law in people who think they're above the law, and as a matter of justice, they're there, waiting for you.

Read this book. It'll tell you were to look.

*Larry Beinhart is an American author, best known for the political and detective novel **American Hero**, which was adapted for the political-parody film **Wag the Dog**.*

***No One Rides for Free** received the 1987 Edgar Award for Best First Novel. His most recent book, **Salvation Boulevard** is a novel focused on the religious Right. An earlier book, **Fog Facts**, examines why some important, even striking truths, are overlooked by the media and the culture at large.*

DANNY SCHECHTER

PROLOGUE

"Denial is the refusal to acknowledge the existence or severity of unpleasant external realities or internal thoughts and feelings."

— *Encyclopedia Of Mental Disorders*

I N July 2009, President Barack Obama held a press conference focused mostly on health care. At its conclusion, in response to a provocative question, he made a provocative remark, "Cambridge police acted stupidly in arresting somebody when there was already proof that they were in their own home," referring to the arrest of a friend of his, Harvard Professor Henry Louis "Skip" Gates.

The media exploded charging that he unfairly judged the conduct of the police in Cambridge, Massachusetts, who had arrested Gates inside his house. It was a comment Obama later regretted and withdrew, well-aware of how any reference to race quickly can be distorted and become a polarizing hot button issue.

Yet, earlier at the same media event, he made another comment that might have triggered a bigger media storm but was ignored, perhaps because it did not involve the current media circus. When asked about his financial reform package, he insisted that Wall Street firms knew what they were doing when they made predatory loans. No one called him on that, not even Wall Street.

Here's what he said. "We were on the verge of a complete financial meltdown. And the reason was because Wall Street took extraordinary risks with other people's money. They were peddling loans that they knew could never be paid back."

If this is true, as I believe it is, it is certainly illegal. Yet no one has stepped up to the plate to deny it. Certainly not the relentless right-wing which fell on Obama like a ton of bricks, even accusing him of being a racist because of his concern about racial profiling in the Gates incident.

If it was a smear by the president, you'd expect an uproar in the Wall Street-Real Estate complex responsible for millions of families losing their homes. After all, this is a mass crisis, not a mere problem. A large proportion of those targeted were people of color. Their lives have been handcuffed, not just their wrists. Even worse are reports that foreclosures are rising, and now impacting commercial real estate, despite all the talk of economic recovery. This is not a problem amenable to resolution over a beer.

Sadly, the explainer-in-chief did not elaborate, did not remind the country that Wall Street firms made billions of dollars securitizing these loans, and then restructured them into exotic products with misrepresented values.

After financing rip-offs of homebuyers, they ripped off investors by selling their infected "tranches" and "bundles" worldwide. The president did not refer to FBI investigations that called mortgage fraud "an epidemic." He also did not announce any plans to prosecute those financing the frauds. So far, some small fish have been caught, but the big ones have swum away. According to economist James Kwak, for banks:

There is no contradiction between fleecing customers and making lots of profits (which is what makes you safe and sound):

1. Originate bad loans

2. Pocket fees

DANNY SCHECHTER

3. Sell bad loans to an investment bank for distribution

4. Repeat

What threatened to bring down banks was the fact that they held on to too much of the risk of those loans, either on their balance sheets or in their off-balance-sheet entities.

There was no follow-up on this far more explosive subject at the press event, just as there was none in the endless media coverage that followed. Is it that they don't know, or don't want to know?

Yet the facts here are well known, wrote investigative reporter Greg Palast:

According to exhaustive studies by the Federal Reserve Board and the Center for Responsible Lending (CRL), African Americans are 250% more likely to get a loan with an "exploding interest" clause than white borrowers – and notably, the higher the income and the better the credit rating of a black borrower, the more likely the discrimination ...

Yet, not a peep from the Obama administration about ending this Ku Klux lending practice which has laid waste black neighborhoods and taken a hunk of white America's housing values with it.

And not a peep in our media except for the occasional lawsuit, such as one in Illinois where State Attorney General Lisa Madigan sued Wells Fargo for unfair lending and racial discrimination against Hispanics and African Americans.

As a professional media critic with a long and frustrating tenure in the trenches, I have been especially sensitive to, and critical of, our media's failure to monitor this aspect of the financial crisis, failure to delve into the many crimes behind it, and failure to warn us about what was coming.

There has been a media failure, as well as a financial failure. I am not the only one to write about this. Charlie Beckett of the London School of Economics (LSE) spells out the problem, in an introduction to "What Is Financial Journalism," a thoughtful academic report about these failures:

"For once, we can't blame the news media for creating this mess or for the cost of clearing it up. However, it does make us ask about the ability of journalism to report upon financial affairs in a way that lets the public know what is really going on. In that sense, the limits of financial journalism may have contributed to the present disaster."

At the same time, I have drawn on experience as a "news dissector" to separate the wheat from chaff, referencing useful reporting by diligent and concerned journalists in this book that is both an investigation into criminality and an effort at media analysis. There may be journo-geniuses covering this world, but I don't claim to be one of them. While I tap a wide range of diverse insights and information from bloggers as well as the financial press, I try to put key information, including the quotes I cite and facts I find, in a context and a narrative.

It's also more than that because this book is a companion to a documentary called *Plunder* that I have spent more than a year making, drawing upon the interviews I did with a wide range of people in the know: Wall Street insiders, economists, experts, advocates, law professors and more. *Plunder* synthesizes my findings as a filmmaker with the information I collected as an investigative reporter and researcher. The result is, of course, my own interpretation of what I believe we need to know and for which I am, of course, responsible.

DANNY SCHECHTER

This work is my fifth on aspects of a catastrophe that is certainly bigger than me, bigger than all of us. I can only hope it will have more impact than my earlier work. Some of us have a problem giving up on issues we care about, when our passions and a sense of urgency drive us to testify to the era of a rapid economic decline in which we live. Even when, it seems at times, that no one wants to know.

This book builds on earlier reporting and also breaks some new ground with a focus on the financial collapse as a crime story. I realize some will find this a narrow frame for a story which is complex, multi-layered and that has built in intensity over time. Some readers may consider this frame more as a thesis, rather than a legally enforceable indictment.

It is one thing to allege crime, another thing to prove it. In this arena, there is a mushy minefield of conflicting laws, subject to a mish-mash of precedent, regulations, rules and judicial findings.

It is nearly impossible to craft a clear and compelling case that would stand up in all courts since many judges are already compromised by political appointments and a pro-business orientation. However, there have been successful prosecutions of corporate criminals but usually only after prosecutors and grand juries subpoena documents, cross-examine witnesses under oath and mount forensic investigations. That is beyond the scope of any journalistic inquiry. Journalists usually go after the small stories to illustrate larger points. Remember, neither the government nor the media brought down Bernard Madoff. He did it himself.

Some in the media have drawn on watered-down standards of proof, likely because the so-called proof of criminal intent may be too high to meet. That's why prosecutors prefer to bring conspiracy charges under the RICO laws. Yet, it is one thing to bring them against organized crime capers, and another to go after sophisticated companies with legions of lawyers, some of whom are ex-prosecutors themselves.

White-collar criminal prosecutions occur based on whether it can be proven that the companies involved in predatory lending and securitization knew what they were doing was wrong. What do you think they will say? ("Of course not!") Only as a result of digging through their internal emails and memos, does a more incriminating picture and real evidence emerge.

As this book was being finished, there were reports that investigations based on this type of documentation are already underway. The *Daily Beast* featured a report from the *Wall Street Journal* revealing, "A Senate panel has subpoenaed financial institutions, including Goldman Sachs and Deutsche Bank, seeking evidence of fraud in last year's mortgage-market meltdown … The congressional investigation is focusing on whether emails and other internal communications reveal that bankers privately doubted whether the mortgage-related securities they were facilitating were as sound as their public reports suggested. Washington Mutual, now owned and integrated into JPMorgan Chase, has also been subpoenaed.

"The investigation is the latest in a series of moves by Congress to examine the roots of the economic meltdown. Spokesmen from the banks have yet to comment." There will, no doubt, be more revelations as these probes proliferate and dig up revealing documents.

Is this financial crisis as big a threat to our country, as serious an emergency as the terror attacks, where authorities suspended normal case law to go after a special class of lawbreakers? Should they be?

In my view, these upright, high status white-collar crooks are as deadly, or deadlier, with a much more serious impact on the lives of hundreds of millions worldwide. Regrettably,

DANNY SCHECHTER

our laws convey more protection on investors than consumers, more on bankers than borrowers or homeowners.

Theft and crime is a political, as well as a legal, concern. Those who champion have-nots see the transfer of wealth in America, from the poor and middle class to the rich, in political terms and have little faith that our legal system will or can address it.

In *The Audacity of Greed: Free Markets, Corporate Thieves, and the Looting of America*, Jonathan Tasini, a labor activist, framed the crime issue in socio-economic terms, perhaps more broadly than I have, exploring how pervasive greed leads to widespread theft:

> Over the past quarter century, we have lived through the greatest looting of wealth in human history.
>
> While billions of dollars streamed into the pockets of a few elites in the corporate and economic class, the vast majority of citizens have lived through a period of falling wages, disappearing pensions, and dwindling bank accounts, all of which led to the personal debt crisis that lies at the root of the current financial meltdown. This "audacity of greed" was legally blessed by the ethos of the "free market," a phony marketing phrase that covered up the fleecing of the American public.

The case I lay forth in these pages, does make an indictment and encourages condemnation and a political response. The indictment is clear, even to those of us who are not lawyers, or play them on TV. I am also not a believer in "mob justice," but I do think that, when asked, Americans in large numbers would agree that what's happened to them – their lives, families and livelihoods – is a crime.

Economists tend to debate fiscal and monetary policy,

the role of the Federal Reserve Bank and the dynamics of a globalized world of investment, trade and production. Politicians disagree on regulatory frameworks and the decisions of elected officials.

Investigative reporters like myself are inclined to "follow the money" in more specific ways, all the while realizing that this is only part of the story but invariably one that tends to be ignored by weightier eminences.

My learning curve on these issues took off back in 2005 with research for my film, *In Debt We Trust*, somewhat prophetically subtitled, *America Before The Bubble Bursts*, warning of what could happen to our economy alongside many far more enlightened seers than myself.

We saw the growing wall of debt encouraged by massive predatory lending and mindless consumption.

We worried about the financialization of the commanding heights of the economy, a concentration of wealth and power in a wild west-like financial services industry that came to dominate the economy with 40% of all corporate profits. I was distressed by the failure of our media to track the – now obvious – signs that it all could come tumbling down.

The wall I ran up against was also a wall of indifference. I was asked: How could you be so negative about what was then so clearly an economic boom enriching so many? Was I a doom and gloomer, or an alarmist? I was told: "Your apartment has gone up in value. Why be so negative?" I soon felt ignored and marginalized when other perhaps more "sexy" issues, mostly partisan and often personality driven, drove the public discourse.

As I toured for *In Debt We Trust*, I met audiences who resonated with its message, who confessed to how hard they were struggling to survive economically because of the debt traps in which they had become ensnared. Their concerns crossed partisan, racial and generational lines. Once they heard others admitting how they were manipulated into taking on too much credit, or were fooled by lenders, they started telling their own stories. They saw that they shared common experiences. Others blamed themselves and the silence produced by stigma. They also asked questions that led me to try to respond and explain. So I kept and keep learning more, and began writing about the issues, as well as filming them.

To follow-up the film, I kept writing columns on these issues. My writings were later collected by ColdType.net into an e-book titled, *Squeezed: America As The Bubble Bursts*. It soon seemed like the economy was in a free-fall and getting worse. (Federal Reserve Chairman Ben Bernanke would later say he acted out of fear that we were about to plunge into a depression.)

With the bubble finally "bursting," I received some advice on finding a more "traditional" book publisher. So I updated and reworked my columns, found an agent, and came up with a more provocative title, *Plunder* (a name I later used for my current documentary). My new and very experienced agent was a bit worried that I might be too far ahead of the curve since we were not then, officially at least, in a recession, and any talk of something worse was not taken seriously in polite company.

Thirty publishers read it. Some said they liked it, but all "passed." The consensus was I was too far out there or lacked the proper credentials. One book buyer told us it would never sell because it lacked stock tips, *de rigueur* in the business book genre. Others didn't think there was a market because there was no evidence that large numbers of people would be interested. They didn't want to gamble on a subject that was perceived of as "of limited interest and impact." Honest!

Cosimo Books and its gutsy publisher, Alexander Dake, was

not deterred and *Plunder* came out just a week before Lehman Brothers was allowed to go bankrupt. It couldn't have been timelier but was perceived as still too far ahead of its time for many who were preoccupied with other issues like the 2008 election and the war. The emerging economic crisis was labeled a "business" problem and not considered of broad public interest.

A year later, the shelves are stocked with new books about aspects of the crisis, but few echoed my analysis or delved into the role played by crime. Satyajit Das, author of *Traders, Guns & Money*, wrote:

> The number of books on the Global Financial Crisis (GFC) has reached pandemic proportions – the World Health Organization (WHO) is investigating. With the decorum of vultures at a carcass, publishers are cashing in on the transitory interest of the masses (normally obsessed with war, scandal or reality TV shows) in the arcane minutiae of financial matters.

The availability of these acres of print does not necessarily mean that the nature of the crime of our time has yet been told. Most of these books follow similar stories in formulaic ways. Ironically, this inundation of expertise obsessed with "minutiae" could have the effect of turning people off even more about a subject that is often so intimidating and foreign to most of our lives.

I was well aware of all the years of predictions of the coming collapse of capitalism. I, too, had scoffed at it as the mechanistic and apocalyptic fantasies of conspiracy nuts. And yet, now I was being lumped by some into that same world of weirdos and world-enders. (On the left, an article of faith was that the workers would topple capitalism; in this crisis, it seems as if

DANNY SCHECHTER

the capitalists themselves are doing a better job.)

As a blogger and a columnist I began looking at the signs of the deepening crisis by following what the people in the know knew. I read the business press and then discovered some thoughtful blogs offering a counter-narrative to the electronic optimism oozing daily from cable TV outlets, such as CNBC.

A journalist for decades, I also knew that the devil is in the details and that you can only dig up hidden truths if you focus your attention appropriately and sharpen your skepticism. Most traditional reporting is more superficial and unquestioning. This work is not only time-consuming but demands a sense of mission, which easily morphs into obsession.

This is not always an easy world to decipher either, as I came to discover first as a student of Industrial and Labor Relations at Cornell, and later, while pursuing an advanced degree at the London School of Economics.

Not only is grasping the fundamentals challenging, but you soon learn that the finance world is shrouded in secrecy, riddled with complexity and increasingly dominated by "quants" and experts in financial market algorithms. Its whole message to non-experts like myself is go away – *it's too complicated for mere mortals like you. This is the province for only the most savvy specialists.*

If what you don't know will hurt you, keeping information from you will also harm you – and the people who do so know it. When knowledge is power, a lack of knowledge quickly turns into powerlessness.

So here I go again, into the fray, ready to bang my head against the walls of exclusion and indifference with a documentary version of *Plunder* focused on the crisis as a crime story – and this book you hold in your hands, *The Crime Of Our Time*, that makes the argument with even greater detail. It is all based on my interviews with insiders and outsiders alike. I am mindful of Albert Einstein's admonition that my colleague Sharon Kayser reminded me of: "Insanity is doing the same thing over and over, and expecting a different result." She applies it to our government which seems to think it can solve all economic problems by throwing money at them.

These issues must be pursued by investigators with more resources than I can summon. We need to hear from more whistle blowers among those with insider experience in this irresponsible industry. We will update our progress as this probe continues online at plunderthecrimeofourtime.com.

Your comments, documents and insider tips are always welcome, please email: dissector@mediachannel.org.

DANNY SCHECHTER

MUSICAL PROLOGUE

The *Plunder* Theme Song by Polar Levine

The shine on America's shoes got dulled
When Wall Street stepped into the Fuld
Congress paid off, workers laid off
Stanford, AIG and Madoff
Credit swaps and credit stops
Empty wallets, empty shops
Dead bank walking is triple-A
Grampa loses 401k

[CHORUS]: Plunder
It's a capital crime
Will anybody do the time?

Money for nothing. Nothing for money
The housing bubble and the Easter bunny
The free market, Santa Claus
Fairy tales and a nation of laws
Bankruptcies, commodities
Retention bonus, credit freeze
We're all paying for the bailout
Shaking the pitchfork, calling for a jailout.

Clueless experts, clueless news
Waitin for the sound of dropping shoes
One shoe drops, the other shoe drops
One parachute drop ahead of the cops
Over-levereged, over-paid

Hard cash too easily made
Easy credit for easy crime
For the American dream – death by subprime

Greenspan serving up the Kool Aid
Timebomb ticking on every trade
The mirror flatters; the razor … sharp
On the company jet tootin' up the TARP
Masters of the universe … the master's voice
Greed is the creed … the drug of choice
Toxic assets … the master plan
Greed is the asset of the toxic man

[CHORUS]: Plunder
It's a capital crime
Will anybody do the time?

PLUNDER © 2009 Polar Levine – Sine Language Music/BMI

INTRODUCTION

OUR TIME AND FINANCIAL CRIME

1. IN WALL STREET WE TRUST

THE daily grind of the financial industry is masked with a secret language of exotic financial instruments and magical trading regimes designed to be understood only by its creators, the cognoscenti of insiders. As with journalism, it pretends at a higher objectivity, with terms like strategic analysis and due diligence defining its work protocols, yet transparency is not its strongest suit.

Its outer facade may be cheering "trust us" but its inner logic is hissing "we will do whatever we want until you stop us." At the same time, there are rare moments of candor as when the head of equities of a large bank in the UK told the *Financial Times*, "It feels as if we are 15 minutes away from the end of the world." Or when President George W. Bush blurted out: "If money isn't loosened up, this sucker could go down."

Many believed the "credit crunch," as it was originally described, would only affect Wall Street players and speculators. They were used to ups and downs – so-called business cycles – and would probably weather the storm, which was viewed as some sudden onset of turbulence that goes as quickly as it comes.

Yet just a few years later, mere quarters in economic terms, a report by the University of Tennessee found millions coping with what has happened to them in intensely personal terms:

While the World Bank estimates that globally 90 million more people could be living in extreme poverty by the end of next year, bankruptcies, foreclosures, evictions and layoffs have taken a heavy toll on Americans.

In response, a range of extreme acts including suicide, self-inflicted injury, record levels of child abuse, murder, and arson have hit the news. The National Suicide Prevention Lifeline logged a record 568,437 calls in 2008, compared to 412,768 the previous year.

Not surprisingly, the economic meltdown has also strained marriages and, according to experts, is contributing to a rise in domestic violence. A spokeswoman for the National Domestic Violence Hotline notes that calls increased 18 percent between October 2007 and October 2008 and attributed the spike to the poor economy.

As social and civil unrest seethes, it is no surprise that the Department of Homeland Security now considers the main threat to the country as economic, even as the CIA rushes to employ financial analysts who can make sense of the continuing economic storm.

Millions of people are impacted by various financial frauds. One out of five credit card holders have been victims of credit card and debit card fraud in the last five years worldwide. In one survey, 22 percent of the respondents said they would change financial institutions, and a further 27 percent would consider changing financial institutions.

In some countries, victims of financial frauds are organizing to fight back. CTV reported in Canada:

A rally for victims of white-collar crime is scheduled for the same day that Earl Jones, the financial advisor who disappeared, leaving questions about $30 to $50 million of investors' money, is scheduled to appear in bankruptcy court.

Organizers say they want to send a message to politicians that they want changes to the laws that deal with this kind of crime. "We can no longer passively sit back and watch as these financial hustlers receive a mere slap on the wrist after having defrauded our hard working and most vulnerable citizens of their entire life savings," read one press release.

As banks and big businesses continue to pay out large bonuses, public anger grows. It seems to be the only financial crisis-related issue that infuriates people, especially when the companies paying large amounts have also received government bailout monies. A study by New York Attorney General Andrew Cuomo found that at some financial institutions the total amount of the bonuses exceeded the net income of the banks themselves. This is looting. Said Cuomo:

> There is no clear rhyme or reason to the way banks compensate and reward their employees … [pay] … has become unmoored from the banks' financial performance.

As for the bailouts, losses on TARP payouts stood at $148 billion as of June 2009.

The public was not wrong to be upset. A later study by the Institute of Policy Studies found, according to the *New York Times*:

> The top five executives at 10 financial institutions that took some of the biggest taxpayer bailouts have seen a com-

bined increase in the value of their stock options of nearly
$90 million.

It's also the latest in a string of studies showing that despite
tough talk by politicians, little has been done by regulators
to rein in the bonus culture that many believe contributed to
the near-collapse of the financial sector.

When the implosion deepened, as businesses and banks
melted down, as billions were spent on bailouts and stimulus
packages, as ordinarily optimistic commentators began to fear
a systemic collapse. President Bush spoke openly of the danger
of a "great depression, greater than the Great Depression."

The arc of political punditry didn't change much in the fall
and winter of 2008, but it was clear something very mysterious
and serious was going on.

We were in crisis mode, but what was behind it? A string
of failures were cited – a failure of judgment, an industry failure, a risk failure, a regulatory failure, a policy failure, et cetera. The blame game had begun. The media frame morphed
into, "We are all to blame, guilty of greed, over-spending and
under-saving."

And when it's everyone's fault, no one can be held responsible. No wonder the circle closed so quickly.

As the crisis lurched forward, from bad to worse, from Wall
Street to Main Street and then from America to the world,
the story became even more challenging to understand and
explain. Its causes are still being debated.

A financial crisis was creating a social crisis. The public,
quiet at first, uncertain of what was happening, or why, was
ready to let its new president handle things. The only exception to a pervasive passivity occurred when AIG brazenly
gave large bonuses to its executives after the government

saved it from collapse. Somehow, the huge bailouts themselves did not provoke as much anger or what the media labeled "pitchforks" of resentment. ("Pitchforks" is a reference to what peasants and street mobs carried when attacking land owners and protesting the rich in earlier times.)

But then, as more strange anomalies appeared, there was a growing desire from law enforcement to investigate patterns of fraud and white-collar crime. This was not unexpected, given the recent history of high-profile intersections of corporate behavior and corruption.

At the local level, media outlets focused more on bank robbers rather than the banks robbing, as if a "if they can do it, we can do it" culture of fraud had spread in the country at large. Here's an example from KRQE News, Albuquerque:

> Thirteen banks and financial institutions around the state are missing a lot of money – $1 million, to be exact – ripped off in a scam broken up by the U.S. Secret Service.
>
> The scam involved 10 people fraudulently applying for loans, according to the Secret Service which reported seven of those people are on the lam.
>
> A local bank president described the group as clever and thorough. It's unusual for such frauds to scam so much money, but this group did it in "little bits and pieces" over a period of time.

This occurred as our society developed an amnesia problem with yesterday's news about far pricier crimes, such as the S & L (Savings & Loan) crisis or the fall of business giants like Enron and WorldCom. The very thought that recent history could be a guide to contemporary events apparently

6

still doesn't resonate that widely. Our news cycles are firmly grounded in the moment of now, the "breaking news" present, and have little time or interest in context, background or connecting the dots.

It took me awhile to realize that the inquiry into how this could have just happened was largely missing and that the best our top media outlets could do was come up with lists of factors that were always somehow unrelated.

There was now broad disagreement on what and who was to blame. Economists on the left, like Walden Bello, argued crises like this happen again and again, and are built into the structure of capitalism's propensity to overproduce, engage in neo-liberal restructuring and promote globalization. These crises are often used to redistribute wealth to the rich boosting the financial sector, while draining the real economy.

On the *Casino Crash* blog (www.tni.org/article/casino-crash-0), Bello argues it went beyond greed with many on Wall Street outsmarting themselves, "Financial speculators outsmarted themselves by creating more and more complex financial contracts like derivatives that would securitize and make money from all forms of risk – including exotic futures instruments as 'credit default swaps' that enable investors to bet on the odds that the banks' own corporate borrowers would not be able to pay their debts!"

Donald Trump, that icon of American capitalism, called today's financial collapse an "Act of God" and blamed bankers for intensifying it. He used that argument to try to persuade a court to allow him to default on a construction loan to the Deutsche Bank under the *force majeure* clause of his contract. Trump claimed his financial problems were not his fauly because he did not create the crisis, as if his financial reverses ever are his responsibility. His financial marauding has long been sanitized through massive media exposure.

DANNY SCHECHTER

Brazil's President Lula, noting that poor people the world over were suffering through no fault of their own, condemned "white people with blue eyes on Wall Street."

The *New York Times* offered neither a racial view nor a divine assessment. Instead the "Gray Lady" devoted thousands of words to explain six "errors" behind the crisis. (Oddly, eight months later, President Obama unveiled a financial reform package to fix what he, also, called "mistakes.") The *Times* offered up this list endorsing a "How We Blew It" analysis:

1. Wild Derivatives

2. Sky-High Leverage

3. A Subprime Surge

4. Fiddling On Foreclosures

5. Letting Lehman Go

6. TARP's Detour

Nowhere did this list reference predatory lending or "white-collar crime." Challenging this view was Professor Michael Hudson, a former chief economist at the Chase Bank (and, as it turns out, a cousin of the late Leon Trotsky, a relationship of which Chase was probably unaware).

He told me: "In practice, fraud is what has brought down almost every single expansion, every bank take over, the saving and loan crisis in the 1980s, the stock market crisis in the 1920s ..." In fact, a closer look at what happened in these events reveals substantial corporate larceny.

Months later, top journalists at the *New York Times* began

to intimate that criminal behavior was pervasive in the finance world. Columnist Bob Herbert wrote in July 2009 of "malefactors" in the financial industry: "The people running this system remind me of gangsters who manage to walk out of the courthouse with a suspended sentence, and can't wait to get back to their nefarious activities."

For every journalist willing to acknowledge pervasive criminality, others obscure the issue, as in a *CNN Money* article that asked, "Who caused the financial crisis, villains or jerks." You can't be both?

The article scoffs at the tone of a story by writer Matt Taibbi, excoriating the investment firm Goldman Sachs in *Rolling Stone* magazine as a "great vampire squid wrapped around the face of humanity." Then it reinforces a characterization of an AIG executive described as an "egotistical jerk" as opposed to being a "diabolical mastermind," and in the words of the author "as trapped as anyone else in the bubble he helped create."

"Though Taibbi may find it hard to believe, that's how it usually is," this lecture concluded as if it is naïve to think that big institutions would flout the law in their own interests.

There Big Media goes again: Everyone gets turned into a victim, even the victimizers. Walter Cronkite's famous dicta "That's the way it is," has become "That's how it usually is," with no clarity on what "usually" is supposed to mean.

Some top journalists recognized pervasive criminal activity but few admitted, as did Gillian Tett of the *Financial Times*, their own ambivalence on punishing wrongdoers. She wrote, "On a personal level, I have little taste for seeing hordes of bankers heading for jail, or facing massive fines. Nor do I have any illusion that public or private prosecutions will resolve bigger structural flaws. A witch-hunt might be a media distraction. But, on the other hand, if there is no retribution against financiers, it will be very difficult to force a real change in behavior."

DANNY SCHECHTER

Why is this? Could journalists identify more with the people they write about than their victims? Is it a class thing or just solidarity between the corporate financial and corporate media elite?

There have been defenses of Goldman by respected financial writers like Michael Lewis who argues that the squid reference is "transparently false." He wrote on Bloomberg, "For starters, the vampire squid doesn't feed on human flesh. Ergo, no vampire squid would ever wrap itself around the face of humanity, except by accident. And nothing that happens at Goldman Sachs – nothing that Goldman Sachs thinks, nothing that Goldman Sachs feels, nothing that Goldman Sachs does – ever happens by accident." Oh!

In August 2009, the *New York Times* reported that former Goldman CEO Henry Paulson was in close touch with his former employer despite an ethics pledge not to do so. "During the week of the AIG bailout alone, Mr. Paulson and Mr. Blankfein spoke two dozen times, the calendars show, far more frequently than Mr. Paulson did with other Wall Street executives.

"On Sept. 17, the day Mr. Paulson secured his waivers, he and Mr. Blankfein spoke five times. Two of the calls occurred before Mr. Paulson's waivers were granted." Ach, so!

2. THE EXPERIENCE OF A BANK REGULATOR

William Black was one of the bank regulators who disentangled the S & L crisis. He told Bill Moyers that many of the banks that failed then were deliberately brought down.

"The way that you do it is to make really bad loans, because they pay better. Then you grow extremely rapidly, in other words, you're a Ponzi-like scheme. And the third thing you do is, we call it 'leverage.' That just means borrowing a lot of money, and the combination creates a situation where you have guaranteed record profits in the early years. That makes you rich, through the bonuses that modern executive compensation has produced. It also makes it inevitable that there's going to be a disaster down the road."

Moyers asked, "So you're suggesting, saying, that CEOs of some of these banks and mortgage firms, in order to increase their own personal income, deliberately set out to make bad loans?"

William Black: "Yes."

As an investigator and enforcement officer, Black is credited with jailing 1,000 executives in the aftermath of the S & L collapse. He said that a subsequent federal investigation found fraud in every bank that collapsed. The head of one of the banks he closed, Charles Keating, who was later jailed, sent his lawyer a letter – covered, unfortunately, by attorney-client confidentiality – urging him to "Get Black, Kill Him Dead." (Keating became infamous because of his links with five senators – the "Keating Five" – including John McCain.) He also sued Black for $400 million and hired private detectives to discredit him.

A government study at the time confirmed Black's claims of a now forgotten wave of mass incarceration. The *Financial Times* asked in September 2009:

> How many financiers do you think ended up in jail after America's Savings and Loans scandals? The answer can be found in a fascinating, old report from the U.S. Department of Justice.

> According to some of its records, between 1990 and 1995 no less than 1,852 S & L officials were prosecuted, and 1,072 placed behind bars. Another 2,558 bankers were also jailed, often for offenses which were S & L-linked, too.

> Those are thought-provoking numbers. These days the West-

ern world is reeling from another massive financial crisis, that eclipses the S & L debacle in terms of wealth destruction.

Yet, thus far, very few prison terms have been handed out.

Black's agency was later downsized and defanged by Congress. He tells this story in his book, *The Best Way To Rob A Bank Is To Own One.* (I did a an earlier story on S & L fraud for ABC's *20/20* program with a similar title.)

By the time, the current crisis rolled around, there were no tough enforcement mechanisms in place. The *Financial Times* explained, "In part that is because of the sheer complexity of the financial deals in the recent crisis, and the fact that these deals were often deliberately and cleverly constructed to 'arbitrage' the law (i.e. skirt, but not break it).

"Another big issue is the sheer number of powerful parties that typically participated in complex finance deals. Few private law firms have the resources or desire to go head to head with numerous Wall Street banks at one time."

The failure of IndyMac, the 7th largest S & L lost more money than all the earlier S & Ls that were closed. According to Black, IndyMac sold over $200 billion dollars worth of subprime "liars' loans." Most had "triple-A" ratings, 80% lost all value. (In 2009, 87 banks had failed by August with financial analysts expecting 300 more. One of the banks that was closed, Colonial Bank of Montgomery, Alabama, with $25 billion in assets was being investigated for criminal fraud.)

Then, non-public Guaranty bank, according to the Associated Press, "The second-largest U.S. bank to fail this year, after the Texas lender was shut down by regulators and most of its operations sold at a loss of billions of dollars for the U.S. government to a major Spanish bank."

A corporate computer expert emailed me this:

This "could" begin the "Domino Effect" because of non-public financial relationships, that is direct financial interconnects below the radar. So far most of the banks have been using SWIFT (a global financial transfer software linking banks worldwide) to move money instantly to create an illusion that everything is OK. SWIFT is the worldwide software that allows for instant transfers of funds.

For example JPMorgan owns 234 other banks, they are all considered one, and named as such, except they also still appear as separate entities for stock and financial purposes. With SWIFT that allows instant transfer, thus a "master" shell and pea game, much more sophisticated than any accounting firm can address. The "pea" could actually be in one individual bank, but because of the speed of the software, it changes in real time to somewhere else. "Cyber games" at their finest.

Guaranty is one of the "key" insider cogs. But it gets even more complicated in that there are additional relationships by direct connections to thousands of other areas from banks to retail. Twenty core banks have their own little private groups, plus tentacles into the smaller banks, meanwhile the money "churns" retail; it's directly interconnected to CVS Pharmacy, Limited Brands and the 2nd largest grocery store chain, for example.

Each of those also have their own "spinning" operations. One might compare all of this to the older workings of a clock, each gear turns another to create a time picture. Guaranty is a cog such as the "minute" hand driver. Minutes shutter, hours fail. Therefore all commerce has to be monitored in real time since in reality all are direct components of the real picture. The old saying "for the want of a nail ... the war was lost" has reached total reality.

This was all "inevitable" argues Howard Wachtel in his history of Wall Street's first century of recurring crises, *Street of Dreams, Boulevard of Broken Hearts*:

Whether it be railroads, new industrial products or commercial shipping, there was Wall Street offering two forms of services: a vehicle for raising funds for the launch of these new ventures and a means for speculative profit-seeking. Each of the functions needed the other but, in reality, the one – the dream of speculative riches – undermined the other.

The requirement of a liquid financial market that enabled the bundling of large sacks of financial capital for investment in new products inevitably led to a speculative thrust that undercut the investment's initial purpose in launching a new product. This existential force on the Street reappears regularly, most recently in the dot.com's over-valuation and implosion at the turn of the twentieth century. Thus, the "street of dreams" of an easy road to riches inevitably unravels and becomes a "boulevard of broken hearts."

Flashback to the Great Crash of 1929 and you have legendary economists like the late John Kenneth Galbraith (whom I met and interviewed before he died at age 97) arguing that it occurred largely because capitalism is inherently unstable and plagued by widespread "corporate larceny."

Galbraith cited the findings of the Pecora Commission, which in 1932 investigated the causes of the 1929 crash. It uncovered a wide range of abusive practices on the part of banks and bank affiliates. They were widespread, fostered by many conflicts of interest involved in the underwriting of securities. This was later recognized as an unsound way to pay off bad bank loans, as well as fund "pool operations" to support the price of bank stocks.

There was outrage then, when banker J. P. Morgan admitted he had paid no taxes for two years. He was one of the richest men in the country.

Historian Steve Fraser discussed how the con men and criminals of this period were regarded:

> With the crash of 1929, some fled the country; others committed suicide. The president of the New York Stock Exchange, Richard Whitney, whose blood lines went back to the Mayflower, whose brother was a senior partner at J. P. Morgan, who had been educated at Groton and Harvard, who hunted foxes and took for granted his right to rule, was carted off to Sing-Sing after being convicted of fraud and embezzlement.

> From Duer [an early American speculator who went bankrupt and ended up in debtor's prison] to Whitney, the sorry doings of these businessmen inspired two public responses. One was to lock them up (sometimes preceded by chasing them through the streets). The second was to attempt to treat the institutional roots of the problem through government regulation.

In the 1930s, the commission's chief counsel, Ferdinand Pecora concluded, "Legal chicanery and pitch darkness were the banker's stoutest allies."

DANNY SCHECHTER

3. THE CRIME WAVE IS STILL WITH US
And today?

Legal chicanery has taken a giant step with a total rewriting of the laws themselves creating a deregulated environment that allowed formerly illegal practices to be considered legal.

This environment was promoted through the expenditure of hundreds of millions of dollars for lobbying legislators and campaign contributions. There was extensive collusion between the financial services industry and politicians of both parties.

Cutbacks in government monitoring of financial practices became the norm with fines and "settlements" (with some exceptions) replacing vigilant oversight and the prosecution of wrongdoers at the federal and state level. Fraudsters were largely punished with fines their companies paid as a cost of doing business. Examples include In August 2009, General Electric settled a government claim on accounting fraud for $50 million. In the same week, AIG founder Hank Greenberg agreed to pay $15 million to settle the U.S. Securities and Exchange Commission's investigation into his role in accounting fraud at the company from 2000 to 2005.

This environment was enabled by privately controlled institutions that the public believed were government agencies, like the Federal Reserve Bank, operating in tandem with the Treasury Department; both staffed by industry veterans.

Today's "pitch darkness" or information gap, is enabled by many media institutions that disregarded or ignored the growth and fusion of shady securitization practices supported by subprime and other predatory practices.

Foreclosures are still growing in number. Government programs to help homeowners have so far failed, barely denting the problem. Even demands that mortgages be modified to keep people in their homes have led to minimal changes. The

Washington Post explained why:

> Government initiatives to stem the country's mounting fore-
> closures are hampered because banks and other lenders in
> many cases have more financial incentive to let borrowers
> lose their homes than to work out settlements, some econo-
> mists have concluded.

By July 2009, only 200,000 at-risk homeowners were in federal loan modification programs, a sign of how slow the response by lenders and the government has been to a deepening crisis.

Mortgage servicers, including Litton, owned by Goldman Sachs, have put many roadblocks into doing what are called "loan mods." Reuters reported at the end of July 2009, that these companies that profited in the subprime boom warned, "U.S. officials that a key program to slow foreclosures may push some financing costs higher and derail their efforts."

Additionally, there's been the creation of a "shadow banking system" operating outside and above the law, with trillions of dollars unregulated, and in some cases unaccounted for, going to offshore financial hideaways. In the summer of 2009, the U.S. government reached an agreement with Switzerland to disclose the names of 5,000 Americans with money stashed in the UBS bank. A UBS "whistleblower" who disclosed that UBS bankers smuggled diamonds in toothpaste tubes was jailed when it was learned that he had benefited by some of the schemes. Another banker with Credit Suisse was indicted for fraudulent practices in the U.S.

The top firms and their "counterparties" have not been regulated or restrained from committing crimes and rip-offs of massive proportions. Market values are their only values.

Some banks continue to put us all at risk. Jeff Nielson

wrote on *Seeking Alpha* (www.seekingalpha.com):

> Fitch Ratings released a report disclosing that just five banks (all U.S. banks) hold 80% of all derivatives risk: Bank of America, Goldman Sachs, JPMorgan, Morgan Stanley and Citigroup. Keep in mind that the global derivatives market has a notional value somewhere around 30 times global GDP. Put another way, each one of these five banks has derivatives risk that is much greater than the entire value of global GDP.
>
> In 2008, when the reckless gambling of these greedy banksters destroyed their sector and threatened to destroy the entire international monetary system, the banksters (and their servants in the U.S. government) coined the phrase "too big to fail." This implied that such banks were so "important" that they had to be saved at all and any cost (i.e., the $10 *trillion* in hand-outs, loans and pledges to the biggest banks).

With their high salaries, training programs, bonus and perks as well as ties to top business schools, the investment houses and financial industries, fostered a culture of entitlement and wealth, creating a superwealthy, self-conscious elite cut off from most Americans. This elite supported politicians who promoted their values while politicians sought their support, perhaps best reflected in the words of former President George W. Bush who told an $800 dollar-a-plate fundraiser, "This is an impressive crowd — the haves and the have-mores. Some people call you the elites; I call you my base."

With personal wealth as its goal, these self-conscious professionals learned to get along by going along, to cut corners in an already deregulated environment. Military metaphors abounded — kill or be killed, wipe out the competition. The bottom line became their only line. They read about satirical labels like "Masters of the Universe" invented by writer Tom Wolfe and took them literally, as if that was a status to aspire to in an ethics-challenged environment.

Inequality mounted as these magicians of mega-wealth creation did their thing. Wealth was transferred from working people and the middle class to the rich. It was vacuumed in one direction – up! One impact: according to a *Wall Street Journal* analysis of Social Security Administration data, more than one-third of all pay in the U.S. now goes to executives and other highly paid employees.

As the crisis worsened, Curtis Lang wrote on *Satya Center* (www.satyacenter.com) in March 2008 that the coming sub-prime meltdown would also bring down globalization:

> It is worth noting that the Bush years also saw a resurgence of leveraged buy-outs (LBOs) financed with junk bonds, a kind of financial '80s retro chic moment, and these junk bonds were fashioned into high performance financial instruments that pieced together bits and parcels of many, many LBOs that were then 'insured' and given a AAA investment rating. There is every reason to believe that these LBOs created companies loaded with debt that are unlikely to meet their financial obligations. The junk bonds and junk financial instruments created to finance their operations are also surely worth much less than face value. This will certainly lead to corporate bankruptcies and further ugly problems for big banks and other big holders of corporate junk.

> More ominous are the problems in the esoteric market for credit default swaps (CDS) that were engineered by computer wizards to manage the risks entailed by the investments in junk bonds. Dr. Roubini estimates there are approximately $50 trillion worth of such instruments, and says that losses

of somewhere between $20 billion and $250 billion are quite likely, with his guesstimate being much closer to the high end of the range predicted. These losses will impact Wall Street firms, hedge funds and insurers of financial instruments, with the potential to destabilize the entire stock exchange.

These shaky, shady credit default swaps became a big issue after the crash. When the White House and members of Congress sought to regulate the traffic in derivatives, *Zero Hedge* (www.zerohedge.com) explained why the industry mounted a major lobbying effort to block reforms:

> The real reason that they don't want CDS regulated is because it will narrow the spreads, and they will make a little less money. In addition, transparency would reduce the market, because investors would see CDS as the snake oil that they are (outside of some very narrow, specific uses) …
>
> As Nobel prize-winning economist George Akerlof predicted in 1993, the financial giants would use CDS until the system crashed, knowing that the taxpayers would bail them out when the crash happened.
>
> They know the same thing will happen tomorrow …
>
> The bottom line is that we are now in a system where gains are privatized and losses are socialized. The debate over CDS is really one part of the larger debate as to whether that system will continue or not.

Bloomberg News confirmed that these highly praised instruments promoted as "financial innovation" were anything but:

The unpalatable reality that very few, self interested industry participants are prepared to admit is that much of what
passed for financial innovation was specifically designed to
conceal risk, obfuscate investors and reduce transparency.

The process was entirely deliberate. Efficiency and transparency are not consistent with the high-profit margins that are
much sought after on Wall Street. Financial products need
to be opaque and priced inefficiently to produce excessive
profits or economic rents.

Could *intentionally* creating these very risky and dangerous
products later sold as safe and highly rated be characterized
as criminal? You bet.

Some of this was new, but not without historical precedent,
especially the way government facilitates corporate crime. It
was a phenomenon denounced centuries ago by the French
free market apostle Frederic Bastiat who argued that laws
were rewritten to protect and advance plunder: "The law has
placed the collective force at the disposal of the unscrupulous
that wish, without risk, to exploit the person, liberty, and
property of others. It has converted plunder into a right, in
order to protect plunder."

But just because this crime has happened before, in a system
that has little interest in learning from history, does not make
it any less urgent to reframe and redefine the crime that's happening now. To come to the view, as I have, that the financial
crisis is at its origins a crime story involved interviewing financial insiders, as well as economic experts and historians. This
research is ongoing as each day seems to bring new arrests and
charges by regulators and courts who can no longer ignore the
stench in their midst.

4. "THE BIGGEST CRIME IN THE WORLD"

When I started moving in this direction, I felt very alone because book after book by insiders purporting to explain the collapse of a "house of cards" – the *cliché du jour* – avoided or minimized the criminal aspects discussed in this book.

But there were many who saw it, too.

Nomi Prins was a former banker at Goldman Sachs and Bear Stearns who helped fashion some of the derivative products at the center of our economic collapse.

On a freezing December day, I interviewed her on Wall Street as large Brink's document-destruction trucks prowled alleys behind the stock exchange and nearly hit our cameraman. She saw where I was going at once and joined in.

> This is the most expensive takeout, the biggest crime in world history. We're talking about a crime we can't even quantify because so many assets were created and so much money was borrowed on the idea that they would exist and so much of that has disappeared. You're talking double-digit trillions of dollars – minimum – already in the beginning of 2009, and we are nowhere near done with finding out how much loss there really is.

One estimate of monies lost, value depreciated, and money spent to try to stabilize the system came to $197.4 trillion, and that may be low. In mid-July 2009, the *Politico* reported that the chief congressional investigator on the Troubled Asset Relief Program (TARP) said:

> "**... a series of bailouts, bank rescues and other economic lifelines could end up costing the federal government as much as $23 trillion,**" the U.S. government's watchdog over the effort says – a staggering amount that is nearly

double the nation's entire economic output for a year.

When challenged the watchdog couldn't back up the number and said that it was an unexpected worse case scenario.

At the same time, back in 2008, the year of the meltdown, the number one crime story on cable television was the case of Casey Anthony and her missing 2-year-old daughter, Caylee, which had captured the attention of the nation as no other in recent history. O. J. Simpson's recent arrest rated second, the Jennifer Hudson family murders were third, and so forth.

Lists like these define crime in terms of perpetrators and victims. Financial crimes, despite their size and volume of damage didn't make the list.

Yet, you would think that a crime of this proportion would not escape media attention.

It didn't, at least in the eyes of one editor of a slick upscale monthly that covers the elite, and which carried many articles on aspects of this crime. *Vanity Fair*'s Graydon Carter wound up and pitched this *j'accuse* down the middle but few of his colleagues swung at it.

Carter's words deserve to be etched on the wall of the well-protected New York Stock Exchange:

> It can fairly be said that the chain of catastrophic bets made over the past decade by a few hundred bankers may well turn out to be the greatest nonviolent crime against humanity in history. They've brought the world's economy to its knees, lost tens of millions of people their jobs and their homes, and trashed the retirement plans of a generation, and they could drive an estimated 200 million people worldwide into dire poverty.

DANNY SCHECHTER

In other words, never before have so few, done so much, to so many.

Harvard Business School Professor Shoshanna Zuboff, goes even further comparing some Wall Street financiers to the Third Reich's Adolph Eichmann in the sense that there was a "banality of evil" in both eras.

"The economic crisis is not the Holocaust," she wrote, "but I would argue it derives from the same business model that routinely produced a similar kind of remoteness and thoughtlessness by a widespread abrogation of individual moral judgment. As we learn more about the behavior within our financial institutions, we see that just about everybody accepted a reckless system that rewards transactions but rejects responsibility for the consequences of those transactions."

Commenting in the *Atlantic* magazine, Denis Arvey wrote:

This was criminal in any serious definition of criminality, but all perfectly legal in the lawyer-crafted vermin-nourishment clauses under which our economy was looted. And will continue to be looted without fundamental revolutionary change. The way that the banking industry recently gutted foreclosure-protection indicates the thieves are still running the show, with the help of a thoroughly corrupted government.

Many Americans have intense contempt for the elites who happily created this disaster, and that includes their government allies, in both parties. For decades, these people were presented as heroic "innovators," creating a 21st century economy and an "ownership society." Now we see them for the corrupt and sleazy manipulators they have always been.

I wondered how a convicted white-collar criminal would feel about this indictment. I turned to Sam Antar, once the CFO of the long-closed Crazy Eddie, a New York electronics chain, who said he and members of his family stole millions until he was caught and turned by federal prosecutors.

He didn't say, "Crime, what crime?" Quite the opposite. He "got it." He went in to considerable detail in a distinct Brooklyn accent: "This crime has been ten, fifteen years in the making. It's been going on at least that long. We're only finding out about it for one specific reason: the tanking economy. Imagine if the economy didn't tank? Imagine if this was allowed to go on for four or five, six, seven years? Imagine how big it would've gotten then?"

How did they get away with it, I asked. Antar spoke to me as if I were a little boy who was naïve about the big, bad world.

"The white-collar criminal has no legal constraints. You subpoena documents, we destroy documents; you subpoena witnesses, we lie. So you are at a disadvantage when it comes to the white-collar criminal. In effect, we're economic predators. We're serial economic predators. We impose a collective harm on society."

Period.

Moreover, he said many "legitimate" businessmen are, at heart, opportunists and will break the law when they think they can get away with it or when they are feeling pressure to make or drive up revenues

"Yes. Everybody lives with sin and temptation. There are two types of criminals. I call them the born criminals like me; and the crossover criminals, those that succumb to sin and temptation, depending upon the circumstances."

I asked, "How common is white-collar crime in, let's say, Wall Street?"

"I think white-collar crime has always been there; it just

goes more noticed or less noticed. Like today we're hearing about all of these white-collar crimes. But actually, it's just that we're finding out about them because of a faltering economy. A faltering economy makes most white-collar crimes unsustainable, and therefore they implode."

Now a blogger on white-collar crime for *White Collar Fraud* (www.whitecollarfraud.com), Antar cited research: "The ACFE, the Association of Certified Floor Examiners, does a study every year. About 90 to 95 percent of all white-collar criminals have no previous criminal record. And the higher the economic value of the crime, the less likely white-collar criminals will have a criminal record. So therefore, it's very hard to profile these guys."

How do they get away with it?

Continues Antar, "Most white-collar criminals are pillars within their communities. They've never had criminal records; most of them are very good parents; most of them give money to the arts. Enron's Ken Lay built stadiums and gave millions to the arts. But most people are fooled by the wall of false integrity that white-collar criminals build around them."

How will we fill in the blanks in our collective knowledge about practices that are deliberately camouflaged and kept secret? As I write, new white-collar crime cases are trickling out of the bubble. Usually, they appear one at a time, with little connecting them. This is because our collective public mind has an attention span defined by distraction, occasionally interrupted by a focus on individual bad guys, not institutional practices and patterns. A network producer chastised me, "You're too institutional, Schechter. People want names of bad guys. Just tell their stories."

At the same time, you hear complaints of prosecutors being too aggressive. Historian Steve Fraser comments on that canard: "Complaints about overzealousness on the part of government prosecutors are not only the height of hypocrisy, they betray a willful blindness to the lessons of the past, even when the past is repeating itself all around us."

We need a new Pecora Commission with subpoena power to investigate the causes of this crisis – and it's too bad that a leader with the stature of John Kenneth Galbraith is not alive to chair it.

Senator Bernie Sanders has called for just such a commission complete with an investigative staff and subpoena powers. Why don't all progressive groups, media, unions, and concerned organizations endorse this call? (Probably because most are not paying attention.)

Yet, even if a commission is formed, there is no certainty that it will get at the truth. Economist Dean Baker fears that already a proposed commission to assess blame is being undercut, stating "there is a real possibility" that the commission appointed by Congress may cover-up the real criminals.

"Instead of striving to uncover the truth, it may seek to conceal it," he fears.

Context is critical. As Tom Frank wrote in the foreword to Baker's book on the crisis, *Plunder and Blunder*, "The history of the last decade is a history of asset bubbles. The pattern repeats itself again and again, the same millennial rhetoric, the same crooked insider behavior …"

In this book, I won't be glossing over that "same crooked insider behavior" but spelling it out with as many dirty details as I can find.

5. INSIDERS WANTED

We need investigations by insiders who know where the bodies are buried, and in many cases, not yet buried. We need to engage professionals like former New York State's attorney general, turned governor, Eliot Spitzer who had denounced predatory lending crimes just before he was outed in a sex scandal. It seems clear that you need people who have been on Wall Street to see through the tricks on Wall Street.

We need to know which politicians took their payoffs and did, and continue to do, Wall Street's bidding.

We need details, documents and proof.

Then, we need a jailout, not just a bailout.

We need to remember Balzac's insight: "Behind every great fortune lies a great crime." But he was not the only great thinker with insight.

"In a closed society where everybody's guilty, the only crime is getting caught. In a world of thieves, the only final sin is stupidity," wrote Hunter S. Thompson. And that does not just apply to the perpetrators.

We need, most of all, a sense of outrage. I am hoping that my own work will help build a sense of outrage with what is the "crime of all time."

As Robert Johnson of the Roosevelt Institute argues, we need outrage if the financial system is to be reformed, and if wrongdoers are to be brought to justice. He quotes the great John Kenneth Galbraith from his book, *A Short History of Financial Euphoria*, as confirming the importance of anger and activism and the link between rage and reform.

> The final and common feature of the speculative episode – in stock markets, real estate, art, or junk bonds – is what happens after the inevitable crash. This, invariably, will be a time of anger and recrimination and also of profoundly unsubtle introspection. The anger will fix upon the individuals who were previously most admired for their financial imagination and acuity. Some of them, having been persuaded of their own exemption from confining orthodoxy,

will, as noted, have gone beyond the law, and their fall and, occasionally, their incarceration will now be viewed with righteous satisfaction.

There will also be scrutiny of the previously much-praised financial instruments and practices – paper money; implausible securities issues; insider trading; market rigging; more recently, program and index trading that have facilitated and financed the speculation. There will be talk of regulation and reform.

But will that talk lead us anywhere, like to the deeper changes we need? Can we even make the case for these changes by laying out the case against what has been done to all of us in the interests of a few. That will be for you to decide after reading this book.

So, ladies and gentlemen of a jury, that doesn't exist, yet, this is the opening statement of the case I proffer in these pages – pursuant to an indictment that has yet to be brought, under the powers vested in me by the Founding Fathers and as a citizen of the United States – against "those few who did so much to so many."

I realize I can only bring it now in a virtual venue where the currency is made up of ideas and where the only derivatives are the values enunciated by the founders like Thomas Jefferson who is said to have said, "I believe that banking institutions are more dangerous to our liberties than standing armies." Our generation has read President Eisenhower's farewell address warning of the power of the military-industrial complex, but far fewer have studied an earlier farewell by President Andrew Jackson railing against the "moneyed power."

That power is with us still, and if anything, is now stronger and more arrogant than ever. Critical voices must be expressed, even as crime and punishment remains at the centerpiece of the American experience. From the days of Al Capone, who began his career as a gangster in racketeering – a form of criminal "accounting" – through a bombardment of Hollywood-made heroes like John Dillinger, Bonnie and Clyde, the Family Corleone and, most recently, the Sopranos.

Entertainers regularly make fun of the practices I write about, but comedians like Jon Stewart and Bill Maher, to cite two, are often on target. Filmmaker Michael Moore calls his hard-hitting film on capitalism "A Love Story," because he probably thinks that portraying his work as entertainment is the best way of getting attention for his ideas. Documentaries like mine may tell, but films like Moore's sell. Moore understands how show business trumps the news business in our culture.

But, to me, this is not funny at all. It is a predictable tragedy, the crime of our time.

In the spring of 2009, the hit TV series *Law And Order* was renewed for its twentieth season. By chance, I was able to film one of its shoots outside a New York courthouse. On that same day, an unlikely poster boy for corporate crime was confessing to a federal judge just around the corner.

It is his story with which I begin.

CHAPTER 1

THE MADOFF MOMENT

BEFORE: Madoff's cell phone message according to his long-time secretary was, "Hi, you've reached Bernie Madoff. I'm unavailable right now. If you need me, you can call my office at (212) 230-2424. Or just leave a message and I'll get back to you." (Please note this phone number is no longer in service.)

AFTER: Madoff became *Prisoner Number 61727-054*. He was sent to a federal prison in Atlanta for processing. That's the place that once housed Charles Ponzi, the man after whom the Ponzi scheme was named, but also such giants of dissent as Socialist Party leader Eugene Victor Debs and Jamaica's black nationalist hero, Marcus Garvey. He was later moved to a federal prison in Butner, North Carolina, which has a hospital. (There's a rumor he may have cancer.) He has now been slated for release on November 14, 2139 – 20 years less than his full sentence. Two weeks later, Madoff's accountant, David Friehling, pled "not guilty" to any wrongdoing.

His phrase, "**indeed**, criminal," was uttered in open court in the spring of 2009 by the arch-financial fraudster Bernard Madoff after he confessed to running an illegal Ponzi scheme.

indeed *(adverb)*

• *used to emphasize a statement or response confirming something already suggested*: It was not expected to last long, and indeed it took less than three weeks.

• ORIGIN: *(Middle English)* as "in deed"

"I knew what I was doing was wrong, indeed criminal," was the whole statement. Later Madoff's CFO, Frank DiPascali, would confess to another federal judge, "I knew it was criminal, and I did it anyway." He pled guilty to ten felony counts, including conspiracy and tax evasion.

For his candor and his *chutzpah*, this market genius credited with popularizing computer trading and chairing the NASDAQ exchange, will be spending the rest of his life behind bars as one more example of a big man taking a hard fall, as well as a symbol of all financial crisis crime, even if Madoff was not really connected to the crimes that shattered our economy.

Some of the details of how Madoff's firm operated came out in Frank DiPascali's testimony. The *New York Times* reported that "he and unidentified others helped Mr. Madoff perpetuate the crime – using historical stock data from the Internet to create fake trade blotters, sending out fraudulent account statements to clients and arranging wire transfers between Mr. Madoff's London and New York offices to create the impression that the firm was earning commissions from stock trades."

The SEC complaint alleged, "DiPascali helped generate bogus annual returns of 10 to 17 percent by fabricating backdated and fictitious trades that never occurred. The SEC further alleges that DiPascali helped Madoff cover up the fraud by preparing fake trade blotters, stock records, customer confirmations, Depository Trust Corporation (DTC) reports and other phantom books and records to substantiate the non-existent trading.

"DiPascali and Madoff ran an extraordinary and massive counterfeiting operation that concealed their fraud from investors and regulators alike," said Robert Khuzami, director of the SEC's Division of Enforcement. The site *Seeking Alpha* added, "DiPascali declined to identify any accomplices other than Madoff. To date, only Madoff, DiPascali and the firm's outside accountant David Friehling have been charged in connection to the $50-billion fraud, though authorities are said to be investigating at least ten other people."

Bernie, as he came to be known – as if his status as a folk character came straight out of a Woody Allen movie – had merged into popular culture after the media at first reported he committed a $50-billion-dollar scam, a figure few New Yorkers could wrap their minds around. Bear in mind that his criminal practices began years before the economy crashed, although it mirrored its get rich psychology. Madoff is thought to be in a league of his own: the Ponzi process itself now has a new name: "Madoffication."

As the courts looked into the details, that figure climbed to $65 billion. On the weekend before his sentencing the judge ruled he would have to give up his interest in all his properties. He then issued a whopping $171-billion-foreclosure order, three times the alleged size of the crime when it was first revealed.

His lawyers then said the "$177 billion" demand – it apparently went up after the first press reports – was exaggerated, as if differences in billions had no meaning.

The judge left his wife Ruth with a mere $2.5 million.

His lawyers argued he should only get 12 years in prison because of his age, (71), cooperation and his expression of "shame." They even denounced an "atmosphere of mob vengeance" even though his most vociferous critics were his own victims. Prosecutors rejected the argument, demanding instead a whopping 150-year prison term, the maximum.

The federal probation department recommended 50 years.

Finally, "M Day," July 30, 2009, came and Bernie went – sent away for a long, long time. Judge Denny Chin threw the book at him – the maximum sentence – to set an example, to warn others, to express how pissed off everyone was. Madoff said he will not appeal the sentence.

DANNY SCHECHTER

In his statement, Judge Chin explained that punishment has several purposes: First "retribution" for crimes that he characterized as "extraordinarily evil." Second, deterrence "and the symbolism is important here because the strongest possible message must be sent to those who would engage in similar conduct." And, finally, it was for the victims because, "Mr. Madoff's very personal betrayal struck at the rich and not so rich, the elderly living on retirement."

The media focused on well known victims like film director Steven Spielberg, who claimed to have lost $300 million, but tax returns uncovered by muckrakers at *Web of Deception* (www. webofdeception.com) found that he earlier reported $126,093 in income from Madoff. Many prominent people gravitated to Madoff because he was known for his consistent and, unusually high returns. Many assumed he had "insider" knowledge.

The judge referenced 133 letters he had received from victims as a basis for his decision.

The *Wall Street Journal* reported the day before Madoff's sentencing that just $1.2 billion, of some $13.2 billion in estimated net losses suffered by investors since December 1995, had been recovered.

Although Mrs. Madoff got to keep $2.5 million for her living expenses, she had to give back millions in property, and fur coats said to be worth $48,500. The government is suing some investors who took large amounts of money out through so-called clawback actions. Some of these investors, who want more, are suing the government.

Every report on the details seemed to dish up different numbers: The Associated Press reported: "At the time of Madoff's arrest, fictitious account statements showed thousands of clients had $65 billion. But investigators say he never traded securities, and instead used money from new investors to pay returns to existing clients."

Prosecutors said the total losses, which span decades, haven't been calculated. But, they said, "1,341 accounts opened since December 1995, alone suffered losses of $13.2 billion. The sheer scale of the fraud calls for severe punishment," the prosecutors demanded.

In a high-profile case such as his, the public and the media would not accept another normal Wall Street "settlement," where fines are paid to avoid incarceration. In this case, the judge did not just rule on the law but branded Madoff's action "evil." At the same time, Madoff's lawyer called the sentence "absurd" and writer Michael Wolf suggested on his *Newser* website (www.newser.com) it was because he is Jewish:

> The notion is that Bernie has come to represent the financial meltdown; he's symbolically paying for the whole thing. He's going to jail not just for the $15 billion he stole but for the other $6 or $7 trillion lost in the collapse.

Actually there were many Jews who opposed Madoff. *Vanity Fair* reported:

> Laura Goldman of the Tel Aviv-based LSG Capital decided not to invest with Madoff. She even sent anti-Madoff articles to members of the Palm Beach Country Club. "I was expecting a thank you, all I got back in return was a hostile response. Some of the Madoff investors said I was behaving unprofessionally and was bad-mouthing a competitor. Oh, they were nasty. Nasty! ... People called me an anti-Semite. I'm not only a Jew, I live in Israel."

Madoff's victims were not all rich or celebrities, despite the impression fostered by the victims. One of them, Lawrence Velvel wrote on *OpEdNews* (www.opednews.com):

Most of Madoff's victims are not the billionaires, "centa-mil-lionaires," hedge funds, and banks that the celebrity-driven mass media has focused on, thereby causing the public to believe that the victims of Bernard Madoff are all wealthy plutocrats. Most Madoff victims are, instead, "small people." They are people who usually started with little or nothing, as members of the working class or lower-middle class, as immigrants, as children of holocaust survivors. They are people who worked like dogs all their lives, finally saved up enough money to make an investment in Madoff, and now find themselves wiped out.

WHO ELSE WAS INVOLVED?

When Madoff told his sons, and then, the FBI about his crimes, the speculation was immediate: Who else was involved? Did he act alone in the spirit of that "lone gunman" who is blamed for all U.S. assassinations? Soon, sure enough the men operating the "feeder" funds that kept him in business, and others who profited through his largess, were being accused of crimes by financial regulators, who looked the other way when "Bernie" became one of the richest operators on the Street.

He was known for impeccable balance sheets and cozy associations with the big shots of the Jewish world of New York, Palm Beach, and even, Tel Aviv. In the shock of the disclosure of his perfidy, the *Ha'aretz* newspaper said he had done "more harm to Israel than Hamas." (He had been seen as a big shot, a big *macher* in Yiddish, and a respectable philanthropist.)

Sam Antar recognized a criminal technique in the way Madoff ingratiated himself to leaders in his community, with a veneer of philanthropic activity. Antar told me, "He built a wall of false integrity around him. He was the guy that, that was in with every single social crowd. In with, with all the charities. So everybody thought of Bernie Madoff as some kind of a god. Nobody questioned him.

"The SEC investigator that did that audit ... she says, 'How am I supposed to find the second set of books?' Well, you weren't trained to find the second set of books, which is another problem that we have. We don't have trained investigators, and we don't have trained experienced investigators working with the government authorities to be able to prosecute these criminals. And you can't just send one investigator to find out what's going on; you need sometimes a team of investigators."

The people he ripped off denounced him in court even as many had, for years, welcomed his reassurances of the high returns they thought he was getting for their money. Many had lobbied their *landsman* to please manage their money, secure in the belief he would come through for them. Some went to him believing insider (i.e., illegal) connections were the source of his success. In short, many were no less greedy, assuming that the only way he could deliver high returns so consistently was because he was flaunting the law by engaging in insider trading. As long as their neatly prepared monthly statements kept coming, no questions were raised.

Madoff's crimes received the media attention they did, not just because of their scale, but because he had also ripped off the rich and famous. The millions of poorer subprime borrowers who have lost homes because of Wall Street scams were not, in contrast, considered sympathetic enough victims.

In Madoff's case, 15,400 investors filed claims. That number had skyrocketed to meet a deadline, the end of June 2009, set by Irving H. Picard, the court-appointed trustee in charge of the claims process.

The *New York Times* reported: "The claims tally adds a new metric to the enormous fraud, which was already remarkable for the amount of paper profits wiped out ($64.8 billion), the amount of cash that flowed through the Ponzi scheme since its inception ($170 billion) and the number of years the fraud continued undetected (nearly 30, according to the government prosecutors)."

The list of victims even included his sons Mark and Andrew who said they were out $15 million in compensation and investments. Andrew reportedly called this a "father-son betrayal of biblical proportions."

Many investors believed his sons were in on it. His secretary told *Vanity Fair* that her boss carefully planned the final act of his Ponzi scheme, confiding supposedly in no one, insulating his family from responsibility. Suspicion surrounded his wife Ruth who eventually issued a statement expressing sympathy for those who were defrauded, sounding like a betrayed woman:

> From the moment I learned from my husband that he had committed an enormous fraud, I have had two thoughts — first, that so many people who trusted him would be ruined financially and emotionally, and second, that my life with the man I have known for over 50 years was over … I am embarrassed and ashamed. Like everyone else, I feel betrayed and confused. The man who committed this horrible fraud is not the man whom I have known for all these years.

Despite her statement and profession of innocence, Ruth Madoff would be sued too, as this release from the Trustee's office explained:

> Irving L. Picard, the Trustee appointed to liquidate the business of Bernard L. Madoff Investment Securities LLC (BLMIS), filed suit today against Ruth Madoff, the wife of Bernard L.

Madoff, seeking to recapture at least $44,822,355 in funds that were transferred from BLMIS during the past six years directly to Mrs. Madoff or for her benefit to companies in which she was an investor.

In the Trustee's complaint, filed in bankruptcy court in Manhattan by the Trustee's law firm, Baker & Hostetler LLP, Mr. Picard details 111 transactions which he alleges were fraudulent transfers or conveyances recoverable under the bankruptcy code.

Noting that "for decades, Mrs. Madoff lived a life of splendor using the money of BLMIS's customers," Mr. Picard states in the complaint that "regardless of whether or not Mrs. Madoff knew of the fraud her husband perpetrated" money she received from BLMIS should be recovered "to the extent possible for the benefit of BLMIS and its defrauded customers."

"Under pressure by investors claiming that not enough money has been recovered, Picard is clearly playing to the public," business journalist Gary Weiss commented on his blog (www. garyweiss.blogspot.com), "Certainly Ruth is not the first wife to have benefited from the thievery of her husband. Down through history, from Mrs. Jesse James to Mrs. Lansky to Mrs. Gotti and, of course, our beloved if fictional Carmela Soprano, wives have enjoyed lavish lifestyles because of their husbands' criminality, and I imagine they could have been sued by the feds by the same logic that Picard is using. I guess there might have to be a bankruptcy involved, but maybe not. Prosecutors can be creative, after all."

The court would order Mrs. Madoff to file a monthly financial report itemizing all personal expenses above $100. Picard had found a hundred and a eleven wire transfers from the Madoff firm to her bank account, and noted that she was listed as holding an interest in her husband's British affiliate.

Ruth Madoff was known as a serial shopaholic, addicted to almost unlimited consumption of luxury items. She bought an expensive cashmere sweater the day after her husband was arrested. She made charitable donations with the company's credit card financed by stolen money, money stolen from other charities, "Even after Bernie was behind bars, Ruth was out spending like there was no tomorrow," wrote Jerry Oppenheimer in his book *Madoff With the Money*, an examination of the family's criminal background that contends he was obscenely materialistic with no redeeming values.

"The evidence of Ruth's piggishness was in black and white," Oppenheimer concluded after studying court records itemizing their American Express account. "Her charges in December 2007 to January 2008, after the markets melted down, were $29,887.94. The total Amex bill for the Madoff clan was $100,121.99." No wonder the trustee Irving Picard would later sue her and her sons for millions more.

Later, when a juicy book came out by Sheryl Weinstein, a Madoff client and executive of the Jewish charity Hadassah, claiming she had an affair with Madoff for twenty years, Mrs. Madoff's attorney commented that this fresh scandal within a scandal, "Stands as a powerful reminder to those who say that Ruth must have known of her husband's criminal scheme, that there are some things that some spouses – however close they are – do not share with each other."

Weinstein's book is among many to come probing Madoff's personality, and upbringing in a family that also ran illegal stock schemes. Some focus on his personal history; others show him as emblematic of "lax" times, and as an arch criminal even though his actual operation was pedestrian if systematic. It's much easier to indict an errant, and now larger than life individual, than probe the entangled institutional environment in which he operated. Some even ask who will play him in the inevitable movie to come?

He swam in a swamp of like minded-operators. Jailing him does not drain the swamp.

A new lawsuit against Madoff, filed in October 2009, contends he promoted a "culture of sexual deviance" at his New York headquarters that featured vast quantities of cocaine and drug-fueled parties with topless waitresses.

"Madoff's affinity for escorts, masseuses and attractive female employees was well known in the office culture," the complaint filed by California lawyer Joseph Cotchett on behalf of dozens of fraud victims read. It charges that "a significant amount of the money stolen from investors went towards these lavish indulgences as well as other expenses for his employees, family and favorite feeders."

The suit charges that a number of the "feeders" brought investors to Madoff and also took part in the "sexual revelry" including trysts on his office couch. It also contends that coke was so rampant in his Manhattan headquarters that it was known as the "North Pole."

This lawsuit is not just about his alleged sexual practices. It also charges that he was in cahoots with major financial institutions including JPMorgan Chase. It suggests that a conspiracy to defraud involved many more key players.

Bernard Madoff's psychology led to even more speculation, as a blog called *The Real Wolf of Wall Street* asked, "What was his motivation? How did he rationalize things? How did he look in the mirror each day and make sense of it all? Did he feel guilty? Remorseful? Was he conflicted? Was he worried about getting caught?"

Actually, in at least one conversation when Madoff talked publicly about his business on the Internet, he comes off very self-assured, even cocky. Among his comments:

I suppose you could program a computer to violate a regulation, but we haven't gotten there yet …

I'm very close to the regulators … my niece married one.

Now, no one is going to run a benefit for Wall Street, so whenever I go down to Washington and meet with the SEC and
complain to them that the industry is either over-regulated or
the burdens are too great, they all start to roll their eyes, just
like all of our children do whenever we talk about the good
old days.

Today, basically the big money on Wall Street is made by taking risks. Firms were driven into that business – including us
– because you couldn't make money charging commissions,
primarily because the rates were lowered and because of the
regulatory infrastructure you had to have dealing with clients.

So what's clear here is that he understood that regulations would
cost him money, and like many in the industry, opposed them.

And what about the victims? What the hell were they thinking? Why did they ignore the obvious warning-signs of a Ponzi
scheme? These aren't widows and orphans, after all; they're
the wealthiest and most sophisticated investors in the world.
So why would they blindly trust someone, without doing even
the slightest bit of due diligence? Was it plain old greed that
blinded them, or was there something more profound at work
– some basic human frailty that makes all people, both rich
and poor alike, susceptible to bubbles, Ponzi schemes, and
irrational exuberance?

Madoff targeted people like himself, reported Reuters:

While basically insolvent from the start, it feeds, fraudulently, on the natural desire to obtain financial gain.

"It's human nature and psychology, it's preying on individuals that are vulnerable," Maria Yip, a forensic accounting expert at Yip Associates, told Reuters. "Successful Ponzi schemes prey on close-knit communities of victims, so-called affinity groups, [to] which the perpetrators of the frauds are either already linked to or can tap into."

And so the process or rationalization goes into high gear, or so suggests the *Real Wolf* blog:

At first, when he looks in the mirror, he feels sick to his stomach. But slowly he becomes desensitized; he gets "used to" things. As the years pass, he maintains his sanity by tucking his scam into a tiny corner of his mind – barricading it behind walls of rationalizations. He says to himself, "Everyone on Wall Street is a crook, so why am I any worse? Merrill Lynch bankrupted Orange County, for Chrissake; Prudential Bache stole a billion dollars from grandmas and grandpas; Salomon Brothers rigged the Treasury market! My scam is mere child's play compared to those!"

He even rationalizes taking his friends to the cleaners. "It's no big deal," he says to himself. "They're rich anyway, so they can afford to lose a few bucks."

For years Madoff remained in the shadows even as a shadow banking system emerged on a giant scale building his network of victims through referrals and from so-called feeder funds which sent him customers for part of the take.

Of all the reporting on Madoff, few have probed as deeply as Mark Mitchell, a reporter with controversial businessman

Patrick Byrne's *Deep Capture* blog (www.deepcapture.com). (Sam Antar and Gary Weiss, with whom I have spoken, both have denounced Patrick Byrne and claim he is engaging in nefarious practices.) While I have no way of verifying Mitchell's allegations that link Madoff to other criminal enterprises, they deserve to be scrutinized by financial reporters with far more access. Mitchell wrote:

> Madoff's brokerages engaged in naked short selling (offloading stock that had not been borrowed or purchased – phantom stock), likely on behalf of miscreant hedge funds looking to drive down prices. In fact, Madoff successfully lobbied the SEC to enact a rule that allowed market makers, such as himself, to engage in naked short selling. At the SEC, this rule was called "The Madoff Exception."

> … in other words, Madoff's operation was not just the largest known swindle in history. It was also a phantom stock machine. And that makes it but one participant in a much bigger scandal – a crime that might have brought us to the brink of a second Great Depression.

> … it was no surprise to learn that one of Madoff's most important "feeders" was Fairfield Greenwich Group, part-owned by a "prominent investor" named Philip Taub. Philip's father, Said Taub, a "prominent investor" from Europe, had been an important "feeder," along with Michael Milken's cronies and other people affiliated with the Genovese Mafia, for the Investors Overseas Services Ponzi.

> Another Madoff "feeder" (and a partner with Madoff in a brokerage called Cohmad) was a "prominent investor" named

> Robert Jaffe. Previously, while working for E. F. Hutton, Jaffe ran money for the Anguilo brothers, the Boston dons of the Genovese organized crime family ...

I am not endorsing these claims without my own deep investigation of them, but surely Madoff's other business associates besides his high-profile "victims" deserve to be probed.

There was one more name in his list, according to Mitchell:

> This is the sad story of the French aristocrat Monsieur Rene Thierry Magon de La Villehuchet ... this French aristocrat also raised billions of dollars for the greatest Ponzi scheme the world has ever known – a Ponzi scheme that entailed illegal naked short selling that probably helped topple the American financial system.

A few days after the Ponzi scheme became public, police entered a luxurious office in a New York skyscraper. On the desk, there were pills (what kind of pills has not yet been revealed). On the floor, there was a box cutter. There was no note.

But there he was – Monsieur Rene Thierry Magon de La Villehuchet.

Dead.

They said it was "suicide."

On October 25, 2009, another Madoff associate, Palm Beach, Florida billionaire Jeffrey Picower, was also found very dead at the bottom of the pool at his mansion alongside the Atlantic Ocean. According to Reuters, "The trustee handling the Madoff fraud case, Irving Picard, said in court documents filed in U.S. bankruptcy court that Picower, newly listed as one of the 400 wealthiest Americans by *Forbes* magazine, was complicit in the fraud." He was being accused of being the biggest beneficiary of Madoff's scheme, "having withdrawn either directly or through the entities he controlled more than $7.2 billion of other investors' money." He had denied the charges as false.

Soon, Madoff's invisibility turned into super-visibility.

He got the full celebrity treatment with more than one hundred TV crews and ten satellite trucks staked out to "go live" with any "breaking news" outside one of his court hearings. His trip to the courtroom was shadowed live by TV helicopters offering a hyped up play-by-play. In one encounter there was almost a physical altercation between Madoff and a pushy TV cameramen outside his Upper Eastside building.

I spoke with one correspondent from Fox News who asked me "What are you doing here?"

I said, "I'm making a film in part about the role of the media in exposing this story."

He quipped, "That will be a short documentary."

His comment was a humorous admission that most of the media has been late to the story if not complicit in keeping it covered up so long. Once the media made it a big deal, the public went ballistic: Standing outside the courthouse in Lower Manhattan with hundreds of journalists and TV crews from around the world, I spoke to Richard Friedman who lost over a million dollars. I asked, "How did he get away with this for so long?"

"I wondered that myself," he replied, "how a person could run a scam for so many years without being detected – that was one of the players who do as much business with each other (with few questions asked) as they compete against each other. It can't be a scam. Nobody can successfully run a scam for that long," suggesting that the government was in on it.

His answer to my question about that: "Of course there is a cover-up. The government does not want people to know how grossly negligent the SEC was in investigating him. The largest fraud in history and they didn't know about it."

Actually Madoff appeared before the SEC on more than one occasion. His niece, Shana Madoff, even married an SEC investigator, Eric Swanson. Court documents showed that the SEC closed an investigation in 2006 after Madoff responded to questions with false testimony.

The SEC's chief watchdog in New York, Meaghan Cheung, said that she missed it too, telling the *New York Post*: "Why are you taking a mid-level staff person and making me responsible for the failure of the American economy?"

The agency's former head, Harvey Pitt, said, "The U.S. Securities and Exchange Commission should have apologized for missing Bernard Madoff's $65-billion Ponzi scheme."

In early September 2009, the SEC issued a report that reviewed its failed investigations into Madoff's crimes. Madoff said he was "lucky" that they blew their probe. The AP reported:

> Disgraced financier Bernard Madoff tried by turns to bully and impress the federal examiners who looked into his business, but the investigators managed by themselves to botch the probes and enable Madoff's multi-billion-dollar fraud to continue for nearly two decades, a new report shows.
>
> A trove of revelations came to light in the report by the Securities and Exchange Commission inspector general, David Kotz ... The 477-page document paints in excruciating detail how the SEC investigations of Madoff were bungled over 16 years – with disputes among agency inspection staffers over the findings, lack of communication among SEC offices in various cities and repeated failures to act on credible complaints from outsiders that formed a sea of red flags.

DANNY SCHECHTER

NBC reported on Madoff's version of the event:

> One portion of the report shows how Madoff thought he was toast in May 2006, but got away scot-free thanks to SEC investigators who dropped the ball on his case.

> "I thought it was the end game, over," Madoff was quoted as saying in the report. He also said he felt fortunate SEC officials didn't call to check up on the account number he'd provided to the investigators.

> "After all this, I got away lucky," Madoff said.

The SEC's reportedly admitted incompetence on the agency's part but some financial bloggers think it may have been an act of "self-exoneration," covering up something more insidious. Wrote Professor Jayanth R. Varma on his blog (www.iimahd.ernet.in/~jrvarma/blog):

> I think the report pushes the incompetence story a bit too much to the point where it almost reads like a whitewash job. I counted the term "inexperienced" or "lack of experience" being used 25 times in the report and that count excludes several other similar phrases. When an investigator is a good attorney, the report complains that the person had no trading experience; when the person had trading experience, it complains about his lack of investigative experience.

> I am a firm believer in Hanlon's Razor: "Never attribute to malice what can be adequately explained by stupidity," but the report's furious attempt to document incompetence makes one wonder whether it is trying to cover up something worse than incompetence.

In an essay on one of the many recent books about Madoff, the *Financial Times* reviewer John Kay noted, "The SEC, is populated by box-tickers whose job is to assess procedure, not to raise queries. Most importantly, the downside for junior SEC officials from annoying rich and powerful Wall Street figures was far greater than the upside in exposing the fraud of the century. Until that changes, there will be little to prevent another Bernie Madoff."

A month after he was sent to federal prison, Madoff met with two lawyers to whom he admitted that he was surprised that his scheme lasted so long. "There were several times that I met with the SEC and thought 'they got me,'" Madoff told his visitors, according to ABC News.

The agency had many files and documents alleging guilt. A Boston-based investigator blew the whistle on Madoff nine years before his admission of guilt.

Harry Markopolos testified before Congress of his own ordeal in trying to stop the Ponzi scheme. He submitted a report of over 100 pages explaining:

> I find it difficult to compress my testimony because there were so many victims, the damages have been vast, and the scandal has ruined or harmed so many of our citizens. I feel that by writing this testimony in narrative form, the public will better understand what steps my team and I took, the order in which we took them, along with how and why we took them. The details will also afford the committee the information necessary to ask the right questions and hopefully aid the committee in ferreting out the truth and in restructuring the SEC which currently is non-functional and, as witnessed by the Madoff scandal, is harmful to our capital markets and harmful to our nation's reputation as a financial leader around the globe.

If you are thinking it was "All in the Family," you may be right. But it wasn't a Mafia-type family but an extended financial one, a global community often operating on the edges of, or outside, the law.

Madoff was one of the players who do as much business with each other as they compete against each other. The notion of counterparties is pervasive in the financial industry where risks and deals are shared. No wonder there is the suggestion that much of this industry runs like one big Ponzi scheme.

Clearly the regulators had no interest in shutting him down even though for ten years this one Boston-based investigator petitioned the SEC to do so.

I asked John Coffee, the Columbia Law School's expert on corporate crime about Madoff: "I think our regulatory system failed, and failed badly over basically the last six or seven years, in failing to spot a Mr. Madoff," he explained, adding, "although in fairness Mr. Madoff has been a crook for almost 20 or 25 years, and we can't just pick on the last couple of years there."

One of my other experts on corporate crime, Sam Antar, said we still don't have all the facts about with whom he wheeled and dealed. "What's happening with Bernie Madoff," he told me, "is that he's protecting the second, third, and fourth tier from not just criminal liability, but civil liability in particular. He's protecting family members and close friends from possible civil liability, from having to pay back money to the victims."

A debate about Madoff's own personality has emerged due to a slew of tell-all books. One is by Jerry Oppenheimer of the *New York Post*, which milked the story to the max. The *Post* quotes him: "Many Madoff acquaintances were stunned by his massive con, as they considered him 'the dumbest man on Earth.'"

Oppenheimer also claims the case is far from over, with "the Russian mob, the Israeli mob and people." His book suggests he was mentored by members of the Chicago mob. And what of rumors about other government and international connections? A widely quoted financial website, *International Forecaster* (www.theinternationalforecaster.com) suggests there is much more to investigate:

> Americans are well aware of the Madoff scandal, but procedures used in his conviction leave many unanswered questions.
>
> Conspiracy charges were never brought against Mr. Madoff. We had information we published just prior to the story breaking of what Mr. Madoff had been doing. Our contacts not only gave us the story, but details of how the funds were transferred from NYC to Israel and other offshore locations, such as the Cayman Islands, Belize and Switzerland. There were many wire transfers and also the physical transfer of bearer bonds to these locations.
>
> What was interesting was Mr. Madoff's association with veteran officers in the U.S. military. That leads us to intelligence sources that have told us that Mr. Madoff was operating his scheme with elements of the CIA, the Russian-Israeli mafia and the Mossad. This would explain Mr. Madoff's closed trial.
>
> A number of banks were used in the operation. The Israeli Discount Bank, Bank Leumi, Bank of New York, Chase and Citibank's private banking facility.
>
> There is no question funds were being used by government agencies just as were those of AIG.

These suggestions may or may not be true, but a real life conspiracy like the Madoff scam inspires many other conspiratorial suggestions.

We live, of course, in a globalized economy where financial crime is also often international. Critics in the U.S. challenge a "shadow banking system" but, outside the U.S., there are reports of Italian financiers working with the mafia, and even underground banks. *Financial Crime Online* (www.financialcrimeonline.com) reported on one, suggesting there may be many others available for laundering illegal transactions like the ones documented in the Madoff affair:

Police in south China say they have broken up an underground bank that illegally sent 10 billion yuan (1.46 billion in U.S. dollars) of laundered criminal cash abroad since 2004. Around 200 police officers raided the underground bank in Fangchenggang in May this year and seized 70 deposit books, 590 bank cards, two cars, six computers and 680,000 yuan of cash. They also froze 327 banking accounts involved in the money-laundering case with book value of 47.5 million yuan ...

The group acted as a bank and offered financial services to criminals that wanted to move their money out of the China. Since the group had no real financial network, they had to rely on the infrastructure of other banks to wire transfer funds. All they did is open accounts and use these to funnel criminal funds for third (criminal) parties.

Some Chinese investors who want to speculate in foreign real estate and other markets have turned to underground banks, such as the one run by the alleged gang, to evade government restrictions on money transfers. But such limits have been eased in recent years. Criminals have always been drawn to similar setups since they allow for a anonymous shell that hides their own identities.

The real question is: will we ever get to the bottom of the larger financial crime wave that caused much of this crisis with encouragement from government agencies and politicians? Madoff may put a human face on one aspect of the corporate crime wave, even as more money disappeared through institutional practices, not just individual wrong-doing.

In June 2009, the head of the FBI said the bureau was investigating 1,300 securities fraud cases, including many Ponzi schemes, as well as more than 580 corporate fraud cases. Most of these cases get little attention. One investigator told the press "there is a 'Ponzimonium' underway."

Putting Bernie Madoff behind bars may satisfy national indignation, but it won't solve the deeper problem argues online columnist Eric Lotke of the *Campaign for America's Future* (www.ourfuture.org):

> This isn't just about Madoff. This is about the system in which Madoff's scam took place. This is about systemic fraud and malpractice, the cultural trade of due diligence for easy profit. It's about conflicts of interest where companies paid ratings agencies for their ratings. It's about ideological blinders that let regulators and the Federal Reserve look the other way while banks turned into betting parlors.
>
> So Madoff got 150 years for breaking into the bank. Fine.
>
> But what about the guard who was asleep out front? What about the clerk who forgot to lock the door? What about the $300 billion that Citigroup walked out with from one vault,

and the $200 billion that AIG took from another? Does anybody know where that money went or what we got for it? Don't they get in trouble too? Did you know that, or do you know why, Goldman Sachs is paying its biggest bonus payouts in its 140 year history?

Actually, Madoff did not receive the longest sentence for financial fraud. He was only in fourth place in the seriousness of sentence sweepstakes. Number 1 was Sholam Weiss who got 845 years for his role in the collapse of an insurance company. His co-defendant, Keith Pound, drew 740 years for the Number 2 spot. At Number 3 was Norman Schmidt who ran "high-yield" investment schemes. When convicted, he drew 330 years. None of these long sentences appears to have deterred Mr. Madoff.

Just before he arrived at his new home at Building No. 1 at the federal prison in Butner, North Carolina, the *New York Post* spoke to inmates. Some expressed admiration according to their unnamed source: "He got a lot of respect from other inmates because he didn't tell on anybody, he didn't take everybody down with him. Some of the inmates admired that."

There are still many unanswered questions about where the money went and even the possibility that Madoff was part of some larger plot.

Investigative reporter Wayne Madsen reported: "The failure of federal prosecutors to bring conspiracy charges against Bernard Madoff, the mega-billion-dollar Ponzi scammer, who pleaded guilty March 12th to eleven counts of fraud and other crimes in U.S. District Court in Manhattan, is providing cover to those who pulled the strings on Madoff's illegal operation."

Madsen spoke to a former close aide to Madoff who related how he handled a number of transactions personally for the man. The source said that Madoff was running a special type of "pump and dump" scheme. The source said Madoff would "pump money out of the system and dump it out to another place." When asked what that "other place" was, the source replied, "Israel."

In Israel, the newspaper *Ha'aretz* reported:

> A number of quite worried clients have shown up at the doors of the best-known Israeli law firms specializing in tax law in the past few days asking for an urgent consultation. The fears that Picard will reveal the names and amounts, or be forced to reveal them as the result of a lawsuit, has caused the large number of requests.

> "Already at this stage it is possible to say that large sums of money reached Madoff's funds from Swiss banks and various tax havens," said Dr. Avi Nov, a lawyer specializing in tax planning. "Usually the money there is not money that the owners are interested in reporting to the authorities.

> "Here there was an excellent linkup of sophisticated investors who knew how to avoid paying taxes in Israel, and funds specializing in hiding their true purposes. Private investors in Israel always spoke about Madoff's returns. European banks recommended investing with him, and when they heard the success stories, they asked to increase their investment," said Nov.

The *Guardian* noted that billions are still unaccounted for:

> So far Irving Picard, the court-appointed trustee of Madoff's collapsed firm, has recovered just $1.2 billion on behalf of investors. It is a small return for a six-month investigation that involved the U.S. Justice Department, the financial regula-

tor, the Securities and Exchange Commission, Picard's office and the U.S. marshals.

If Picard is to narrow the gap between asset recovery and escalating investor losses, it now seems likely that he will have to focus more on those who did business with Madoff rather than rely on tracking down his personal assets.

Although those assets give a fascinating insight into the fraudster's lifestyle they cover only a fraction of investors' losses.

Canadian columnist Diane Francis also wonders where the money went. She consulted a tax expert knowledgeable about offshore maneuvers, who told her:

My guess is that the money is probably in the Cayman Islands where most of these funds go from Anglo Saxon economies. The Cayman Islands cooperates with law enforcement officials from other countries and will surrender information if there's a search warrant involving a beneficial owner. But in this case, I would suspect that Madoff's wife, sons or a trusted relative have signing authority or beneficial ownership. If they haven't been charged, the Cayman Islands won't disclose or surrender any information about what they may have on deposit there [or may have received and transferred elsewhere] without search warrants.

According to this source, here's a crook get away with stashing money in secret havens:

1. He sets up a company to act as advisor to his funds in the Cayman Islands [or another secrecy haven]. This company has a management role – call it Ffodam [Madoff back-

wards] Limited. Ffodam earns 10% in fees on the capital raised and puts this money into Ffodam Limited.

2. The beneficial owner is not Bernie Madoff. So when Bernie pleads guilty and a search warrant is served all over the world asking for any and all information and assets in his name, nothing happens unless he is the beneficial owner which he won't be for obvious reasons.

3. They can't touch these assets or even find out if anything is there. It's the perfect crime.

But beyond the actual losses, there was another surreal dimension to his conviction. With Madoff getting what may or may not have been his just rewards, there was a sense that somehow corporate criminals are getting theirs. He's become a larger than life symbolic substitute for those vast institutional practices that now may not be pursued.

When *Portfolio*, a now defunct business magazine, convened its own panel of experts, it ran up against considerable equivocation in legal circles – a sense that the massive theft by many Wall Street firms did not meet a prosecutable standard. "The problem isn't a lack of targets. Hatred of financial executives comes cheap these days. Instead, we're missing something bigger: a Leader (capital L) with the ego, hubris, and imagination to bring Wall Street to heel."

Many of the experts the magazine reached out to seemed jaded, as lawyer Stanley Arkin did, insisting that "… most current and former top executives are guilty not of criminal behavior but of poor judgment. It's surely hubris, but how is that actionable?"

Hubris? Maybe. But public rage is likely to press for more prosecutions. *Portfolio* concluded, "If the executives do go to trial, look out. Justice depends upon the willingness of a jury to weigh facts without fear or favor. And it's going to be difficult to find a group of people who are unaffected by the economic collapse. The law, therefore, is not the executives' biggest enemy. Anger is."

Look what happened to Madoff. His sentence drew cheers in the courtroom and widespread approval in a media that has not been as zealous about crimes against lesser victims. Some even suggested that he be tortured, too.

Did he deserve a 150-year sentence? His lawyer called it "absurd." But many in the media were far more punitive in spirit. John Gapper of the *Financial Times* said such a long sentence was very rare:

There was a moment during Bernard Madoff's sentencing hearing in Manhattan on Monday when it became obvious that the 71-year-old fraudster was going down for a very, very long time, indeed.

It was when Judge Denny Chin cited the case of a woman who went to see Mr. Madoff after her husband's death to be reassured that his legacy was safe. The avuncular titan put his arm around her shoulder and assured her that all would be well; she could trust him.

Fraud is often a difficult crime to prosecute, and for which to obtain punitive sentences. It is complex and hard for juries to understand and the harm it causes – the losses to investors in the companies involved – are intangible compared with violent and physical crimes.

If someone is mugged and robbed in the street, both the damage and the way in which it was caused are obvious for all to see. In cases where a chief executive fiddles [with] the accounts to cover losses, how it was done and the way that it hurts mutual fund investors are harder to grasp.

So Bernard Madoff was a prosecutor's dream – the Hollywood incarnation of a white-collar criminal. He dealt face-to-face with many of his victims and looked them straight in the eye; he did not merely taint the value of the investments but squandered the cash they entrusted to him.

But was the sentence fair? Not according to the *MacDoctor* blog (www.macdoctor.co.nz):

The absurdly long sentence makes no particular sense as a punishment (Madoff, at 71, will be unlikely to make 15 years, let alone 150) nor does it make much sense as a deterrent (this kind of crime is committed by people who think they are too smart to be caught and who would be terrified of 150 weeks in prison, let alone years). It does not even make sense as a protection of society as Madoff is never going to be in a position to do this again. Therefore a punishment of this length can only be put down to one thing: Revenge.

People have been embarrassed. I don't mean financial embarrassment, although there is that, too. I mean true 100% "egg on your face" and "call me a donkey" embarrassment. And least we get all self-righteous and blather on about all the mom-and-pop investors who have been financially destroyed (and who have a legitimate grievance against Madoff), the people we are talking about here are bankers, lawyers and politicians. People who should have known better.

DANNY SCHECHTER

Yet there is so much more to look into in this case. Many unanswered questions. And does the U.S. government want the full story out?

Many believe that since he has been convicted and sent away, the story is over.

In the *New York Times*, Frank Rich said Madoff's sentence had a ho-hum response because his crime didn't seem so spectacular and because of what else was going on: "The estimated $65 billion involved in Madoff's flimflam is dwarfed by the more than $2.5 trillion paid so far by American taxpayers to bail out those masters of Wall Street's universe. AIG alone has already left us on the hook for $180 billion. It's hard for those who didn't have money with Madoff to get worked up about him when so many of the era's real culprits have slipped away scot-free. Already some of those same players are up to similarly greedy shenanigans, again, now that the coast seems to be clear."

Economist Loretta Napoleoni, who appears in my film, *Plunder*, asked in her book *Rogue Economics*, "What if the root of the Madoff scandal and of the credit crunch which crippled the world economy and revealed the nakedness of capitalism … is something much worse defining the system itself, not just a few bad apples or culprits." She believes that Wall Street became a Ponzi scheme which "can be described as the best formula for creating and inflating a financial bubble."

Futurist James Howard Kuntsler believes major crimes are pervasive but probably won't be exposed:

Something like $14 trillion worth of nominal dollars is being sucked into a cosmic vortex never to be seen again. It was last seen in the spectral forms of so many collateralized debt obligations, credit default swaps, so-called structured investment vehicles and other now-obvious frauds. That giant sucking sound we hear means the process is still underway, and the "money" disappearing into yawning oblivion will out-pace any effort orchestrated by the Federal Reserve and the U.S. Treasury to replace it ...

Notice the two words largely absent from whatever public dis-cussion exists around these matters – "swindle" and "fraud." The reason they're missing is because if they happened to enter the conversation, something would have to be done about them, namely investigations and prosecutions.

Once again, it is up to the public to demand accountability. One big fish is in the tank; many others are swimming away.

CHAPTER 2

THE WHITE-COLLAR PRISON GANG

M ove over Ayran Brotherhood and Blackstone Rangers, there's a new prison gang forming on cellblocks across America. Here are some of its possible members:

- **Jeffrey Skilling:** age 55, former CEO of Enron, 24 years

- **Andrew Fastow:** age 47, former CFO of Enron, 6 years

- **Bernard Ebbers:** age 67, former CEO of WorldCom, 25 years

- **Dennis Kozlowski:** age 62, CEO of Tyco International, 25 years

- **Joseph Nacchio:** age 60, former Qwest CEO, 6 years

- **John Rigas:** age 84, founder of Adelphia Communications, 12 years

- **Timothy J. Rigas:** age 53, former CFO of Adelphia Communications, 17 years

- **Conrad Black:** age 64, former newspaper magnate, 6.5 years

- **Walter Forbes:** age 66, former chairman of Cendant Corp., 12 years and seven months

- **Martin Frankel:** age 54, investor who looted insurers, 17 years

- **Samuel Israel:** age 46, Bayou Group, securtities fraudster, 20 years

- **Sholam Weiss:** age 55, $125-million-insurance thief, 845 years

Note that none of the felons on this list were implicated in the crimes connected to the current financial crisis. The *Financial Times'* Gillian Tett worries this may be sending a bad signal:

> After all, no amount of twiddling with Basel rules or pious statements about bonuses will ever scare a financier as much as the thought of jail.
>
> Moreover, without some retribution it will also be hard to persuade voters that finance is really being reformed, or has any credibility or moral authority. That is bad for politicians and regulators. However, it is also bad for bankers too. So, in the months ahead, keep a close eye on what happens to the legal cases in the system and, above all, watch to see just how many do (or do not) quietly die, compared to those S & L days.

Bear in mind as well how corrupt practices encourage a corruption of a society's values leading to the acceptance of a "whatever works" outlook. Here's a sobering example from China, a country that often executes corrupt businessmen:

A six-year-old girl has become a media darling in China on her first day of school by expressing her aspiration to become a "corrupt official" when she grows up, state media said.

The young student stated her aspirations in a televised interview that was posted on a southern China website, leading bloggers to describe her comments as "a reflection of social reality," the *Southern Metropolis Daily* reported.

"When I grow up I want to be an official," said the girl, whose face was blurred to protect her identity.

"What kind of official?" the interviewer asked.

"A corrupt official because corrupt officials have a lot of things," she replied.

CHAPTER 3

THE CRIMES OF WALL STREET

f the *New York Times* is able to come up with a list, so can I. Only mine is longer and itemizes some (but I am sure not all) of the shadowy practices on Wall Street:

• Fraud and control frauds

• Insider trading

• Manufacturing asset bubbles

• Theft and conspiracy

• Misrepresentation ("cooking the books")

• Ponzi schemes

• False accounting and "relaxing" reporting requirements

• Embezzling

• Diverting funds into obscenely high salaries and obscene bonuses

• Bilking investors, customers and homeowners, lapses of fiduciary responsibility

- Looting of companies by private equity firms

- Conflicts of interest

- Mesmerizing regulators

- Manipulating and monopolizing markets

- Tax frauds and "phantom" assets

- Making loans and then arranging that they fail

- Engineering phony financial products and statements

- Misleading the public and lobbying for bailouts to subsidize shady speculation

Financial frauds and other crimes are on the rise in the United States, reported the *Economist*, citing figures from 2008. (Bear in mind, these statistics probably underestimate the scale of the problem.)

Over 730,000 counts of suspected financial wrongdoing were recorded in America last year, according to recent data from the Treasury Department's Financial Crimes Enforcement Network. Institutions such as banks, insurers and casinos are required by law to report suspicious activities to federal authorities under 20 categories.

Financial institutions filed nearly 13% more reports of fraud compared with 2007, accounting for almost half of the increase in total filings. The number of mortgage frauds alone rose by 23% to almost 65,000.

Not all of these crimes were related to activities on Wall Street, but increasingly many are. It is no wonder that there are a growing number of "forensic accountants" being hired to try to detect and stop the frauds. The *Arizona Republic* reported:

> There are about 37,000 certified fraud examiners working to uncover an estimated **$994 billion in fraud schemes in the United States** [in 2008], according to the Association of Certified Fraud Examiners.
>
> **$175,000**: Median loss among reported fraud cases
>
> **27 percent**: Percent of fraud cases from financial institutions or government agencies
>
> **17–30 months**: Estimated duration of a typical fraud scheme before detection

Those monitoring fraud say it is on the rise. Kelly Jackson Higgins reported on *Security Dark Reading* (www.darkreading.com) in October 2009:

> A former Wachovia Bank executive who had handled insider fraud incidents says banks are in denial about just how massive the insider threat problem is within their institutions. Meanwhile, the economic crisis appears to be exacerbating the risk, with 70 percent of financial institutions saying they have experienced a case of data theft by one of their employees in the past 12 months, according to new survey data.
>
> Shirley Inscoe, who spent 21 years at Wachovia handling insider fraud investigations and fraud prevention, says banks

don't want to talk about the insider fraud, and many aren't aware that it's an **"epic problem."**

David Russell who, worked on Wall Street for 20 years, said the culture there rationalized pushing the limits and skirting the law: "Wall Street hires extremely smart people, these are people who have gone to the best business schools. These are people who have been trained and over-trained. They have been licensed and all this stuff. You can't tell me after you've learned how to digest a financial statement, like these guys have, that you didn't see something wrong with those books. That's bull. Absolute bull."

Despite protestations, he said the people on the inside knew what was happening but didn't care as long as they got big payouts: "They saw it but their attitude is, man, that's not gonna hit me, let me see if I can get a couple of more of these checks and then once I'm gone, if the house of cards falls apart, who the hell cares?"

Russell believed that these bankers had been getting away with this for so long, they started to forget it was illegal in the first place: "These people knew they were putting out infected stuff but because the system was rigged for such a long time they got used to getting away [with it]. They were allowed to be illegal for so long that they didn't even know that they were illegal until somebody called them on it."

The *Clusterstock* blog (www.businessinsider.com/cluster-stock) confirmed Russell's point this way:

There is a sick psychology of entitlement on Wall Street that was created during the bubble years. Many simply cannot believe that they do not deserve huge pay packages. Their brains have not caught up with the idea that they are working in broken institutions that would be unable to pay to keep the lights on if not for the fact that Washington has given them billions of taxpayer dollars.

It seemed hard for Russell to talk about it because he had benefited from the system and was once an admirer of Bernie Madoff because he was considered a market leader. In the end he was shocked: "I think that none of us, including myself who worked on Wall Street for 20 years, I never ever expected, I didn't think that they, how could they, I couldn't believe that they could be so careless, how they could be so heartless."

Yet Wall Street investors are better protected than ordinary consumers. Crimes against investors are punished; crimes against consumers are often not. These crimes certainly affect more people – shady lending practices that are calculated and often illegal, deepening debt, exploiting customers, overcharging borrowers with arbitrary late fees, and imposing other hidden costs that bilk consumers. Most of these practices are calculated and done deliberately.

A few examples: "loans by payday lenders" sometimes charge 400 percent APR (Annual Percentage Rate) – which means the average borrower pays $800 for a $500 loan. Experts say unauthorized bank overdrafts strip $17.5 billion from consumers each year. The spillovers from foreclosures (due to poor upkeep, theft and the like) in which occupied houses next door lose value have already cost lenders $502 billion in 2009. Also, no limits have been imposed by the credit card reform bill (signed by the president in 2009) on ever-rising interest rates.

What's worse, debt collectors continue to illegally harass customers. Consumer groups report collectors are urging people to sell their blood to pay down their credit card debt. These practices have been exposed for years but have yet to be fully outlawed or prosecuted.

DANNY SCHECHTER

Worldwide financial crime has become a growth industry with law enforcement running fast to keep up. Whole websites are now devoted to cataloging financial arrests. I asked corporate crime specialist John Coffee why we haven't seen more prosecutions. His response: "Well first of all, we may, yet. It takes a good deal of time."

One reason that the Obama administration has put forward a package of financial reforms and Congress has passed new regulations is to head off public outrage. The politicians could see which way the wind was blowing – in their faces.

Coffee explained, "We have a virtual revolutionary mood which partly explains the dramatic action taken by the president to restrict compensation and bail out firms. So I'm not surprised there is now anger."

When the lead story in the *New York Times* was, "Financial Fraud Rises as Target for Prosecutors," one of its columnists reported, "The fury of ordinary Americans was bubbling up at those who continue to plunder our economy."

Suddenly the word plunder was in wider use as protests, demanding justice, spread worldwide.

Many firms prefer to settle complaints rather than admit wrongdoing. Goldman Sachs paid Massachusetts $60 million rather than admit they had designed their mortgages to fail.

Investigative financial journalist Gary Weiss, who has investigated Wall Street crimes in several books told me, "That's standard. It's standard when Wall Street firms negotiate, what are in effect, plea-bargains with regulators, so the firms do not have to admit guilt."

Part of the problem, said Professor Coffee, is the way laws are written: "Any criminal prosecution for fraud requires that you show not only that investors lost and investors were outraged but you have to show a level of culpability by the manager that you wish to indict. You must show either a specific intent to defraud or, what federal law calls, willfulness which means a real intent to deliberately defraud someone and engage in misconduct that you realize was causing injury."

I pressed him, "So if somebody had the best intentions in the world but still defrauded large numbers of people they can't be prosecuted?"

"Not criminally."

So there you have it – the same argument the conservative Supreme Court justices used in the June 2009, decision on the New Haven firefighter affirmative-action case. You have to show intent. People who practice discrimination, or defraud investors, rarely admit they have any deliberate intent to discriminate or cause harm. Apparently, it just happens. So you can't prove it. Case closed.

Weiss added: "It's hard to prosecute somebody for white-collar crime because of the necessity to prove intent … that's what you have to prove, is knowledge. You have to prove criminal, guilty knowledge of what you were doing. You knew what you were doing was a crime. And that's why, you know, so much of what you see happening in the financial industry which is criminal, is not always prosecuted criminally.

"And that's why prosecutors sometimes hold back. However, certainly, under certain prosecutors in the past, going from Tom Dewey to Rudy Giuliani, the fact is that you did have criminal prosecution of Wall Street misconduct. So, you know, you can, in fact go after Wall Street in a criminal way and it has been done. But it's hard."

I asked Weiss, "Why did it stop? Why did they stop the vigilance? Why did they basically pull their punches?"

"Well, one of the reasons that criminal prosecutions stopped after Giuliani was that Giuliani's successors weren't interested. They simply were not particularly ambitious and ruthless as Giuliani was, but they simply were not interested in taking on the Street the way he did. You [did] see this to a certain extent with Eliot Spitzer, you know, although I think his successor's started to step up to the plate a bit more."

I asked a prosecutor, Richard Aborn, a five year veteran assistant district attorney (ADA) in Manhattan, why prosecutors dropped the ball.

"It was mistake," he told me. "They saw this as a problem of regulation, not criminality. They seem to be realizing their error and we are now seeing more criminal indictments and prosecutions."

Conservatives want to block this by reinforcing the intent standard which they say can lead to wrongful conviction. A research group at the Heritage Foundation (www.heritage. org) argues against new laws because:

> ... under these new laws, the government can often secure a conviction without having to prove that the person accused even intended to commit a bad act, historically a protection against wrongful conviction.

This is just one more sign of how right-wing ideology informs efforts to shape the legal environment, and limit prosecutions of the "wrong people" from their point of view.

Whatever the standard, often, prosecutors prefer cutting deals with corporate wrongdoers rather than imprisoning them.

Under the Bush administration, the Justice Department preferred to seek cash settlements for most corporate crimes rather than pursue remedies in court. Advocates of this approach argued that harsher penalties sought by Congress were unlikely to have a serious impact on corporate offenses. In 2007, Bloomberg News reported:

Sixty-one percent of defendants sentenced in the Bush administration's crackdown on corporate fraud spent no more than two years in jail, escaping the stiff penalties given to WorldCom and Enron executives.

In the past five years, 28 percent of those sentenced got no prison time and 6 percent received 10 years or more, according to a review of 1,236 white-collar convictions.

The victims of corporate criminals rarely get the same treatment, argues the former Texas Agriculture commissioner, populist Jim Hightower:

If you got caught robbing a bank, chances are excellent that you'd be facing some serious time in the pokey. But what if a bank *robs* you?

Corporate executives and their lawyers like to claim that a corporation is a "person" with all of the rights of an actual human being. Yet when one of these outfits goes bad and gets caught violating laws, then the lawyers drop the pretense of personhood, insisting that while this entity might be fined, it can't be put in jail or given a death sentence, because, well, because it's a financial structure, not a human.

Embracing this game of now-you-see-us-now-you-don't, the Bushites have devised a neat way to go soft on corporate criminals. Called "deferred prosecution agreements" (DPAs), this ploy allows corporations and banks that are guilty of everything from robbery to bribery to be given a get-out-of-jail-free card.

DANNY SCHECHTER

Of course, such judicial favoritism creates an incentive for criminal behavior, since corporations now know that they can likely avoid prosecution if caught. And fines are no deterrent – multi-billion-dollar corporations can simply absorb them as a necessary cost of doing business.

Unspoken, or unexplained in most media accounts, is how Wall Street money was responsible for the softening of the laws including higher standards triggering prosecution. Part of the deregulation of the industry involved the defanging of the power of prosecutors.

It also happened by design when Wall Street firms, who benefited by this transfer of wealth, invested in a major lobbying and political campaign to loosen regulations allowing them to pursue their self-interest at other's expense.

Ex-investment banker Nomi Prins spelled it out for me this way:

> When we think of regular crime – someone stealing something in the dead of the night – you know, or sort of law-and-order, murder-type crime scenes or larceny-type crime – you think of covert taking. Whether it's a material of life or whatever, it's an extraction that's illegal.

> On Wall Street a lot of the extraction tends to be very borderline legal, because the people extracting tend to be the ones setting up the legal framework. So you're creating a crime scene, and you are creating the crime, and you are effectively buying the police officers, all at the same time only in the form of a regulatory body or a politician.

Yet, this also didn't just happen. It was engineered by some of the smartest minds in the business world working with some of the slickest high-billing law firms.

This seems to be recognized by some journalists even though there have been few probes into the combo of crime and the crash. The suspicions are almost subconscious but sometimes surface in strange ways.

Perhaps that's why *Time* magazine's story of the top twenty-five people they considered responsible for the crisis – financiers, regulators, politicians and officials – carried a photo shoot staged against the backdrop of a police line-up.

On July 9, 2009, to pick just one day, the *New York Times* was reporting three major fraud cases, all as separate unconnected stories.

One was about a firm called Sky Capital, a Wall Street retail broker, charged with securities, wire and mail fraud in a $140 million fraud scheme. The head of the firm Ross Mandell was arrested. In 2005, *Forbes* ran this item on an earlier incident in which he was involved:

> Mandell, while denying the problems, blamed his troubles on a cocaine addiction from which he was recovered.
>
> Despite Mandell's checkered record, his companies have attracted a slew of illustrious former politicians and government officials to advise and sit on their boards. Among them: Former House Majority Leader Richard K. Armey; former presidential envoy to Iraq, L. Paul Bremer III; and former Senator Larry L. Pressler. Mandell and his employees are also contributors to politicians, including Eliot Spitzer.
>
> Is Ross Mandell a changed man? Pressler, a Republican from South Dakota, thinks so. "I've come to know Ross Mandell personally," he says. "I concede that in the 1990s he made some mistakes, but I believe in second chances

for people. He's an entrepreneur and a businessman, honest and good."

Another case, in Manhattan, involved 13 real-estate professionals including lawyers and bank workers accused of a multi-million-dollar mortgage fraud. A prosecutor was quoted as saying that if the mortgage firm "had a legitimate side, it was by accident." In this case $12 million in mortgages were falsified and home values were fudged.

Finally, Marc S. Dreier, a prominent lawyer, was facing a 145-year sentence being proposed by prosecutors for elaborate frauds estimated at $400 million. He had already pled guilty.

In a pre-sentencing letter to the judge, Dreier tried to explain his own descent into a life of crime:

As I sit here today, I can't remember or imagine why I didn't stop myself. It all seems so obviously deplorable now. I recall only that I was desperate for some measure of the success that I felt had eluded me. I felt that my law firm was my last chance to make a mark for myself, and I was fearful of seeing it fail. I know of course that this amounted to nothing more than self-pity, but this was my state of mind when I became a criminal. I gave in to being overwhelmed by the anxieties of life that we are all expected to cope with every day, and most people do, but I just could not manage to do so. I had no one close to me with whom I could talk. I had isolated myself, both personally and professionally. I lost my perspective and my moral grounding, and really, in a sense, I just lost my mind.

At the beginning, I spent most of the money on growing the law firm. Much of the money also went to servicing the "debt" itself. But, as time went on, I was more and more self-indulgent. I bought extravagant things – a beach house, an apartment, a boat, expensive art. Obviously, other men suffer through divorce and "mid-life crisis" and manage not to steal. And, other people grow their business without resorting to crime. I just wasn't in control of myself.

It is hard to explain how my crimes in 2002 reached the level that they did by 2008. Certainly I never intended, when this began, to steal on the scale I eventually did. I took the first money thinking that I could and would repay it shortly with revenue derived from the law firm. Soon, however, I exhausted the money, and it was evident not only that I would be unable to repay the initial "loans" but that I would need more. I had stepped in a quicksand of spending. By 2008 I had hired over 250 lawyers and opened additional offices in Los Angeles, Pittsburgh and Connecticut. The expenses were more and more uncontrollable, and the "loans" became more and more expensive. As the credit markets worsened, hedge funds were demanding much higher interest rates and, in many cases, substantial discounts to principal. In some cases, when I desperately needed new money to pay back loans becoming due, I was selling loans for 60 to 65 cents on the dollar, meaning that I was paying back far more principal than the hedge funds were actually paying me, which obviously was dramatically deepening the hole I was in.

In this way, without ever actually planning to, I found myself running a massive Ponzi scheme with no apparent way out. No doubt as is typical in Ponzi schemes, there was always the unrealistic expectation, or at least the hope, that I could use the "borrowed" money to eventually make it all work out. Obviously, and predictably, I was unable to do so.

And the beat goes on while new scandals continue to surface daily. Larry Doyle's *Sense on Cents* blog (www.senseoncents. com) commented on a lawsuit filed in July 2009 by New York Attorney General Andrew Cuomo against Charles Schwab, a well known broker, involving charges of fraud in the sale of Auction Rate Securities by salesmen who admitted they didn't understand what they were selling. Doyle wrote:

> The single greatest fraud ever perpetrated on investors is the collective Wall Street enterprise that marketed and distributed Auction Rate Securities (ARS). The ARS market at its peak was a $330-billion market. Of that initial size, those on Wall Street tracking developments within the ARS market project that $165 billion held by thousands of retail and institutional investors remain frozen.

So, no sooner does one scandal erupt with no end in sight than another threatens to push it out of the public eye.

CHAPTER 4

THE CRIMINAL MIND

I n the media, the story of pervasive crime gets reduced to the stories (and the glories) of lone or nefarious con men. Systems are rarely referenced, and cultures that foster criminality are only occasionally analyzed.

This may be changing. The idea that there is a crime wave has now worked its way into the culture with the criminals themselves becoming cult figures. On July 4, 2009 a new *Con Artist Hall Of Infamy* was launched online (www.thehallofinfamy.org/index.php).

The *Con Artist Hall of Infamy* showcases the exploits and crimes of individual criminals. It is the ethic of the clever criminal that the site explains. It reads in part:

> In 1920, Charles Ponzi ran a short-lived but spectacular scam that linked his name to the most classic of all cons. At first, a Ponzi scheme seems too good to be true. Then people start making money. Thrilled by the easy cash, investors keep their money where it can grow or talk up the incredible returns. The scam depends on new recruits – after all, it's their money the con artist gives to earlier investors.

> Other con artists sell or trade things that don't actually exist. To secure a loan or make a profitable deal, they present phony collateral with an air of unflinching honesty. Relying on their superhuman skills at bluffing, and on the gullibility or laziness of their victims, the con artist earns millions out of thin air.

Fraudsters and white-collar crooks run another sort of con. Cooking the books, pocketing huge bonuses, and making inside deals, require less artistry than a con, but these crimes are also rooted in calculated deception. The fraudster plays a role of trustworthy and sure-footed CEO, for instance, and lies without hesitation to shareholders and auditors.

The success of a con artist, broadly defined here to include those who loot and bribe for profit, blooms out of a complex alchemy of character, skills and circumstance.

TOOLS OF A CON ARTIST

Whether he draws on his innate character, or earned and practiced authority, a con artist uses every angle to persuade people to believe in his integrity and his financial prowess.

Con artists draw on a variety of strengths, including:

- **Power & Influence:** When he talks, people listen. He has a position of power and friends in high places. He exudes an aura of success; whatever he touches seems to turn to gold.

- **Charisma:** He appeals to a broad spectrum of people. He makes people feel clever and charmed; he plants the seeds of his con with such cunning, his victims think they've come up with the idea themselves.

- **Strong Cover:** He seems almost incapable of wrong-doing. His cover might be his solid reputation and the loans he's secured for others from big banks and investment firms. Or it might be a persona he adopts: a pious member of the community or a gifted, but naïve, businessman.

CLIMATE FOR A CON

The con artist sees and exploits individuals' vulnerabilities. Likewise, he taps into points of weakness in his environment.

A ripe climate for a con is one that includes some or all of the following:

- **A booming stock market:** When stock prices are high, con artists will do anything to keep them up and to profit from the buzz on Wall Street.

- **Optimistic and inexperienced investors:** A spirit of risk-taking often accompanies a booming market. Investors — including those with little experience — are ready to jump in and make a fortune.

- **Regulatory loopholes:** A good con seems plausible — and has multiple layers of plausible complexity. Cons flourish when they can fly under the weakened or ineffective radar of the SEC.

While this approach is often colorful — and does speak of the "ineffective radar" of regulators — it still treats the phenomenon in individual "crook gone wild" terms. The insights of novelists who have written about the culture of greed and arrogance in a "greed is good" culture get short shrift.

Some individual criminals, or a former criminal like Sam Antar, have a more philosophical view. "White-collar crime has always been there; it just goes more noticed or less noticed. Like today we're hearing about all of these white-collar crimes. But, it's just that we're finding out about them because of a faltering economy. A faltering economy makes most white-collar crimes unsustainable, and therefore they implode. But a lot of these crimes that we're hearing about today, they've been going on for years."

"What's the mentality of the white-collar criminal in your view?" I asked him.

"White-collar criminals are economic predators. We consider you, humanity, as a weakness to be exploited in the execution of our crimes. In order to commit our crimes, we have to increase your comfort level.

"Because we measure the effectiveness, we measure our effectiveness by the comfort level of our victims. And in order to increase your comfort level, we have to build walls of false integrity around us. For instance, while I was a crook – and I may still be a criminal today because you'll never know, but the point is, while I was a crook – I used to walk old ladies across the street, too. I used to give monies to charities. I used to help people out in social causes. But did that make me any less of a crook? I built a wall of false integrity around me."

He went on to explain the obstacles and challenges a prosecutor faces when he or she goes after a white-collar criminal: "Our laws – innocent until proven guilty, the code of ethics that journalists like you abide by, okay, limit your behavior and give the white-collar criminal freedom to commit their crimes, and also to cover up their crimes. We have no respect for the laws. We consider your codes of ethics, your laws, weaknesses to be exploited in the execution of our crimes. So the prosecutors, hopefully most prosecutors, are honest if they're playing by the set of the rules; they're hampered by the illegal constraints."

I pressed him on the matter of crimes committed by institutions. We are all familiar with individuals committing crimes, but institutions can also commit crimes.

He replied: "You're talking about institutionalized crime. You're correct. What the white-collar criminal tries to do is – they don't make it that any single act is a crime in of itself, or an obvious crime in itself. What they do is they basically spread it out and set up different companies, different, uhh, different transactions."

I suggested another potential problem for prosecutors, **the law itself requires, in white-collar crimes, that you show intent.** I wanted to know whether this is easy for the criminals to use to their advantage, a tool to get them off.

He expanded on this matter: "There's a saying: You can't be prosecuted for being stupid. So all white-collar criminals always try to play stupid.

"They don't want to show intent. It's easier to say that this was a result of a mistake or an error in judgment, than to say that I intended to, to victimize or defraud somebody.

"It's relatively easy. What prosecutors try to do to counter that is, they try to use something called the conspiracy counts. Conspiracy counts *are* a prosecutor's orgasm — excuse me, more like a wet dream. That enables them to use hearsay evidence against other witnesses. Other ways prosecutors get around it is by flipping witnesses from the bottom up."

Antar believes that there will be more corporate crime reported in the years ahead as investigators probe into the enormous sums of money spent by government on bailouts and stimulus programs — a view that a congressional investigator shares: "If I have to put myself in the mindset of a criminal, okay? Okay, and it's relatively easy for me. I'll give you that one. If I had to put myself in the mindset of a criminal, the criminal element today is figuring out a way to exploit it.

"There's going to be a trillion dollars in money that's going to be available to buy back distressed assets. The government is printing money like there's no tomorrow. I think the stimulus program is over a trillion dollars, too. I think between the stimulus program and the Wall Street bailout, we're up to about two trillion dollars.

"When they have that much money being disbursed over a short period of time, there's going to be fraud. In the last three years of Obama's administration, I will give you one prediction – that Obama's administration, the Democrats, are going to be accused of being corrupt because of all the fraud that's going to be associated with the stimulus and bailout packages. It's just the natural order of things.

"And the way the Republicans are going to get back into the White House is not going to be three years from now, or three and a half years from now. It's going to be about eight years from now after Obama's second term. Because that's when the corruption will start coming to the surface. When you disperse so much money over a short period of time, without adequate controls, even if five percent of it results in fraud, you're talking about at least a hundred billion dollars.

"And that's the problem that we have. So if I were a criminal today, I'd be looking to take advantage of all of the money that the government is disbursing at relatively short periods of time because I know that the government cannot adequately control that money."

In August 2009, the *New York Times* reported that investigators fear the mafia is moving in on the stimulus funds. "They want their taste," said one investigator.

CHAPTER 5

THE CRIME AT THE HEART OF THE CRIME

T he first challenge you face in making a crime caused it argument is to define the crime because in a world of complicated financial markets and even more complex financial instruments you have to be careful in determining what constitutes fraud and crimes.

As *Baseline Scenario* (www.baselinescenario.com) noted, "There is a deeper phenomenon at work than just the Bush administration's hands-off attitude toward corporate fraud (an attitude largely shared by the Clinton administration). That is the general tendency of people – investors and officials alike – to underestimate the risk of fraud during a boom and overestimate the risk of fraud during a bust."

Or maybe, to not see it at all.

These crimes of our time were not always simple to suss out and often rationalized, even by most of those involved, as business as usual. When you become part of a money making machine, when you embrace market logic, questions about ethics and values and even legalisms are often dismissed or denied. When everyone's doing it, it is assumed that's the way things are done. It is easy to rationalize

The line between legal and illegal can be a thin one or no line at all. It can also be complicated, even hard for government to investigate and prosecute.

Sam Antar explained, "Unless you're willing to put these pieces together, you can't find the crime. These are complicated – crimes, of which the government does not have the resources to thoroughly prosecute. And the – criminals know it; so they set it up, not as a single transaction that's a crime, but a series of transactions, that once it's all put together, makes it a crime.

What was the crime? And was it illegal?

Laws against racial discrimination were clearly violated as mortgage companies targeted minorities. This occurred routinely, and was, according to groups resisting predatory lending, systematic. Redlining – refusing to loan to minorities – gave way to discriminatory lending.

Are there really economic crimes? It is almost as a vague in many respects as war crimes. Do you know them when you see them, or forget them when you don't see them?

The U.S. government did not, at the time consider the My Lai Massacre in Vietnam a war crime, and certainly many do not see the economic crisis we are living through as a crime scene.

Even Nazi war crimes were prosecuted selectively, with different standards of guilt applied. Many offenders were freed when the decision was made to only really go after the men at the top. The United States government applied far stricter criteria when it prosecuted Japanese war criminals in Tokyo in a tribunal in which the U.S. was acting unilaterally as opposed to jointly with three other powers in Nuremberg.

There is no widely accepted definition of economic crime, as I discovered in the *American Law and Legal Information Library* (www.law.jrank.org) where I learned that:

> ... it is impossible to enumerate briefly the various definitions, theories, and offenses included in this category. We focus on the theoretical work that explores three aspects of economic crime: offender motivations, economic outcomes, and economic processes.

There are many theories and it becomes clear that "intent" is often unknowable and unprovable.

This online legal encyclopedia challenges simplistic notions of intent because it assumes that offenders' motivations are readily observable or knowable from the criminal act itself.

Although the motive behind robberies may appear to be the desire for property, perpetrators' primary motivation may be different (e.g., thrill seeking or racial hatred). Some crimes have multiple motives and economic gain may be a secondary goal. Furthermore, offenders themselves are not always conscious of their motives and they may be unable to distinguish between the reasons that precipitated their actions and the rationalizations or justifications that follow them.

In the case of the Nazis, Hannah Arendt found that many of the perpetrators were "normal," treating genocidal strategies as administrative problems, oblivious to the morality or the consequences. Professor Shoshanna Zuboff of Harvard Business School sees a similar pattern in terms of Wall Street business practices. Are its perpetrators any less criminal?

This institutionalized narcissism and contempt for the "Other" found its ultimate expression in the subprime mortgage industry, and the investment business derived from those mortgages.

In far too many cases, the obvious risks to borrowers and investors were simply regarded as externalities for which no one would be held accountable. If there was a family forced to relinquish its home or a retiree exposed to unfathomable risks in her pension, these human beings had not been imagined. Their suffering was invisible to those on the inside: it was so remote that for all practical purposes it did not exist.

In the Nazi case, decisions were coming from the top in furtherance of an ideology based on hate. On Wall Street, free-market ideologies shaped a culture of exploitation and rationalized its excesses. In many cases the laws were changed, or removed, to allow unscrupulous practices.

The law changers enabled the law breakers by limiting liability and shattering regulations.

CHAPTER 6

WHO SHOULD
BE PROSECUTED?

This crisis had its origins in the collapse of the housing market, a product of activity by two separate but interconnected industries: real estate and finance. To pursue them both, you need an overview of how the criminality of one flowed into the other and vice versa.

While individual transactions can be probed, the wrong doing was interrelated, more subject to prosecution under the RICO criminal conspiracy laws used against the mafia, or even civil litigation.

There are precedents for this approach, a history of financial crimes on Wall Street, as reporter Gary Weiss explained to me, "You have many instances in the past where the Street has consciously been accomplices to criminal acts and gotten away with it. So, yes, absolutely, in the subprime area absolutely, they knew what they were doing, and they got away with it. That's the way the system is designed."

Who designed the system this way, and how conscious was its exploitative practices?

For starters, information was rarely fully disclosed so that risks could not be fully calculated and consumers didn't know what was going on. A system built on fraud and deception requires effort to weaken enforcement, and insure that very few people know what was going on.

Lun, a commentator on the *Baseline Scenario* website wrote:

A key factor in this crisis is that when it really mattered, no financial institution could trust another and the public information about it. That, in turn, is powerful evidence that every institution knew its own disclosures were trash. And that reflects woefully bad disclosure and accounting standards.

The absence of good information created an environment where many of the people who ran the securitized mortgage market, were, in all likelihood, consciously parceling bad loans together with good loans. And, in all likelihood, they did that because they knew that their duties of disclosure meant their misdeeds would be very hard to detect. Fraud was probably systemic. So it's not just the mini-Madoffs that need attention in this crisis. It is the Madoffication of the system.

That's a term to write down: Madoffication!

Criminologists rely on examining certain common business models and precedents for detecting financial fraud. William Black focuses on the role of the CEO, faced with pressures to generate mega profits in industries where books were cooked and information hidden. He argues that in any financial bubble, company executives try to generate as much profits as possible by loaning money to people who can't afford it (but pay extra for the money) and then divert revenues to their own compensation and bonuses.

Thus companies are pressured from the top to "grow like crazy" with Ponzi scheme levels of growth. These returns expand through the use of extreme leverage and borrowing in the expansion phase of a financial bubble. This leads to a kind of hyperinflation that ultimately results in catastrophic failure. These CEOS and their CFOs know they are in jobs that have little security – average tenure is three years – so they do all of this quickly. The idea is not to make the business sustainable, but grow the business even if that means killing it.

He said that the institution itself is used to defraud in what he sees as an ethics-free "crimopathic" environment where its easy to justify cutting corners because everyone else is doing it, too. He argues that "bad ethics drives good ethics out of the market place, like some Gresham's law."

When companies fail in these "control frauds" it is usually because of a failure of a number of "layers." Here is Black's paradigm, presented from a public lecture:

1. Corporate governance fails. Power is delegated to CEOs and collaborating members of management.

2. External controls fail through the manipulation of outside auditors and accounting firms (as happened in the Enron and WorldCom frauds).

3. Rating agencies are co-opted and suborned through conflicts of interest.

4. Regulation fails or is defanged with rules softened or changed. This happens in several ways:

   a. Deregulation

   b. No Regulation

   c. Desupervision

   d. Lobbying by companies to undercut regulators which is justified on ideological grounds as support for free markets

   e. Capture: Regulators are drawn from the industry and share its outlook.

The result, said Black, is not just the destruction of companies but of the wealth of working class and middle-class Americans who lose homes, jobs and pensions.

Former Labor Secretary Robert Reich confirmed Black's claim of disproportionate victimization on his blog:

> I keep hearing that the economic meltdown has taken a huge toll on the stock portfolios of the rich. That's true. But the rich haven't lost nearly as much of their assets, proportionately, as everyone else. According to a report from the Bank of America Merrill Lynch, ("The Myth of the Overleveraged Consumer"), analyzing data from the Federal Reserve, the bottom 90 percent of Americans hold 50 percent or more of their assets in residential real estate, which has taken a far bigger beating than stocks and bonds. The top 10 percent of Americans have only a quarter of their assets in housing; most of their assets are in stocks and bonds. And although the stock market is still a bit tipsy, it has rallied considerably since it hit bottom earlier this year. Home values, on the other hand, are down by an average of a third across the country, and are still falling.

Fraud examiner Ann Megan explained a theory called Cressey's "fraud triangle" named after Donald Cressey, a prominent sociologist who studied crime and came up with the approach. Its three elements are opportunity, incentive and ability to rationalize:

Fraud Triangle Point #1: OPPORTUNITY

Fraud Triangle Point #2: INCENTIVE (PRESSURE)
Incentive has also been called "pressure." Pressure can come in the forms of peer pressure, living a lavish lifestyle,

a drug addiction, and many other aspects that can influence someone to seek gains via financial fraud.

Fraud Triangle Point #3: RATIONALIZATION

Rationalization is the grayest area in the fraud triangle but in a culture where "everyone" was doing it and with regulators asleep at the switch, or when formerly illegal practices are justified as legal, a climate for massive fraud exists.

Investigators into the S & L crisis stressed the need for disclosure at all levels to prevent massive fraud, but that lesson was not applied.

In his book *Wall Street*, Doug Henwood of the *Left Business Observer* (www.leftbusinessobserver.com), reminds us that fraud was pervasive and acknowledged by the *Wall Street Journal* and the whole business press. He wrote:

> Every institution that was supposed to watch the S & Ls botched the task.

> Topping the roster of failures are the regulators, federal and state, in the grip of the early Reagan-era euphoria, who failed to supervise the institutions – often run by dim provincials – that they had just set free to enter businesses they'd never been in before. Congress had long been in the industry's pocket ...

> But it's wrong to blame only the government, despite the American habit of doing so. Virtually every high-end profession around was involved (a point made well by Martin Mayer. Auditors repeatedly certified fictitious financial statements, lawyers argued on behalf of con artists and incompetents, investment banks bilked naïve S & L managers, and

consultants testified as character witnesses for felons. One of these character witnesses was Alan Greenspan, then an undistinguished economist from whom "you could order the opinion you needed."

Now that a new collapse of the system has occurred, we realize how much we didn't know because the information was kept from us. At the same time, we think about how a criminal tribunal or special court might subpoena documents and take testimony under oath.

But even in the absence of such an institution or process, prosecutors can make a *prima facie* case, based on what we already know to get indictments. If the people behind the scams and swindles continue to avoid detection, obscure the issues, and sidestep prosecution in real courts, then it's time for a "people's court." This is a case that even a televison courtroom like Judge Judy's can handle.

All the while, the business world and media were debating how to treat accused white-collar criminals in their midst. *Money* magazine even offered advice about socializing with colleagues accused of fraud:

> Seriously, we're as offended as you are by white-collar crime and the people who commit it. But until a person stands trial – until the prosecution presents its case and the person accused of the crime has an opportunity to defend himself – you shouldn't rush to judgment. Once the evidence is in, though, feel free to let the judgment flow. And if what you learn convinces you that this guy is a crook, there's no reason you shouldn't treat him as one, regardless of how your friends behave toward him.
>
> What you mustn't do, however, is use a friend's party as an

opportunity to act out your disapproval. When you accept an invitation to someone's home, you have an obligation to be pleasant with all the other guests. If you aren't willing to do this, you should decline the invitation. You might even want to tell your hosts why, in the hope they'll reconsider before again extending their hospitality to this man. But making a friend's guest feel uncomfortable, while not in a league with securities fraud, is still out of bounds.

Forbes, meanwhile was running tip pieces like, "How to Get The Best Deals in Prison." It reads in part, "So, you're relocating from the boardroom to the prison cell. You certainly won't be needing that country club membership. But even in Club Fed, there can be perks for those in the know. That's why prospective inmates hire experts like ex-con Larry Levine of American Prison Consultants."

Before the worst of the crisis hit, *Business Week* was offering up-beat counsel: "Does corporate crime pay? The record can seem pretty arbitrary. Tyco International Ltd.'s, L. Dennis Kozlowski and WorldCom Inc.'s Bernie Ebbers got hammered for their misdeeds. But plenty of other corporate and financial titans at companies engaged in chicanery have come away only mildly bruised."

CHAPTER 7

INVESTIGATING FINANCIAL CRIMINALS

Criminal investigations are usually the province of police agencies and attorneys general. The FBI, for example has taken the lead on mortgage fraud cases. But there has also been a clamor for a special commission modeled on the Pecora Commission that looked into the wheeling and dealing and corruption on Wall Street that led to the crash of 1929 and the depression that followed.

Congress agreed to organize a body like this, but independent analysts fear it will go nowhere now.

Economist Dean Baker is uncertain about its potential impact: "Unfortunately, there is a real possibility that the commission appointed by Congress may follow a different precedent. Instead of striving to uncover the truth, it may seek to conceal it."

Robert Kuttner, of the *American Prospect* magazine, also fears that partisan politics would derail an aggressive independent probe:

> Perhaps it was too much to hope that this commission would be a chance to investigate root causes and mobilize public sentiment behind the sweeping reforms that are needed and not yet forthcoming. Obviously, Republican House Leader John Boehner and his Senate counterpart, Mitch McConnell, are not about to put serious critics of deregulation on this panel.

For the new Pecora Commission, Pelosi and Reid need to do better than finding a predictable list of retired and safe Democratic politicians. This is a rare chance to light a real fire on behalf of deep reform.

Baker suggested what a real truth commission might do:

What questions does the commission have to ask? How about putting all the 7- and 8-figure executives under oath and ask them if they were really too dumb to see an $8 trillion housing bubble. For a follow-up, the commission can ask them what exactly they do to earn those multi-million-dollar paychecks. Those questions should make for some very informative testimony.

Unfortunately, it is more likely that the commission will get buried in obscure details of collateralized debt obligations and credit default swaps. That would be a serious distraction from the real story and a waste of the taxpayers' money.

In a review on the *Naked Capitalism* blog (www.nakedcapitalism.com) of Pecora's book *Wall Street Under Oath*, "Doctor Rx" explained the commission's role:

Roosevelt felt he needed an energized public to push through financial reforms, and Pecora delivered the goods. The Pecora Investigation is given a great deal of credit for creating the momentum for the signature legislation between 1933 and 1935 that helped save Wall Street from its own excesses …

In his book, Pecora himself wrote:

... if you now hearken to the oracles of the Street, you will hear now and then that the money-changers have been much maligned. You will be told that a whole group of high-minded men, innocent of social or economic wrongdoing, were expelled from the temple because of the excesses of a few. You will be assured that they had nothing to do with the misfortunes that overtook the country in 1929–33; that they were simply scapegoats, sacrificed on the altar of unrea-soning public opinion to satisfy the wrath of a howling mob blindly seeking victims ... These disingenuous protestations are, in the crisp legal phrase, "without merit."

He also issued a warning that couldn't be more relevant:

... It is certainly well that Wall Street now professes repen-tance. But it would be most unwise, nevertheless, to under-estimate the strength of hostile elements. When open mass resistance fails, there is still the opportunity for traps, strata-gems, intrigues, undermining all the resources of guerilla warfare ... More than ever, we must maintain our vigilance. If we do not, Wall Street may yet prove to be not unlike that land, of which it has been said that no country is easier to overrun, or harder to subdue.

In the end, the reviewer was not hopeful that the Obama administration is up to the battle that must be waged:

Let us recall that no Congress since the passage of Sar-boanes of 2002 has passed important legislation to limit or prevent the housing and credit bubbles or, the power of Big Finance. We note that the president's two main finance and economic advisers are Robert Rubin protégés.

It therefore would appear that the chance that this administration and Congress will truly take on Big Finance in any way, shape or form as did Ferdinand Pecora in alliance with Franklin Delano Roosevelt will remain vanishingly low unless, perhaps, a yet greater calamity engulfs our financial system and it would then be expedient for politicians to turn on their current allies in Big Finance.

So it may be that we cannot depend on the government and need to consider creating a "people's inquiry" instead, something like the tribunal Nobel Laureate Bertrand Russell organized in 1967 to get at the truth about Vietnam War atrocities when they were not being reported in the media.

There is no reason why top economists, labor leaders and intellectuals couldn't do their own probe. It may not get the media attention that a government panel like the 9/11 Commission received, but it may be able to do more honest probing.

The public has to be educated and mobilized to demand more criminal prosecutions, and the issue itself has to be reframed. It is unlikely that the government and the media would do that without a lot of outside prodding. Wrote Charles Burris on the *Campaign for America's Future*:

> Barack Obama, Rahm Emanuel, their key administration functionaries, and the leading congressional figures who call for and would direct a new investigation of Wall Street's complicity in bringing on the present crisis, are all captives of the very Wall Street banksters at Goldman Sachs they would be investigating. Such a farcical investigation, if it comes off, will make the bogus 9/11 Commission, Warren Commission or Senator Joe McCarthy's controversial hearings on Communist spies in government, exercises in veracity and moral clarity.

And all the time, the real culprits of the crisis at the Federal Reserve will remain ensconced and undisturbed. Greenspan and Bernanke will continue to enjoy uninterrupted nights of slumber and blissful hubris.

The *New York Times* has called editorially for a probe into all the banks: "Some banks may try to argue that although they received assistance, they were never in danger of failure, and thus are off limits to commission investigators. But all of the major banks are implicated in the crisis, and none should be outside the commission's purview."

One problem I see is that the Obama administration has already asserted executive privilege and may withhold documents from the commission. This may be its first battle – not with the banks but with the administration that called for its formation.

As for Goldman, Joel S. Hirschhorn wrote in the online magazine *Toward Freedom* (www.towardfreedom.com):

If there was ever something that should have sparked a Second American Revolution it is the Goldman Sachs story in this recession. Goldman Sachs reported that it earned $3.44 billion in the second quarter, and is preparing its largest bonus payout in history. Did this company with so many former executives running the federal government's financial system manage this strictly on its own merits? Not exactly! It received a $10-billion injection of TARP funds to help it handle the fiscal crisis.

It was allowed to convert itself into a commercial bank and member of the Federal Reserve System, gaining access to low or zero-cost capital at the Fed discount window and access to federally guaranteed borrowing through the FDIC

Temporary Liquidity Guaranty Program. And it had the good fortune (literally) to receive a $13-billion payout of federal dollars at one hundred cents on the dollar for its outstanding credit default swap contracts with AIG.

It is actually more than that, explained Nomi Prins, the former Goldman executive I interviewed for my film, *Plunder*. She wrote in *Mother Jones*:

Keep in mind that by virtue of becoming a bank holding company, Goldman received a total of $63.6 billion in federal subsidies (that we know about – probably more if the Fed were ever forced to disclose its $7.6 trillion of borrower details). There was the $10 billion it got from TARP (which it repaid), the $12.9 billion it grabbed from AIG's spoils – even though Goldman had stated beforehand that it was protected from losses incurred by AIG's free fall, and if that were the case, would not have needed that money, let alone deserved it. Then, there's the $29.7 billion it's used so far out of the $35 billion it has available, backed by the FDIC's Temporary Liquidity Guarantee Program, and finally, there's the $11 billion available under the Fed's Commercial Paper Funding Facility ...

Which brings us back to these recent quarterly earnings. Goldman posted record profits of $3.4 billion on revenues of $13.76 billion. More than 78 percent of those revenues came from its most risky division, the one that requires the most capital to operate, Trading and Principal Investments. Of those, the Fixed Income, Currency and Commodities (FICC) area within that division brought in a record $6.8 billion in revenues. That's the division, by the way, that I worked in and that Lloyd Blankfein managed on his way up the Goldman totem pole. (It's also the division that would stand to gain the most if Waxman's cap-and-trade bill passes.)

Of course, Goldman did pay back the U.S. government which made a profit on the deal but at the same time, supposedly, lost any possible leverage on the firm according to President Obama on PBS, "Now, there are some companies, like Goldman Sachs, that have paid the money back and that means that we don't have the same kind of levers on them that we might have."

Why did Goldman pay even more than was expected? David Reilly of Bloomberg News explained they were worried about mounting public hostility: "The danger for Goldman is that it becomes a focal point for populist bailout ire, leading the government to take a tougher stance on regulation. Treating too-big-to-fail institutions as financial utilities, for example, would curtail Goldman's ability to generate returns on equity in excess of 20 percent."

The hostility to Goldman Sachs can be found plastered all over the Internet. Just one example, from Ilargi on *Automatic Earth* (www.theautomaticearth.blogspot.com): "Two consecutive U.S. governments, both with economic teams led by 'alumni' from Goldman Sachs and other Wall Street firms, have put $23.7 trillion in U.S. taxpayer money at risk to rescue their former – and often future – employers. This has bought the main banks the chance to be left intact for a while longer (but only for a while), because the only thing people now can see is the veil the banks hide behind, the most costly layer of veneer in history."

The truth is, the government didn't have many levers on Goldman in the first place. It seems as if Goldman was the dominant party in that relationship.

Financial analyst Reggie Middleton offers more details in his *Boom Bust Blog* (www.boombustblog.com):

As readers know, I have stated many times that Goldman is nothing but a gigantic, taxpayer guaranteed, government protected hedge fund. They have taken more risk than any large financial institution in this country, nearly failed but for a massive government bailout, and have benefitted multiple times from government assistance: ranging from expedited bank charters, government guarantees on their debt, ZIRP, TARP, open access to the discount window (without being a bank), and 100% payout on 50% devalued assets that they voluntarily purchased from Merrill and voluntarily insured with a soon to be insolvent counterparty.

Despite all of this, they are actually being lauded as supermen! Hey, give me $95 billion of cash, guarantees, impunity and immunity from prosecution and associated assistance and I'll blow my quarterly numbers out as well. What's to prevent me from maxing out risk when I know I keep the rewards and the taxpayer keeps the losses?

It is significant that major media organizations are not raising or advancing the concerns posed by financial insiders like Middleton. These are the type of questions which should but are not being posed by Big Media and members of Congress. Edward Harrison of *Credit Writedowns* (www.creditwritedowns.com) asked:

Why is Goldman Sachs allowed to maintain leverage ratios significantly higher than the large legacy bank holding companies like Wells Fargo, Bank of America, JPMorgan and Citigroup?

Why is Goldman allowed to operate like a private equity company, holding large stakes of foreign non-financial corporations? (I should note that financial-holding companies do have ten years in which to sell their stakes)

Why is Goldman (and other large banks) allowed to operate like a hedge fund and take outsized risks with capital via large proprietary trading operations? Most of Goldman's profits are coming from this area. At least Deutsche Bank has offloaded these bets onto hedge funds in which it invests. Given the fact that the large too-big-to-fail financial institutions have received a large backstop from the taxpayer, the fact that they are loading up in "prop trading," shows that regulation in the U.S. is non-existent.

Why is Goldman allowed to have an interest in the failure of other financial firms? We now hear that Goldman has an interest in the failure of CIT, a major lender to small and medium-sized businesses. These perverse incentives are everywhere in the derivatives world and were an enabler of the financial meltdown and the principal reason AIG was bailed out with taxpayer money.

Commenting on the various conspiracy theories about Goldman, former New York Governor Eliot Spitzer, while not subscribing to one said, "Just because it's a conspiracy theory doesn't mean it isn't true." In late October 2009, financier George Soros matter of factly told the *Financial Times*, that the recent wave of high profits were only possible because of "hidden gifts from the state."

The *Open Secrets* website (www.opensecrets.org) that monitors corporate lobbying clout noted: "[Goldman Sachs] closely monitors issues including economic policy, trade and nearly all legislation that governs the financial sector. It has been a major proponent of privatizing Social Security as well as legislation that would essentially deregulate the investment banking and securities industry. The firm tends to give most of its money to Democrats." Political donations in 2008 came to nearly $6 million dollars.

Earlier, at one point in the debate over the first bank bailout, Congressman Dennis Kucinich pointed at Goldman's power in Washington by asking his colleagues, "Is this the Congress of the United States or the boardroom of Goldman Sachs?"

What are the odds now that Congress is authorizing a serious investigation of Goldman?

So it may be that, in the end only an extra-governmental people's inquiry of distinguished and credible eminences will be able to educate us about these relationships. That's why I cited an entity like the tribunal Bertrand Russell organized in 1967 to get at the truth about Vietnam War atrocities when they were not being reported in the Western media. It was very controversial at the time, condemned or ignored by mainstream media, but it did bring out a side of the war that was not being reported. History has vindicated most of its findings.

It would still be better, however, if at some point, as the economy continues its decline, that these issues are brought to some court where evidence can be presented, and witnesses required to testify under oath.

Given the highly negative global impact of this criminally engineered crisis, a major case should probably be referred to the International Criminal Court in the Hague. Imagine what the reaction on Wall Street and in Washington would be.

DANNY SCHECHTER

CHAPTER 8

COUNT ONE: PREDATORY SUBPRIME LENDING

ndictments always follow investigations, and once under subpoena and tough grilling, executives say the most revealing things. Here's how I believe the crime of our time played out.

The original crime was played out in the housing sector, where massive predatory subprime lending – what I call "sub-crime" – over the years got millions of families into mortgages they couldn't afford, and that the lenders knew they couldn't sustain. It was enabled by artificially low interest rates from the Federal Reserve and active support and collusion from top financial institutions.

Here's just a few of the investigations underway and some of their findings. If I, as just one person, can locate these sources, there must be far more to find. All it will take is a serious well-funded effort by experienced professionals.

According to an investigation by the Center of Public Integrity (www.publicintegrity.org), twenty-five of the sleaziest subprime lenders were backed by the biggest "blue chip" banks in the country: CitiGroup, Wells Fargo, JPMorgan and Bank of America.

Together, the *Financial Times* reported, they originated $1 trillion in subprime mortgages issued from 2005 to 2007, almost three-quarters of the total. (By the way, these same banks, also received the vast bulk of the $700 billion in Troubled Asset Relief Program (TARP) funds issued since October 2008. At the same time, most had supported a well-funded lobbying effort to prevent tighter regulation of the subprime market.)

The Center also reported that earlier warnings were ignored: "Washington was warned as long as a decade ago by bank regulators, consumer advocates and a handful of lawmakers that these high-cost loans represented a systemic risk to the economy, yet Congress, the White House, and the Federal Reserve all dithered while the subprime disaster spread. Long-forgotten congressional hearings and oversight reports, as well as interviews with former officials, reveal a troubling history of missed opportunities, thwarted regulations, and lack of oversight."

Housing activist Bruce Marks, CEO of the Neighborhood Assistance Corporation of America (NACA), calls this a deliberate "scheme."

All of this money was pumped into a housing market dominated by a network of mortgage brokers, lending institutions and loan originators working together to attract buyers with mortgage products most knew were designed to fail.

A vice president of the New York Mellon Bank spoke at a business breakfast I attended. He said, "… in Ohio alone, a study found that 18% of the mortgage industry was made up by people with criminal records."

A comment on *PBS NewsHour*'s Paul Solman's *Making Sense* blog (www.pbs.org/newshour/economy/makingsense) explained why the brokers took part in frauds:

> When it comes to home mortgages, the information comes from the mortgage broker. The broker makes commission from loans. The *uglier* the mortgage, the more they get paid, so they have every incentive to get the borrower onto the most expensive plan. The loan is then packaged up and sold, so the broker simply doesn't care if the borrower cannot pay. A system that rewards reckless behavior will only lead to disaster.

DANNY SCHECHTER

So how did these subprime marketers explain their products to their customers?

"Not very well," confided Dan Osso, a former loan originator: "The borrowers were not aware of what was happening in terms of the structures of the loan. They did view us as someone who was trying to help them, but from our end of it, our intention was to make as much money as possible."

Osso was one of the few in the industry who blew the whistle on these practices. He had gone from pedaling predatory products to warning the public about them, as part of an effort to encourage financial literacy. I interviewed him at length. He is a straight shooter whose conscience forced him out of the business.

"During that time what I had seen was nothing short of amazing. It was very predatory. The techniques that were being used, the salesmanship that was being used, the gimmicks on the loans and how they were structured. It really disturbed me."

I was intrigued, was it really that *predatory?*

"It was very predatory; it was very much akin to a used car salesman trying to make the best deal that he could. The loans themselves, whether it be for financing a house, reconsolidating loans or debts – the techniques that were used were definitely predatory, in my opinion."

I asked him how pervasive he thought these practices were.

"It was the standard. A question of pervasiveness is one thing, but it was the standard. This was the way the business was run. The idea was to make as much money as possible, not just on the loan but on the different fees that were added onto the loan and even things that they refer to as back-end bumps on interest rates, where the borrower had no idea that the actual loan that he was getting is not necessarily what he was qualified for."

"Is this *criminal*?" I asked Osso.

"Uhh, that's a good question. It's certainly unethical. The catch-all to this and how they could get away with that is that people here think there is full disclosure, but it depends on the lending institution you went to – in other words a bank, a broker, or a lending institution. All three are different. All three have different sets of regulations that govern them. And so full disclosure wasn't always necessary. It wasn't necessarily important to the loan itself, just get them to sign on the dotted line. If they were happy with the numbers, you have a loan."

Later, the FBI would cite massive fraud in many of the transactions that got people into homes – abusive practices of many kinds. They first warned of a "fraud epidemic" in 2004 – also revealing that their capacity to investigate this epidemic was limited because many corporate fraud investigators had been transferred to fight terrorism. When the problem got too big to ignore in March 2008, they launched "Operation Malicious Mortgage." FBI Director Robert Mueller spoke at the first press conference: "Through this operation, more than 400 defendants have been charged. We have attained 173 convictions in crimes that have accounted for more than $1 billion in estimated losses." (By the fall of 2009, FBI investigators started going after accountants and lawyers as well as brokers, when 41 mortgage fraudsters were busted in one October raid in New York.)

At the same time, Congress was told that the FBI had fewer than 250 special agents assigned to financial fraud cases, despite caseloads having more than doubled in the past three years. The FBI admitted it could not investigate the more than 5,000 fraud allegations received by the Treasury Department each month.

In a speech to the Mortgage Bankers Association, the head of the operation charged with investigating mortgage fraud, revealed the numbers were escalating way beyond the extant 5,000 allegations:

> For our first detailed study focusing exclusively on mortgage fraud, published in November 2006, we proceeded to go back to take a closer look at all of the mortgage fraud filings since the inception of the suspicious activity report (SAR) reporting requirements, analyzing ten years of mortgage fraud reporting data nationwide. Depository institutions filed more than 82,000 SARs describing suspected mortgage fraud between April 1, 1996 and March 31, 2006. SARs, pertaining to mortgage fraud, increased by 1,411 percent, the FBI continued, in nearly a decade between 1997 and 2005, compared to a 543 percent increase for SARs overall.

> In the November 2006 study we explained a range of fraudulent schemes in an effort to provide the financial industry with red flag indicators that could help them protect their financial institutions and their customers from being victims of fraud. **The report detailed that material misrepresentations and false statements were reported on approximately 2/3 of reports,** and noted the vulnerabilities posed by automated processing and low and no documentation loans.

> The Financial Crimes Enforcement Network (FinCEN) issued its second study in the mortgage fraud area in April 2008, which provided an update of fraud schemes, with more details on complicit insiders. A key finding was a 50 percent increase in SARs that reported intercepting the suspected fraud prior to funding a mortgage (an indication of growing vigilance and awareness in the financial community). The report also noted that the total for mortgage fraud SARs filed reached nearly 53,000, **an increase of 42 percent from the previous year.**

Their most recent report showed an even larger increase:

> Our February 2009 report looked at 62,084 SARs reporting mortgage fraud. Filings **have increased 44 percent** from 53,000 the prior year. New trends include suspected fraud identified when mortgage purchasers exercise rights to send mortgages back to originators and in the context of foreclosures.

The FinCEN reported: "Through FY [fiscal year] 2007, cases pursued by the FBI resulted in 183 indictments and 173 convictions of corporate criminals. Numerous cases are pending plea agreements and trials. During fiscal year 2007, the FBI secured $12.6 billion in restitution orders and $38.6 million in fines from corporate criminals."

What crimes were they looking into? FinCEN enumerated the problems it monitors:

(1) Falsification of financial information, including:
  (a) False accounting entries
  (b) Bogus trades designed to inflate profits or hide losses
  (c) False transactions designed to evade regulatory oversight

(2) Self-dealing by corporate insiders, including:
  (a) Trading
  (b) Kickbacks
  (c) Backdating of executive stock options
  (d) Misuse of corporate property for personal gain
  (e) Individual tax violations related to self-dealing

(3) Obstruction of justice designed to conceal any of the

above-noted types of criminal conduct, particularly when the obstruction impedes the inquiries of the SEC, other regulatory agencies and law enforcement agencies. The FBI has formed partnerships with numerous agencies to capitalize on their expertise in specific areas such as securities, tax, pensions, energy, and commodities.

The FBI has placed greater emphasis on investigating allegations of these frauds by working closely with the SEC, Financial Industry Regulation Authority, Internal Revenue Service (IRS), Department of Labor (DOL), Federal Energy Regulatory Commission (FERC), Commodity Futures Trading Commission, and U.S. Postal Inspection Service (USPIS). As reflected in the statistical accomplishments of the president's Corporate Fraud Task Force, founded in 2002, which includes the above-mentioned agencies, the cooperative and multi-agency investigative approach has resulted in highly successful prosecutions.

Kat Aaron and Nick Schwellenbach assessed these figures, in a report headlined, "Mortgage Fraud Reports Rise, But Some Fraud May Still Be Undetected," for the Center for Public Integrity. They write:

> Those who are allegedly committing the fraud may be some of the same folks who helped create the crisis in the first place, according to the FBI's 2008 Mortgage Fraud Report. But **the bureau and FinCEN might have trouble catching them** because non-bank mortgage lenders, responsible for almost half of all subprime loans, **don't have to report suspicious activity to the feds**, as other financial institutions do. **Even so, the totals on suspected fraud are alarming.**

The United States Senate has now launched an investigation,

according to the *Wall Street Journal* on July 30, 2009:

> A Senate panel has subpoenaed financial institutions, including Goldman Sachs Group Inc. and Deutsche Bank AG, seeking evidence of fraud in last year's mortgage-market meltdown, according to people familiar with the situation.
>
> The congressional investigation appears to focus on whether internal communications, such as email, show bankers had private doubts about whether mortgage-related securities they were putting together were as financially sound as their public pronouncements suggested. Collapsing values for many of those securities played a big role in precipitating last year's financial crisis.

Investigations like these could inspire new whistleblowers to step forward with their own confessions of wrongdoing. Several books about the Enron and WorldCom frauds relied on the testimony of insiders.

In *Le Figaro*, two prominent French police experts, Jean-François Gayraud and Noël Pons, wrote:

> No one contests that the subprime crisis has both structural (the orgy of credit) and cyclical (the bursting of the real-estate bubble in the United States) dimensions. However, no one appears to see the criminal aspects of this globalized financial crisis. **A surprising omission, since history teaches us that all financial crises "contain" a criminal dimension,** either by the intrusion of organized crime, or by the repetition of criminal operations committed by normal market actors; and sometimes also through the association of these two universes.

Crime accompanies, amplifies and sometimes provokes financial crises. Besides, how can one not be troubled by the strange public alert American Attorney General Michael Mukasey launched in May 2008 on the growing threat to national security represented by "organized crime's penetration of the markets?"

So even as experts outside the United States saw this clearly, the American media and our own politicians played it down. Two other French experts, Bertrand Monnet and Philippe Very, professors at the Edhec Institute for the Management of Criminal Risks, foresaw the fusion of the criminal and "legitimate economies," an area few journalists in the United States investigated.

They explained how this works in "Economic Crisis and Criminality," published in *Les Echoes*:

Organized crime does not launder for pleasure, but to invest a part of those laundered funds in the legal economy to meet two objectives: territorial domination and enrichment. Controlling a business allows a mafia to distribute wealth in the form of jobs or purchases and consequently, to ultimately place whole regions under economic dependency. But investing in the legal economy allows organized crime above all to benefit from the growth of the businesses it controls and the profitability of its holdings, just like any other investor.

The present crisis risks enlarging organized crime's access to the legal economy. In a context of rarefaction of investments, the funds resulting from money laundering are, in fact, mechanically more interesting than ever. The legal and ethical resistance to pressure from questionable investors risks decreasing, in emerging countries, as well as in the heart of the OECD. This is all the more likely, given that organized crime's investment capacities are enormous: even if one cautiously estimated that the mafias invest only half the sums the UN estimates they launder, their average investment capacity would broadly exceed that of the biggest sovereign fund in the world.

There were related industries that also used criminal practices to defraud customers. One example is America's biggest homebuilder, Beazer Homes, USA.

It took years to rein in Beazer, a firm which Floyd Norris, the chief financial columnist of the *New York Times*, later described as **"much more than a builder of houses. It was a veritable crime wave."**

He went on to say, "The company defrauded buyers, particularly poor people being sold homes they could not afford. It defrauded the federal government by getting government-guaranteed mortgages for those buyers. It created subdivisions now dominated by dozens of foreclosed homes.

"And while it was at it, Beazer lied to shareholders about how much money it was making."

The company was not fronted by gangsters but by businessmen. Its operations were poorly monitored and its criminal practices unchecked. It ran a very organized machine that was not considered part of organized crime.

When you look at the structure of the real-estate industry with its brokers, loan originators, financiers and mortgage servicers, there are multiple levels of fraudulent activity that occur: from the issuing of the mortgages in the first place, to scams tailor-made for homeowners facing foreclosure.

The *Calculated Risk* blog (www.calculatedrisk.blogspot.com) cited some of the most common housing frauds:

Short-Sale Schemes: Short-sale schemes are desirable to mortgage fraud perpetrators because they do not have to competitively bid on the properties they purchase, as they do for foreclosure sales. Perpetrators also use short sales to recycle properties for future mortgage fraud schemes. Short-sale fraud schemes are difficult to detect since the lender agrees to the transaction, and the incident is not reported to internal bank investigators or the authorities. As such, the extent of short sale fraud nationwide is unknown. A real-estate short sale is a type of pre-foreclosure sale in which the lender agrees to sell a property for less than the mortgage owed. In a typical short-sale scheme, the perpetrator uses a straw buyer to purchase a home for the purpose of defaulting on the mortgage. The mortgage is secured with fraudulent documentation and information regarding the straw buyer. Payments are not made on the property loan causing the mortgage to default. Prior to the foreclosure sale, the perpetrator offers to purchase the property from the lender in a short-sale agreement. The lender agrees without knowing that the short sale was premeditated. The mortgage owed on the property often equals or exceeds 100 percent of the property's equity.

Foreclosure Rescue Schemes: Foreclosure rescue schemes are often used in association with advance fee and loan modification program schemes. The perpetrators convince homeowners that they can save their homes from foreclosure through deed transfers and the payment of up-front fees. This "foreclosure rescue" often involves a manipulated deed process that results in the preparation of forged deeds. In extreme instances, perpetrators may sell the home or secure a second loan without the homeowners' knowledge, stripping the property's equity for personal enrichment.

The Federal Trade Commission has been documenting the deceptive marketing of loan modification and foreclosure "rescue" schemes, an industry that New York State Attorney General Andrew Cuomo labels as a scam **"in its entirety."**

They have also been closing down and suing violators of "deceptive tactics to market their mortgage modification and home foreclosure relief services," including firms that marketed their services by giving what the FTC calls, "The false impression they were affiliated with the federal government."

In July 2009, even as the growing number of foreclosures were called the **"single biggest threat to economic recovery,"** 25 of the country's top mortgage servicers were dragging their feet or refusing to modify loans despite the fact that many were made in a fraudulent way or that the government had provided them with incentives through a program called "Making Homes Affordable" that would give them $1,000 per mortgage to keep people in their homes.

These companies, which benefited financially because of the pervasive fraud in the industry – even when they didn't commit it directly – were claiming it was not profitable enough for them to bring relief to most at-risk homeowners.

The remedies have been inadequate, as has the monitoring of all this fraud nationwide. The FDIC told Congress in March 2009:

Vice Chairman Martin Gruenberg called for those responsible for the current housing crisis to be held accountable.

Gruenberg noted that there are currently 4,375 mortgage fraud claims (at the FDIC alone) under investigation and an additional 900 civil mortgage fraud lawsuits are expected to be filed over the next three years.

The FDIC representative informed the committee that defendants in civil lawsuit cases have primarily been mortgage brokers, appraisers, closing attorneys and other closing agents, as well as title companies, title insurance companies, and other third parties that participated in mortgage fraud against FDIC-insured banks and thrifts.

The horrendous damage done to individuals by these scammers is documented in the *Mortgage Fraud Blog* (www.mortgagefraudblog.com). One example:

Shawn Corcas, 39, of St. Albans, New York, pleaded guilty to stealing the identity of a 68-year-old man in Jamaica, Queens, who had been disabled as a result of a stroke, and then secretly selling his house out from under him and pocketing the profits.

The victims, as we will see, are everywhere.

Years after, all this came to light – even if housing advocates had been trying to expose it in the press and in front of Congress. Journalists slowly, oh, so slowly, came to see how these mortgage machinations were at the center of the economic collapse. The *financezee* blog (www.financezee.com) reported:

A year-long *Herald-Tribune* investigation into thousands of suspicious Florida flip deals found that lenders of all kinds approved risky deals and ignored obvious red flags for mortgage fraud ... What makes the flipping fraud so egregious is not just that it happened, but that it would have been so easy to stop. Using public records and Internet searches, the *Herald-Tribune* identified hundreds of deals that exhibited classic red flags for fraud.

Gretchen Morgenstern of the *New York Times*, one of the few business journalists to have raised the issue, returned to it on July 12, 2009, and began calling for action against the perpetrators in the industry itself:

> It is hard not to be dismayed by the fact that two years into our economic crisis so few perpetrators of financial misdeeds have been held accountable for their actions. That so many failed mortgage lenders do not appear to face any legal liability for the role they played in almost blowing up the economy really rankles. They have simply moved on to the next "opportunity."

It is hard not to feel that her next paragraph is more important in finally acknowledging a key, but long missing, connection (although it is still not being taken far enough):

> And what of the giant institutions that helped finance these monumentally toxic loans, or arranged the securitizations that bundled the loans and sold them to investors? So far, they have argued, fairly successfully, that they operated independently of the original lenders. Therefore, they are not responsible for any questionable loans that were made. **But this argument is growing tougher to defend.**

This approach still views the problem in terms of "litigation risks," not outright criminality. Since these so-called toxic products were also designed to fail and pedaled fraudulently – in violation of the law – and considering the basic rights that guard against deliberate misrepresentation, this no longer is just a civil matter.

It is criminal, yet the laws were inadequate and also inadequately enforced,

In the *Fordham Law Review*, Kathleen C. Engel and Patricia A. McCoy accused Wall Street of turning a "blind eye" to the way securitization promoted predatory lending. This is from an academic summary:

> As subprime securitization has grown, so have charges that securitization turns a blind eye to financing abusive loans ...
>
> When investors buy securities backed by predatory loans, they face a classic "lemons" problem in the form of credit risk, prepayment risk, and litigation risk. Securitization exacerbates all three risks by unbundling the mortgage process, giving rise to adverse selection. In theory, the lemons problem should cause investors to flee the market for subprime mortgage-backed securities or demand a risk premium commensurate with the worst quality loans.
>
> Instead, securitization allays adverse selection concerns by structuring transactions so that risk-averse investors receive their agreed-upon return without needing to screen out predatory loans. In addition to pricing, the secondary market uses structured finance and deal terms, instead of filtering, to manage credit, prepayment, and litigation risk. Furthermore, structured finance provides incentives to securitize predatory loans.

Translation: The people were screwed and the Wall Street firms were part of it. The professors called for voluntary due diligence. Fat chance.

As another law professor, Christopher Lewis Peterson of the University of Utah, put it in the jargon one finds in law articles:

The reform strategy favored by many legislators and a grow-ing number of scholars – assignee liability law – is only a par-tial solution. While a necessary component of the law, these rules are by themselves inadequate because **they excuse many of the most culpable parties from accountability**.

As for the history of all this, Yuliya S. Demyank of the Fed-eral Reserve Bank of Cleveland and Otto Van Hemert of New York University's Department of Finance write in the *Cardozo Law Review*:

> We find that the quality of loans deteriorated for six con-secutive years before the crisis and that securitizers were, to some extent, aware of it. We provide evidence that the rise and fall of the subprime mortgage market follows a classic lending boom-bust scenario, in which unsustainable growth leads to the collapse of the market. Problems could have been detected long before the crisis …

Another study found that subprime loans were dispropor-tionately channeled into the poorest zip codes. The pattern of exploitation is clear. They knew what they were doing. The researchers document it. The law scholars "tsk, tsk" about it, but where are the prosecutors?

Wall Street loved securitization because much of it oper-ated outside normal regulatory frameworks. A Congressional Research Service report called "Financial Crisis? The Liquidity Crunch of August 2007" explained:

> Securitization allowed mortgage lenders to bypass tradition-al banks. Securitization pools mortgages or other debts and sells them to investors in the form of bonds rather than leav-ing loans on lenders' balance sheets. The MBS [mortgage-

backed security] market developed in part because long-term fixed-rate mortgages held in banks' portfolios place banks at significant risk if interest rates rise (in which case, the banks' interest costs could exceed their mortgage interest earnings). MBS were popular with investors and banks because it allowed both to better diversify their portfolios. But because the MBS market was growing rapidly in size and sophistication, accurate pricing of its risk was difficult and could have been distorted by the housing boom ...

The growth of securitization meant that more loans could be originated by non-banks, many of which are **not subject to examination by federal bank examiners** and **not subject to underwriting guidances issued by federal financial regulators** ...

There you have it – a clear scheme to avoid oversight and ethical standards.

CHAPTER 9

THE VICTIMS ARE EVERYWHERE

The victims of financial crimes and predatory practices are everywhere. Nassim Nicholas Taleb, a professor of risk engineering at New York University Polytechnic Institute, explained: "We have just witnessed a similar phenomenon in the financial markets. A crime has been committed. Yes, we insist, a crime. There is a victim (the helpless retirees, taxpayers funding losses, perhaps even capitalism and free society). There were plenty of bystanders. And there was a robbery (overcompensated bankers who got fat bonuses hiding risks; overpaid quantitative risk managers selling patently bogus methods)."

Millions of families were hurt by taking on dubious subprime loans. Yet, the big money was not made there according to former Wall Street banker Nomi Prins. She identified a more insidious culprit: leveraging:

The biggest crime in all of this is the thing that's the least able to be understood and examined.

The tiny, tiny lowest layer of the crisis that started with subprime defaulting at the homeowner-borrower level which is being examined now to see if mortgages had been frauds or if mortgagors did the right practices whether predatory loans were used – all that stuff is important to know and important to examine and important to investigate. The money wasn't made there.

The money was made because several layers up a pyramid, Wall Street investment firms and commercial bank investment groups decided to repackage those mortgages, create layers of them, that they then resold to investors. They borrowed against those layers, which is the real crime. They would take a little piece of the layer of a security, underneath which somewhere there was a bunch of homebuyers, and they would take it and they would borrow 30 times the amount of money that it represented.

Wait a minute. They seemed to be creating money out of the air even as homeowners started defaulting on their loans. So I asked her about the deception in many of these transactions.

"Didn't they misrepresent the value of what they were selling – you know, it was rated triple-A and they sold it overseas as if it had assets behind them?" She looked at me as if I were totally naïve and then patiently explained:

The thing is that you take a bunch of assets that are mediocre and you say you assume that 10% of those mediocre assets will default, will disappear. That means you can say to an investor 90% of them are going to do completely fine.

And so those 90% – but you don't know which 90% they are – but again this is all generalities in the pitch to the investor and stamped with a AAA marked by the rating agency who's involved as well – and it's a perfectly valid thing to understand. You don't assume 100% of these loans are going to default. So as long as you don't assume that as an investor you believe the reasoning that 90% of them will do okay and for some reason you believed your 90% will do okay and they are effectively perfect and AAA …

"But that was an illusion, wasn't it from many of the banks that bought these securities?"

It became a complete illusion because what wasn't taken into account was first of all, defaults became higher than they were because the people who were being lent to weren't the only people involved in the whole pyramid of debt. Things were packaged and repackaged – there were CDOs [collateralized debt obligations] on Wall Street that referred to themselves four layers down, 20 pages down in their documentation.

They're completely circular so if anything goes wrong at any one point it perforates the whole structure. Anyone who buys it loses and, worse, there was no market for them way before it was publicly known that there was a crisis. These things were not selling. It didn't matter if they were triple-A. It didn't matter whether the defaults were higher or lower than expected. They were not moving so therefore they have no value.

"And then they also insured these investments. Tell us about these credit default swaps. What were they, and how did this contribute to the problem?"

The other thing that was going on, is you would take a bunch of subprime loans, you would package them up into a CDO and you would also write something called "credit default protection" against pieces of the CDO. So a bank for example like Goldman Sachs would create a CDO. It would stick all kinds of subprime loans and packages – packages and packages of them into a package and then it will go off to AIG which has spectacularly failed since then – and AIG had a triple-A rating which was an insured ID, a pristine impact, pristine credit rating – and Goldman would say, "You know what? You take this package of junk we just created and kind of insure it. You basically write a default swap to us. You basically credit insure it. You've got a much better rating than we do so investors will buy it from you without insurance. You make money. We make money. Everybody's happy ..."

"We are talking *trillions* here aren't we?"

We're talking trillions of dollars. So it's $14 trillion worth of asset backs with subprime and other types of mortgages and CDOs created between 2003 and 2007. $14 trillion were created. On that, investment houses and hedge funds and private equity funds could leverage 30, 40 times. Banks could leverage 15 to 20 times. On average they could only leverage 13 times on certain securities ...

My mind was spinning as I tried to decode this secret bankster lingo. My next interviewee was clearer. A former vice president of Standard & Poor's, Mo Sacirbey, agreed that homeowners were unfairly stigmatized. "Someone can talk about a poor homeowner who maybe didn't deserve [a] $120,000 home but on the other hand there was someone on Wall Street making a $12 million bonus because of that deal. So we need to be sure that we allocate accountability properly."

Former loan originator Dan Osso told me that the money that Wall Street was making was obscenely high: "From the Wall Street perspective, they realized that on [a] $100,000 note, they can make $186,000 in real money. So the more loans they had, the more loans they could flip over. If the loan was $100,000 and they sold it for $120,000 they made $20,000 immediately, in addition to getting their capital back."

I pressed him to elaborate, "There were reports that there was, what was called, 'suction' from Wall Street. In other words Wall Street investment houses began to make billions on these securitized loans, on CDOs and other derivatives were pressuring the mortgage people at the local level. Give us more. Give us more. Give us more."

Osso added: "Well the reason why Wall Street was putting the pressure, or the sucking sound that you referred to, on the loan originators is because of the profits that they were generating. When this whole concept first opened up and people realized the money that was to be made on the back end, trading the paper, **they were essentially creating liquid cash from nothing**. There was nothing there to back it up."

So as we see, the first level of the crime driven by massive mortgage fraud led to the second level: manipulation, exploitation and extraction by Wall Street.

CHAPTER 10

WITNESSES FOR THE PROSECUTION

I interviewed many homeowners who told me how they were suckered. Each has a story to tell, but together, they testify to a larger pattern based on false promises and deceptive deals. Many victims like this can be found from public hearings when and if there are any.

From my interviews:

Homeowner #1: Most of the world is sleeping. They are not aware of all the ins and outs of buying a house. They're not attorneys. They don't know. We don't know. It's really up to the guys that do know – the guys that are in those positions of leadership. They should be helping us – the people that don't know. But the sad thing is, they're just doing the opposite. They are taking advantage of our lack of understanding.

Homeowner #2: If I'm paying $2,800 a month for my home I want to live next to J-Lo and Marc Anthony, not where I live.

Homeowner #3: It started at 7%, now it's 9.8. It keeps going up and up. And we have no one to help us. This is the reason I'm here today. I feel that we should not have to leave our dream and our shelter. We don't even understand why it's going up. It's going in somebody's pocket, but not ours.

Homeowner #4: I'm a person that's trying to save my house. I'm in foreclosure right now. I feel like someone's hand is in my pocket, and I just want a fair break, a fair shake at the American dream.

Moe Badnor specializes in forensic investigations of the mortgage documents themselves. Eighty percent of the ones he examined were fraudulent. I watched and filmed one session in which he examined one homeowner's mortgage document. He's pointing at one page of the mortgage:

You have this signature, her actual signature. And this was from 1993, showing a completely different signature. It doesn't take a rocket scientist to see there's something terribly wrong here.

There's an entry here of a consultant fee. That should set off red flags. There are not really any consultants on a mortgage sale. It should have been one fee to Rise Mortgage. [Not to someone else.] This Mark Murphy [the consultant] is someone we need to investigate to find out why he got $7,800 dollars on this loan.

These people fraudulently took this woman's home that she's been living in for 15 years, thinking it was hers, when it hasn't been hers since 1993.

A line-by-line review of the application revealed deliberate misinformation, a pattern later confirmed in many investigations. What's news is Dan Osso's testimony that this was done *deliberately* and *by design*.

He told me, "The fraud and deception that was built into these transactions was a necessary part of the transaction in order to generate the profits. I think what happened is that the gravy train got so fat no one cared. They figured that this thing would never end. This was a train that had taken off. There is too much money being made by too many people, especially big people in the business – so why kill the golden goose? Let's just let it ride. They thought there would be no end to this whole thing."

Economists Tito Boeri and Luigi Guiso, argue on the European site *Vox* that mortage hustlers took advantage of the low level of financial literacy among American home buyers. They knew what consumers didn't know, and knew how to confuse them further. The U.S. educational system and media bear the responsibility for this situation.

> The first ingredient of the crisis is a blend of bad information, financial inexperience and myopia of consumers and investors. They fell for the prospect of getting a mortgage at rates never seen before and then extrapolating these rates out for thirty years.

> This myopia was encouraged and indeed exploited by banks and other lenders eager to attract and retain clients. This is surprisingly similar to what has been seen in the past when banks and intermediaries have advised their clients to invest in financial assets ill-suited to their ability to bear risk. In both cases, a biased advisor is the reflection of a clear conflict of interest in the financial industry.

> Financial literacy is low not only in financially backward countries (as one would expect), but also in the U.S. **Only two out of three Americans are familiar with the law of compound interest; less than half know how to measure the effects of inflation on the costs of indebtedness.**

Financial literacy is particularly low among those who have taken out subprime mortgages. The intermediaries exploited this financial illiteracy.

Mortgage abuse is the easiest component of this criminal enterprise to document and prove, but there's more. Much more.

CHAPTER 11

COUNT TWO:
WALL STREET COMPLICITY

The second level of the crime: The biggest banks and investment houses on Wall Street bought and then securitized loans after bundling and chopping, slicing and dicing them into "tranches" as "structured financial products" and had them falsely rated as more valuable then they were.

Economist Max Wolff explained Wall Street's role, when I filmed him for my *Plunder* documentary, outside the ever shrinking New York Stock Exchange. (The exchange had five trading rooms at the height of the boom; now it is down to two, handling only 30% of the stocks that are traded.)

What Wall Street did was package, sell, repackage and resell mortgages – making what was a small housing bubble – a gigantic housing bubble, and making what became an American financial problem, very much a global financial problem.

These mortgage bundles would be sold worldwide without full disclosure of the lack of underlying assets or risks. The banks that bought these derivative products failed to do due diligence relying on ratings agencies that overvalued their worth and accounting firms that did not do their job. The whole process was corrupt at its core.

Firms securitized. They bought securitizes based on mortgages that had no assets behind them. They must have known what they were doing … there was more than a little bit of fraud and there is more than enough blame to go around.

An insider in the industry, Janet Tavakoli, president of Chicago-based Tavakoli Structured Finance, a consulting firm for institutions, banks and institutional investors on derivatives wrote on CNN.com:

> The biggest crime on the American economy may go unpunished with no consequences to the perpetrators. The biggest crime was not predatory lending, but predatory securitizations, packages of loans that did not deserve the ratings or prices at the time they were sold. They ballooned what should have been a relatively small problem into a global crisis.
>
> Wall Street owes the American public for its key role in bringing the global economy – and in particular, the U.S. economy – to its knees. Goldman is not alone in owing the American public. It is not the worst of all of the Wall Street firms.
>
> **But among all of Wall Street's offenders, it is the most well-connected, and Goldman was the firm that cleaned up the most as the result of government bailouts.**

Political scientist Ben Barber put Tavakoli's concerns in a deeper context: "Capitalism has sort of gone off the rails. It ceased to be capitalism – it's financialization. The fact that it's now all about speculation, the fact that it's about Ponzi schemes, the fact that it's about selling and buying paper.

"We went from an economy of real goods, real commodities and real services to a system where people were buying and selling money, buying and selling assets, buying and selling other firms, where no new value was created."

Mo Sacirbey, once with Standard & Poor's, sees the system changing, too: "I think we had a transition from what truly was a free-market system to something now that is out of control and probably what I would define as a predatory system."

What we do know is that thanks to Wall Street's intervention, vast resources were transferred from the poorest neighborhoods to the richest institutions. Hofstra University real-estate law professor, Ron Silverman, quantified this phenomenon for me this way: "The severity of a problem of home mortgage lending in a predatory way may be quantified in the following terms: you are talking in recent years, of a problem that every year transfers hundreds of billions of dollars."

Taken aback by the statement, I had to check that I hadn't misheard him, "Hundreds of billions? You said *billions?*"

He replied, "I said billions, not millions, from the pockets of the poor to people who are in a far better position than their so-called victims."

A community organizer in Brooklyn, Rick Echeveria, argues that debt is central to this story: "Debt is profitable. One of the questions that we're often asked is, 'Well, Rick, uhh, how is it that a bank would lend $600 or $800 thousand dollars on a property that's only worth $300 or $400 thousand dollars? I mean, what are they going to do if the … if the mortgage borrower doesn't pay the mortgage?' And I explain to them the first lender is selling the debt, and being completely reimbursed. So there's no risk for them."

"Here's what happens," adds Barber: "There are three defaults on mortgages. The bank that holds those [defaults] sells those at 10 cents on the dollar to a second bank. That bank puts those [defaults] together with three other defaults and three other defaults and makes a second package and sells it to a third bank. The third bank sells 6 of these things from 10 different – from five different banks – to a hedge fund. The hedge fund repackages them, bundles them and sells them to some investor who has no idea what he has. And now we have a world of bad debt and no one can even tell you what it's – you know, what it's worth."

This Wall Street interest was fueled by the hunger for profits and bonuses according to Jean-François Gayraud and Noël Pons. "The second period (securitization and insurance derivatives) gave rise to convoluted scams, still caused by the attraction of bonuses and the very complexity of the operations themselves. The fraud changed in nature: conflicts of interest between rating agencies and banks, banks and insurance companies multiplied along with appraisals and contracts.

"Above all, the burdensome loans were leaving balance sheets veritable 'gasworks,' in which the fictive was incorporated with the real, were set up. At the moment of final reckoning, losses must be regularized: balance sheets manipulated and accounting statements falsified. The specter of Enron reappears!"

Former bank regulator Bill Black said many of the frauds on the Street originated at the top of the corporate ladder, when he told Laura Flanders on GRIT TV about his experience during the S & L crisis:

First we learned what was causing the problem, so we correctly identified the epidemic, and it was an epidemic of fraud led by the CEOs, and they were using accounting to commit that fraud. We found there was a distinctive pattern to how they did this so we looked for that pattern.

And even though savings and loans were reporting they had record profitability we made them priorities for enforcement actions if they were following this pattern.

The second thing found was the way they maximized their gains was to act like a Ponzi and to grow extremely rapidly. So we passed a rule that restricted growth to 25% a year which is an absurd number but the frauds were growing at an average annual rate of 50% a year. They couldn't survive unless they grow at least that fast. I mean the Ponzi dynamic is that you have to keep growing faster as the fraud progresses.

So in 2 years we had eliminated either directly by taking them on or once we ran out of money through the rule that restricted growth, all 300 of the control frauds.

Flanders then asked Black to bring the story up to the present, asking if these frauds are still underway:

Absolutely the pattern is very, very similar. The first thing you do is gut your underwriting or due diligent standards because the idea is to grow very rapidly and because people who can't repay loans will agree to pay you a higher interest fee so that combination plus extreme leverage, that means really heavy borrowing by the bank or the saving and loan.

You put them together, really high growth with lending to people who won't be able to pay you back and super leverage, and you are mathematically guaranteed as long as the bubble is expanding that you'll report not just that you're profitable, but you have extraordinary profitability. This is a sure thing this is not a risk.

Flanders asked Black, "Was it just motivated by greed?" Black's response was:

Greed is essential but greed is of course not new to the financial industry. What you have is a situation where now because of modern executive compensation, the greed is channeled in the most destructive way for the economy. So CEOs now make astonishing amounts of money through their bonuses' system overwhelmingly and they get vastly bigger bonuses if they report much, much higher profits.

But of course these are based on very short term accounting games, which are precisely the things you gimmick, by what we in criminology call "control fraud": fraud led by the people that control the organization. And as I said, it's a sure thing so they can guarantee that they get record compensation in a very short number of years. The institution will be destroyed but they'll be left far wealthier than they ever could imagine.

What is significant is that many of the Wall Street firms were doing business with each other and following the same pattern. Most were complicit.

Many of these executives threw their weight around bullying anyone, including their own auditors and boards who might question them.

"It amounts to little more than the temporary dominion of a bully," wrote Lewis Lapham in a special issue of *Lapham's Quarterly* on money. "The bully is bigger than it was, bigger and harder to see in the massive cloud of metaphor circling the globe at the speed of light. How then identify the perp with a name, age, license number and last known address?"

The arrogance of these CEOs is now being used to offer up a psychological rationale for the financial crisis, as writer Malcolm Gladwell wrote in the *New Yorker*: "The first wave of postmortems on the crash suggests a third possibility: that the roots of Wall Street's crisis were not structural or cognitive so much as they were psychological."

Responds James Kwak of the *Baseline Scenario* website:

> I think this is a bit much. The fact that some Wall Street actors were megalomaniacs does not change the facts that regulators did not regulate, or that rules and guidelines were inadequate. Nor is overconfidence inconsistent with incompetence ...

> All of these problems are endemic to modern American capitalism, not just Wall Street banks (although Wall Street trading floors are particularly fertile breeding grounds for overconfidence, given the nature of trading gains and losses, and the amount of money being made). I would tend to put it more in the category of problems that will always be with us than the category of specific causes of the financial crisis.

Neither Gladwell or Kwak even cite crime as a factor, much less *the* factor. That is another problem that will "always be with us."

CHAPTER 12

COUNT THREE:
THE INSURERS

The third level of this interconnected but decentralized criminal enterprise involved insuring these mostly fraudulent practices – in some cases betting against the securitized mortgages by the very people who sold them to guarantee that their investments would be protected when borrowers, who couldn't afford the loans to begin with, defaulted as many expected. They used insurance companies like American International Group Inc. (AIG) and hedge funds. Sometimes the Wall Street firms assumed the risks themselves. They also used credit default swaps to protect themselves against defaults because these lenders knew that defaulting was a likely outcome.

This hedge-fund world was also a pit of fraud. One example: In late July 2009, Bloomberg News reported:

> Hedge-fund manager Mark Bloom pleaded guilty to U.S. charges that he stole at least $20 million from clients and lied to them, and that he helped sell illegal tax shelters while working earlier at BDO Seidman LLP.

> "I committed securities fraud. I committed mail fraud," said Bloom to U.S. District Judge John Koeltl.

Some U.S. attorneys became more aggressive, using informants and then wiretaps to snag more hedge-fund fraudsters. On October 16, 2009, Raj Rajaratnam, a billionaire and founder of the Galleon Group Fund that managed investments worth more than $3.7 billion, was busted for insider trading with six others in a $25-million-dollar scheme. The arrests were said to have "unsettled" the industry while, according to the *New York Times*:

> ... ensnaring a top IBM official and executives at Intel and McKinsey & Company – Preet Bharara, the United States attorney for the Southern District of New York, said "The defendants operated in a cozy world of 'you scratch my back, I'll scratch your back.'"

It was such a serious case that the judge set bail at $100 million dollars. The *Wall Street Journal* quoted colleagues that called him a "star ... he was highly regarded." A U.S. attorney said the arrest should be a "wake up call" for Wall Street where crimes are only acknowledged after people are caught.

AIG burst into the headlines when the government stepped in to stop it from collapse with some $85 billion. It turned out that some of that money was used to make Goldman Sachs whole again – 100% on the dollar on outstanding claims by so-called counterparties. The company triggered a shitstorm of public protest when it announced outsized employee bonuses as the company was being saved by taxpayer funds.

While the bonuses got the headlines and condemnations, other company practices were forgotten. This one was reported on the *White Collar Crime Prof Blog* (www.lawprofessors. typepad.com/whitecollarcrime_blog):

> Five former insurance company executives, four from General Re Corporation (Gen Re) and one from AIG, were convicted of conspiracy, securities fraud, false statements to the SEC, and mail fraud in connection with a "finite insurance" contract

used to make AIG's reserves look stronger than they were. The defendants include the former CEO of Gen Re, Robert Ferguson; the company's former CFO; senior vice president; and the long-time assistant general counsel; in addition to a vice president from AIG. The case revolved around reinsurance transactions in 2000 and 2001 that helped AIG report an increase in its insurance loss reserves, something that analysis had been critical of, negatively affecting the stock price. According to prosecutors, the contracts were a sham transaction because no real risk passed to Gen Re, so AIG's accounting of it as a reinsurance agreement was improper.

An interesting twist in the case was the government's identification of former AIG CEO Maurice Greenberg as an unindicted co-conspirator. Greenberg has never been charged with any crime.

Two years earlier on February 10, 2006, AIG "settled" federal and state fraud claims according to the *White Collar Crime Prof Blog*:

American International Group Inc. reached a global settlement with federal and state authorities, including the civil suit filed by New York Attorney General Eliot Spitzer, to resolve the various investigations of insurance and securities fraud at the company. AIG's total payment will be $1.64 billion, comprised of the following: $700 million in disgorgement and a $100 million penalty to the SEC; $375 million to AIG policyholders; $344 million to states harmed by AIG's practices involving underreporting for workers' compensation funds; and, fines of $100 million to New York and $25 million to the U.S. Department of Justice.

AIG's later role in escalating the financial crisis was even more shadowy and important, as James Lieber reported in the *Village Voice*:

> The heart of darkness was the AIG Financial Products (AIGFP) office in London, where a large proportion of the derivatives were written. AIG had placed this unit outside American borders, which meant that it would not have to abide by American insurance reserve requirements. In other words, the derivatives clerks in London could sell as many products as they could write – even if it would bankrupt the company.
>
> The president of AIGFP, a tyrannical super-salesman named Joseph Cassano, certainly had the experience. In the 1980s, he was an executive at Drexel Burnham Lambert, the now-defunct brokerage that became the pivot of the junk-bond scandal that led to the jailing of Michael Milken, David Levine and Ivan Boesky.
>
> During the peak years of derivatives trading, the 400 or so employees of the London unit reportedly averaged earnings in excess of a million dollars a year. They sold "protection" – this Runyonesque term was favored – worth more than three times the value of parent company AIG. How could they not have known that they were putting at risk the largest insurer in the world and all the businesses and individuals that it covered?

Lieber has more, charging that these subprime-time players knew exactly what they were doing:

> In mid-September, when it was on the ropes, AIG received an astonishing $85-billion-emergency line of credit from the Fed. Soon, that was supplemented by another $67 billion. Much of that money, to use the government's euphemism,

has already been drawn down. Shamefully, neither Washington nor AIG will explain where the billions went. But the answer is increasingly clear: "It went to counterparties who bought derivatives from Cassano's shop in London."

There are more cases than I can count that illustrate this firm's clout.

Criminal law professor, John Coffee, a leading expert on white-collar crime at the Columbia University Law School, sees these insurance dodges and mortgage lending cases as functions of weak regulation. He told me: "I think that [the] regulatory system allowed these offerings when there was evidence that lending standards were being relaxed at the mortgage loan originator stage, when the underwriting standards were being relaxed, and in which credit rating agencies were becoming so conflicted that the really sophisticated person no longer believed their ratings."

Washington's Blog (www.washingtonsblog.com) reported that credit rating agencies took "bribes" for higher ratings:

[Finance professor] **ED KANE:** One has to remember that these are profit-making institutions. Issuers would pay more money for a good rating than a bad one, and issuers are very clear what kind of ratings they want. This is a straightforward way to pay bribes without ever violating the law, it appears, and the credit rating organizations do not take formal responsibility for their incompetence or negligence.

[Prolific financial journalist, Brookings Institution scholar and the author of more than 30 books on financial-market issues] **MARTIN MAYER:** One of the untold scandals of this country is that our museums are stuffed with fake old masters because the people who authenticated paintings for the Mellons and Morgans of this world were paid a percentage of the price for the authentication. If they said it was no good, they got a few hundred bucks. If they said it was great, they got $100,000. Same story in the credit-rating organizations.

Former bank regulator William Black told Bill Moyers these practices were deliberate. (Moyers allowed me to use the interview in my film, *Plunder*):

BILL MOYERS: Is it possible that these complex instruments were deliberately created so swindlers could exploit them?

WILLIAM BLACK: Oh, absolutely. This stuff, the exotic stuff that you're talking about was created out of things like liars' loans, which were known to be extraordinarily bad. And now it was getting triple-A ratings. Now a triple-A rating is supposed to mean there is zero credit risk. So you take something that not only has significant, it has crushing, risk. That's why it's toxic. And you create this fiction that it has zero risk. That itself, of course, is a fraudulent exercise. And again, there was nobody looking during the Bush years.

In his book *Liar's Poker*, Michael Lewis wrote about AIG's role, noting: "Every firm on Wall Street was making fantastic sums of money from this machine, but for the machine to keep running, the Wall Street firms needed someone to take the risk."

Hedge funds were like "Millionaires-Only Clubs," where ungodly sums could be invested in complicated vehicles, in secret, outside the prying eyes of Wall Street regulators. They began popping up more and more throughout the 1990s and exploded in the 2000s.

Bear Stearns' Bill Bamber explained it to me this way, "A hedge fund is designed. It is generally a private pool of capital, generally unregulated, so it has the kind of investors — typically not individual mom-and-pop investors, if it's individuals — it tends to be very-high-net to ultra-high-net-worth individuals and institutions who can afford to make the minimum million-dollar to five-million-dollar investments required to enter into investment and hedge funds."

Soon all the traditional investment firms had their own hedge funds. No wonder so many of these young people wanted in — and at the top.

Leading investor Jim Rogers told my *Media Channel* colleague, Rory O'Connor, how this worked: "Well, if you were going to be in the investment world, and you're a good investor the best way to make money was to have a hedge fund because you get compensated much higher. Hedge funds were being paid 1% of the assets and 20% of the profits in those days. So obviously that was the best way to make money if you were any good at it."

Rogers, with George Soros, started a fund because it was the thing to do, explaining, "A hedge fund is someone who buys things and at the same time hedges himself by selling short. The problem is, most people on the street don't understand selling short."

Terms like "selling short," "collateralized debt obligation" and "credit default swap" were soon everywhere but not really understood outside the financial world. Inside the world of hedge funds, each boasted about the superiority of its own super-secret proprietary investment algorithms.

They attempted to take the risk out of investing by putting large amounts of money in "side bets." While traditional investments grow the "real economy" by providing companies with money to hire workers and produce products and services, **Wall Street began putting more money into bets on the market than were being placed in the actual market itself.**

The side bet that finally blew up the economy was one of those complicated financial instruments, called a "credit derivative." Someone wishing to protect himself on a risky investment would pay regular premiums to a firm that would then agree to insure the investor if a loss were to occur.

An insurance policy on an investment is a smart idea. Chances are you've taken one out on your house – basic coverage against fire or lightning damage depending on where you live, perhaps flood, too. But now imagine that you could take out insurance on someone else's house, and you were permitted to take out multiple policies.

Back in 2005, as I show in my film, *In Debt We Trust*, written with Ray Nowsielski, you might have seen an opportunity and bought as many policies as you could afford on the homes in New Orleans before Hurricane Katrina wiped out the city. You'd have made a lot of money off the misery of those residents. So much for the Big Easy.

That is exactly what happened with credit derivatives. Savvy hedge-fund managers heard the weather report, knew which way the wind was blowing, and took out an incredibly large number of insurance policies on mortgage-backed securities.

When Katrina-like events blasted throughout America, in the form of the poorest in the country defaulting on mortgages in the millions, those policies paid out in the trillions for hedge-fund investors – already some of the richest people in the world. As millions of Americans went deeper into debt, as inequality grew, a small class of financiers prospered.

The *Village Voice* called it a "scheme that smacks of securities fraud," asking, "How could they not have known they were putting at risk the largest insurer in the world and all the businesses and individuals that it covered?"

Was this criminal? Again, it depends on to whom you speak. To John Coffee, "The real fraud in my mind, or the primary fraud, are the victims who were sold these worthless securities that were presented as utterly safe."

Economist Loretta Napoleoni who worked on Wall Street went further, "I would even say that this is racketeering because it took place between a group of real-estate agencies and banks together."

"And don't forget the role of the ratings agencies," adds Coffee. "Wall Street relaxed its due diligence standards, but it did not exercise any kind of scrutiny. He [an investor on Wall Street] was willing to buy almost any portfolio of mortgages because it found that in global markets it could sell these portfolios to a global audience based on credit ratings that were, frankly, the product of conflicts of interest and very strong pressure from Wall Street on the credit rating agencies.

"Taken together, the loans, the securitization and the insurance was part of a transaction pipeline – a highway of fraud and deception."

What do the ratings agencies say? Not much. Elizabeth MacDonald reported on *EMac's Stock Watch* (www.emac. blogs.foxbusiness.com):

> The agencies, which are not government run and are publicly traded, wrongfully gave top notch triple-A ratings to Kryptonite derivatives, (many of them subprime-mortgage bonds) just before that market collapsed …

> Congress at the time released internal memos written by executives at Moody's and Standard & Poor's, as well as email exchanges, instant messages, all pointing to how **insiders at these companies knew** they were botching the

job – and did little to stop the worst credit crisis in history from happening.

According to one internal message, Moody's top executive Ray McDaniel wrote that Moody's "analysts and MDs [managing directors] are continually 'pitched' by bankers, issuers, investors" and sometimes "we 'drink the Kool-Aid.'"

The markets have known about this problem for years. The credit rating agencies were painfully slow to warn investors about the problems at Bear Stearns, Enron and WorldCom, just to name a few calamities.

The fact that Warren Buffet, the so-called Oracle of Omaha and an Obama supporter, had invested in Moody's adds a certain unlikely twist to this issue. You'd think he knew better. He didn't!

At the same time, larger, arguably more important issues are still being downplayed.

What has been the societal impact of so many CEOs and firms making bad loans and then taking excessive salaries by extracting more wealth from investors and customers? This is not a question most media outlets even care about. They are more preoccupied with the well-being of high-net-worth individuals than the rest of society.

There have been few reports on how economic inequality deepened to shocking levels as unemployment and debt skyrocketed.

Economist Michael Hudson summed it up this way: "Ten years ago the upper one percent of the population owned 30% of America's return to wealth (dividends, interest and capital gains). Five years ago, they raised their proportion from 37% to 57%. And today it is estimated that the upper one percent of America population owns almost 70% of the return to wealth.

"It's unprecedented. It makes America look like a third-world banana republic."

"So why isn't the media screaming?" asked former Labor Secretary Robert Reich. "Partly because these job and wage losses are not, for the most part, falling on the segment of our population most visible to the media. They're falling overwhelmingly on the middle class and the poor."

By the summer of 2009, even as top bankers including Federal Reserve Bank Chairman Ben Bernanke projected a recovery right around the corner, unemployment continued to climb, foreclosures to mount, bankruptcies to grow, markets to shrink, firms to fold, and tensions to tear apart families and communities.

New rules are needed, more regulations will help but the media, too, has to wake up to help shift the debate to include the need for deeper changes and a crackdown on white-collar crime. Will our media cover these issues?

CHAPTER 13

CO-CONSPIRATORS: THE ROLE OF THE MEDIA

(Editor's note: Part of this chapter has appeared previosuly in two European journalism reviews)

Most journalists failed to pick up the worldwide crunch that was to shatter capitalism. Were they lazy? Or worse to imagine: Were they embedded with the bankers?

We were just entering the new millennium when I joined a caravan of journalists and business leaders on a mountain climbing trek, from the airport in Zurich to the snowy peaks in Davos, Switzerland, for the annual meeting of the World Economic Forum. It was hardly taxing or dangerous. We went by limo. Even though I am an independent journalist, I had wrangled an invitation as a guest to a special media program, and was given full credentials to mingle with the heavy hitters. I was not there as a mere reporter, consigned to the working press room carved out of a fallout shelter in the basement of the conference center, but as a full-fledged attendee alongside editors of the *Wall Street Journal*, *Time*, *Newsweek* and the *Financial Times*.

We were the chosen ones and allowed to "embed" ourselves into the elite of the multinational corporate culture. The affluence and the elitism were seductive and co-optative on that mountaintop, with many media outlets glowing over a new genre of masters of the universe – the "Davos Man." One of our number, a reporter for CNBC would soon "cross the aisle" and leave reporting for a hedge fund (it later went bust).

At the time, January 2000, the dot-com bubble was unraveling but there was no discussion of what might replace it, or expectation that just a few years later the world economy would collapse into a global crisis. The hype that year was about the promise of globalization, and a capitalist system that could do no wrong. A spirit of "cautious optimism" was as much criticism as was permissible.

Eight years later, Bloomberg News went back to Davos in the heart of Europe and found leaders there willing to concede that they had not alerted us to the problems, and in effect may have contributed to the environment of greed and free-market bullishness. Now, in the riptide of the worst financial crisis since the Great Depression, World Economic Forum (WEF) officials and delegates said that many of the chief executive officers who gathered in Davos over the last five years didn't listen to warnings from their peers. Davos organizers also say they failed to play tough with the financial-industry bosses, opting to accept their funding and let them turn Davos into a rave-up for Wall Street excesses.

"Once upon a time, the World Economic Forum was the ultimate Wall Street jamboree," said Klaus Schwab, the 70-year-old WEF founder and executive chairman, to Bloomberg News. "The partying crept in. We let it get out of control, and attention was taken away from the speed and complexity of how the world's challenges built up."

It was not just the CEOs who indulged and enabled practices that would destabilize the system, but many media outlets that lacked the independence and critical judgment needed to investigate the financialization of the economic system and failed to warn of serious excesses and, sometimes, criminal conduct. When I say the "media," I mean newspapers and TV stations – with some exemplary exceptions – in the United States and Europe.

DANNY SCHECHTER

Others saw the risks and were also ignored. In fact, the economist James Galbraith of the University of Texas said that only eight out of thousands of his colleagues saw what was coming. He noted, "It's an enormous blot on the reputation of the profession. There are thousands of economists. Most of them teach. And most of them teach a theoretical framework that has been shown to be fundamentally useless."

If a top economist will criticize his colleagues, why won't leaders in the media examine how the industry got it so wrong?

Today, we are all alarmed by the rapidly spreading global crisis. My film *Plunder* investigates three aspects of it: the practices of the mortgage industry and Wall Street firms, the regulators who didn't regulate, and the media that was often complicit. Not only were there few investigations of subprime predatory practices between 2002 and 2007, but also, media companies took billions – that's right, billions – in advertising revenue from dodgy lenders and credit card companies. Banks had gone from telling to selling

One of the key sources of revenue for newspapers is real-estate advertising in weekend supplements and classified sections. The newspaper industry became in some communities the marketing arm of the real-estate industry. In some cities you actually had newspapers getting a piece of the action of sales through the ads that they had generated – they were part of the corruption. So of course there was little real scrutiny about what was actually happening in the neighborhoods where mortgage fraud was pervasive, where people who couldn't afford to buy houses were buying them with bogus mortgages. Some newspapers were making money on the sales of these homes.

While coverage in Europe may have been better once the crisis erupted, there had been little reporting on or questioning of the large investments by European and Asian banks in sub-prime securities, many based on shoddy and discriminatory lending practices. Some of those banks would later collapse or write off billions because these "asset-backed" securities had no assets backing them. They would blame the Americans for scamming them – and there is truth to the charge – but surely they had a responsibility to do due diligence and realize that their money was underwriting sleazy practices that has led to a foreclosure crisis affecting millions of families?

Instead many outlets politicized the problem, with the media rarely acknowledging their laziness and superficial coverage. Soeren Kern, a senior analyst for transatlantic relations at the Madrid-based *Grupo de Estudios Estratégicos*, wrote:

> While much of the initial reaction emanating from Europe was self-congratulatory gloating to the effect that Europe's "superior" economic model made it immune to the kind of problems plaguing the United States, the fact that this has now proven to be false has unleashed an entirely predictable populist reaction; European leaders of all ideological stripes are now busy blaming the United States for the financial problems in their home countries, as if anti-Americanism will somehow shield them from the political fall-out from the trouble that lies ahead. Many Europeans are calling for an end to American global economic dominance, with, of course, a correspondingly greater regulatory role for Europe.

> Some of the most virulent anti-Americanism stems, as usual, from Germany, where media soothsayers have had a field day prophesying America's imminent downfall. The weekly news magazine *Der Spiegel*, for example, has a cover showing the Statue of Liberty's torch, extinguished, with the headline: "The Price of Arrogance." The cover of the *Die Zeit* news-

paper shows a Bald Eagle plunging to Earth, feathers flying, with a flag of the European Union clutched in one of its talons. Another *Die Zeit* article titled "USA: Can the Superpower Learn to Step Down?" asks: "How can the land of victory and optimism adapt to life after the imperial moment?" And so on. German politicians have joined in the America-bashing too. Finance Minister Peer Steinbrück predicts that "the U.S. will lose its superpower status in the world financial system." (He also said "the financial crisis [is] above all an American problem," words he ended up eating a few days later while trying, unsuccessfully, to rescue Germany's Hypo Real Estate banking group.)

Global media has a responsibility to do a better job covering the crisis and also acknowledging its own role. I am not the only media critic raising this issue. Howard Kurtz wrote in the *Washington Post*:

As news organizations chase exclusives about the Wall Street meltdown, they also are grappling with a troubling question: Why didn't they see this coming?

"We all failed," says Charlie Gasparino, a former *Wall Street Journal* and *Newsweek* reporter [now of Fox Business Network]. "What we didn't understand was that this was building up. We all bear responsibility to a certain extent."

The shaky house of financial cards that has come tumbling down was erected largely in public view: overextended investment banks, risky practices by Fannie Mae and Freddie Mac, exotic mortgage instruments that became part of a shadow banking system. But while these were conveyed in incremental stories – and a few whistle-blowing columns

– the business press never conveyed a real sense of alarm until institutions began to collapse.

Former business journalist Dean Starkman, once with the *Wall Street Journal*, who now covers the business media for the *Columbia Journalism Review* agreed, telling me, "The business press did not really recognize and understand what they were up against, how dramatically the world had changed, how the lending industry had changed, how out of control Wall Street had become. They were to me extremely slow to recognize, appreciate and confront the changes in the financial system." He also believed there was a relationship between the advertising revenues and the quality of journalism: "They made a lot of money. Again that was a big miss. A lot of time was spent on [reporting] the personalities, but not on how those earnings were being created. The third big miss is the growing financial distress of the middle class generally speaking. To me it was the most frustrating thing to see the coverage of the deterioration of the everyday financial life of Americans."

The *editorsweblog* (www.editorsweblog.org) discussed this issue too, "The media stands accused of failing to foresee the global financial crisis, of a lack of understanding of the issues, and even of having a hand in the problems we now face." The blog interviewed me and the managing editor of the *Financial Times*, Daniel Bogler, who believes the media is "fanning the flames" of the crisis.

I was in Paris in mid-October of 2008 where the word *crise* was plastered all over every magazine, newspaper and newsstand. It's big news and the French public seemed to think that its government acted swiftly to stem it. *Le Figaro* reported a 60 percent approval rate for President Nikolas Sarkozy's strategy of promptly injecting money into banks to make the *crise financiere* go away. Out in *La Défense*, an overdeveloped *arrondisse-*

ment known as the Wall Street of Paris, where the banks and insurance companies are based, I was filming interviews against the background of glass towers, with the *Arc de Triomphe* visible on the far horizon. There, a German businessman assured me that the crisis will be "over by Monday," since his government was busily capitalizing (or is it recapitalizing?) its engines of capitalism (while the German public was making a run on the bookstore for copies of Karl Marx's *Das Kapital*).

One young man had no idea what I was taking about when we asked him if he was worried. He said he didn't really know what was going on and doubted that it would affect him since he had a debit card, not a credit card. Another confided the worst that would happen was a "slowdown." We don't have subprime loans in Europe I was assured. Maybe, I responded, but your banks invested in these bogus products, made billions and now are writing it all down. And then I followed my usual practice of interviewing people in junior positions who don't feel the need to hype their companies. A grad student interning at a large bank that was taken over told me that people who don't follow finance have no clue about what's going on and how serious it is. He added that the companies and the media are not telling them either. He described the atmosphere of panic and uncertainty in the bank he worked for, where the new owner had yet to assert control, and, he said, "Who knows how long our jobs would last?" He spoke of a climate of greed that led a small number of interconnected executives operating in their own bubble to accumulate millions for themselves with no apparent concern about how it affected others.

It is hard for me to be as critical of European media as I am of the media I know best, the media in the U.S. I seem to get interviewed more, in the press and both on radio and television, in Europe. The European mass media seems more diverse

THE CRIME OF OUR TIME

and critical than the U.S. press, whose critics have suggested that a kind of corporate embedding took place in which journalists at leading newspapers and TV channels bought into the ethos and culture of money-making and reckless acquisition.

Hendrik Hertzberg, a senior editor of the *New Yorker*, told me recently, "You could say that **business journalism was in bed with, or embedded, in the institutions, the way that war correspondents were embedded in the units in Iraq.** But you know, that can go both ways. You have a kind of Stockholm Syndrome, you adopt the point of view of the one with whom you're embedded with on one hand; on the other hand, you are seeing it, the reality is coming before your eyes, whether you're reporting it or not, so you can get the kind of reporting we got in Iraq."

In Britain, former *Observer* editor Will Hutton, now CEO of the Work Foundation, sort of echoed that when he lashed out at his former colleagues during a news agencies conference in Spain. Speaking to reporters and editors via video link, he charged media complicity: "General journalists, as well as business journalists, are really guilty in this. They have indulged madness in the last five years — we should have been better at whistleblowing than we were. Journalists for the most part missed the build-up to the crisis and did not warn the public. We all kind of believed that we had fallen upon some kind of alchemy, which capitalism had changed. And I think everyone got carried away. Even skeptics in the end found it was pretty difficult to maintain skepticism in the face of the tsunami of apparent easy money. We lost our senses, all of us journalists, politicians. We suspended our judgment and we are paying a big, big price."

The British press has viewed the crisis through the ideological lenses identified with various media outlets, but in some cases political lines have been crossed. The *Daily Telegraph*, nominally a pro-business, free-market newspaper – an enemy of statist liberals and mechanical Marxists – was the most outspoken in its predictions about a financial Armageddon. So much so that it was denounced as alarmist, even apocalyptic in its projections. Its columnists were often accurate and ahead of the pack.

What started as a kind of anglophile bashing of Wall Street for its lack of regulation turned into the scrutiny of British practices in the Northern Rock affair and its aftermath. This was happening as the paper and others began to deal with the consequences of the crisis by cutting more staff and looking to save money on "extras" elsewhere.

In late January 2009 it was announced that the Treasury Select Committee would take evidence the following month from key figures in the news media, including Robert Peston, the BBC business editor, who broke several stories last autumn when the financial crisis was the most acute. Also called were columnist Simon Jenkins, who in the *Guardian* had written that financial journalists should be more aware of how their coverage can affect sentiment, *Financial Times* editor Lionel Barber, and *Daily Mail* financial editor Alex Brummer. The Select Committee said it would weigh whether financial journalists should exercise greater restraint during periods of market turbulence and whether any kind of reporting restrictions should be applied during such periods. The journalists it mentioned were largely on top of the story; countless others were not. Funny how there was no inquiry about lack of coverage of a pending crisis. Now, suddenly, it's the media's fault.

What accounts for this media failure? I wrote to John Gittelsohn of California's *Orange County Register* whose work on the mortgage fraud issues I admired. He replied by indicting the media's lack of depth and resources and the way our media system has cut back costly investigations because of our own financial crises. He cited another factor – fear of lawsuits. Businesses were eager to silence or suppress "bad press" in an era when so many wealthy companies had invested in sophisticated public relations.

So what's to be done? Hutton calls for the media to ask tougher questions, but that may not be enough – journalists need to be educated, or re-educated, in the dark arts of financial institutions. During an interview recently on *editorsweblog*, the *FT*'s managing editor Daniel Bogler wrote, "It's unfortunate that the financial literacy and understanding of how things work in the city and of basic accounting and so on, is actually very thin in financial journalism."

On the night I wrote this, I chatted with a senior editor of the *New York Times* who deals with news ethics and practices. I set out my critique, arguing that despite a few early strong articles in the *Times*, most of the paper missed the run-up to the crisis just as much of the press was uncritical of the run-up to the war in Iraq. I thought he would argue with me. He didn't.

There is an unfortunate dialectic between financial failures and media failures. We as journalists may not be able to do much about the former but we must become more conscious of, and be willing to do something about, the latter.

We were then at the end of the Bush era. We were expecting a new political order. Can we also hope for a new media order?

DANNY SCHECHTER

CHAPTER 14

WARNINGS IGNORED

I t wasn't just the traditional journalists who missed the crisis. According to economist Robert Samuelson, most economists missed it. In the *Washington Post* in July 2009, he lamented: "One intriguing subplot of the economic crisis is the failure of most economists to predict it. Here we have the most spectacular economic and financial crisis in decades – possibly since the Great Depression – and the one group that spends most of its waking hours analyzing the economy basically missed it. Oh, a few economists can legitimately claim some foresight. But they are a handful. Most were as surprised as the rest of us."

Also in July 2009, the *Economist* acknowledged these problems but rushed to defend the economics profession. Law Professor Linda Beale responded with a blistering critique on her *A Taxing Matter* blog (www.ataxingmatter.blogs.com) characterizing the piece as revealing three disturbing truths about the world of professional economists, it:

1. Helped cause the current economic crisis

2. Failed to see it coming

3. Doesn't know how to fix it

Yet, there were some economists who saw it coming like a freight train, bloggers and many whistleblowers among others. I would like to think that I was among them. As usual, the mainstream media for the most part shut out critical voices that challenged the conventional wisdom.

There were insiders in Washington, including at the Federal Reserve Bank, who warned of danger ahead. They, too, were ignored. One was Brooksley Born, of the Commodities Futures Trading Commission, who raised red flags about the unregulated trade in derivatives. She told PBS's *Frontline* program that she was "puzzled" by the opposition she faced in Washington. "What was it that was in this market that had to be hidden," she asked.

In my own case, I found many in media circles in total denial when I released my film, *In Debt We Trust*, as no major TV outlet would show it, perhaps because of all the advertising money sloshing around supporting them. (The *New York Times* put the figure at more than $3 billion from 2002 to 2007.)

"There is a credit divide in America that fuels our economic divide," I argued in my film, warning of a potential economic implosion because so many Americans are trapped by a debt squeeze. I was not alone in projecting a crisis, although my focus was more on the failure of many media outlets to track the problem and ask deeper questions.

"Ours has become a nation in which the carrot of instant affluence is quickly menaced by the harsh stick of bill collectors, lawsuits, and foreclosures," I contended. "And yet, this bubble can burst and has: the slickest of our bankers and the savviest of our marketers have *not* been able to undo the law of gravity, that what goes up must come down."

One didn't have to be an expert to see the warning signs which have since led to a massive market meltdown, a collapse of the subprime mortgage market, bankruptcies by leading financial lenders, billions of dollars in losses by top banks and financial lenders, and predictions of more pain to come for millions of Americans facing foreclosures.

DANNY SCHECHTER

Many in positions of power downplayed the seriousness of the threat, preferring modest, unrealistic and inaccurate estimates, perhaps so as not to further panic the markets.

Federal Reserve Chairman Bernanke was among those who was way off in his prognostications. As Bear Stearns hedge funds were imploding in July 2007, thanks to the mismanagement by execs who would later be arrested for fraud, he told Congress that he only expected subprime losses in the $50 to $100-billion range.

Economist Yves Smith responded, "I recall gasping out loud when I read that, because no one in the private sector had, had loss estimates like that for a while. The lowest estimates I was seeing around then was $150 billion." Bernanke was telling Congress that this should be seen as "bumps" along the road of market innovation.

A quick Google search uncarthed a *MarketWatch* story on Bernanke's Senate testimony. Not only did it have the estimate I so fondly recalled, but it had doozies like this:

Federal Reserve Chairman Ben Bernanke that there will be "significant losses" associated with subprime mortgages but that these losses should be regarded as "bumps" along the road of market innovation …

He was challenged by Senator Richard Shelby of Alabama: "We have been told the problem is largely isolated and contained, but I am concerned that it may not be …"

It wasn't. Bernanke had drunk his own Kool-Aid. Like many officials, he downplayed the seriousness of a crime when it was unfolding. He saw the massive foreclosures coming but did nothing at the time to stop them.

When I started making my film on the subject, a colleague

warned me that the issue might be too obscure to rate media coverage. "No one likes to talk about money," said a producer friend. "This could be such a downer."

I wasn't the only one running into a wall of media refusing to acknowledge what was going on.

Financier Peter Schiff, a supporter of Congressman Ron Paul's libertarian politics, focused on government responsibility not corporate complicity and yet was also treated with hostility.

He told me "… every time I would find myself in that venue where I was on television surrounded by other supposed experts on economics in the market. They would completely dismiss what I was saying … They would laugh it off; they would snicker, you know."

It was startling to watch a Fox News interview in December 2006, where other guests praised the economy and poo-pooed Schiff's argument, actually laughing at him on air. "It was like there's no way that this could happen," he said about how his forecast of the coming collapse was regarded, "I'm just a pariah of global doom. I'm Chicken Little. This is a fantastic economy."

What also seemed increasingly clear was that Fox was not really a news channel. It looked like one, followed its formats with lots of spice and attractive females designed to reel in its overwhelmingly male audience, but it had more of a political function than a journalistic one as *New York Times* op-ed columnist Paul Krugman told Rory O'Connor: "There's nothing like Fox News. There's no liberal news organization like Fox News. I wrote during the 2000 campaign that if Bush said that the earth was flat, the media would have headlined, 'Some different opinions about the earth's shape.'

"Look we have a situation now in which there are several major parts of the news media that are, for all intents and purposes, part of movement of conservatism. There's the *New*

York Post, the *Washington Times*, which other news organizations are intimidated with these to some extent."

It wasn't just Fox News and the business channels that missed the real story. They all followed the same approach, as Hendrik Hertzberg, a senior editor of the *New Yorker*, told me: "TV financial journalism, particularly the business networks, are sort of like the sports networks. You know [what] they're really there for. And the idea that the stock market is a wonderful game, and it's you're going to win — not lose — when you play it."

Financial journalist Gary Weiss saw the same problem: "The general tenor of the coverage is going to be to celebrate the Street, to celebrate CEOs, and not to give critical scrutiny that questions the way they do business. You know the coverage, when you get there, will be critical scrutiny with the way individual companies operate and critical scrutiny of individual CEOs. But you won't get coverage that looks at what's happening wrong. That you won't, that you don't, really see."

"There's not that much skepticism in business journalism," convicted white-collar criminal, Sam Antar, agreed.

I put it to Antar that the public was not warned about the coming crisis.

Antar replied, "That is, in large part, that is correct, except there were smart people out there. There were smart short sellers out there that saw it coming and made money from it. And when they did publicize their findings, they were either sued, or marginalized, or smeared by public companies, not able to get on television, et cetera. That's the unfortunate part."

Dean Starkman, once with the *Wall Street Journal* and who now critiques business journalism for the *Columbia Journalism Review*, told me: "The business press did not really recognize and understand what they were up against: how dramatic the world had changed; how the lending industry had changed.

That's the thing you've documented. How out of control Wall Street had become. I think it's a contributive problem that led us to where we are today."

Starkman even compares the journalists who cover Wall Street to reporters sent to Iraq. He said that they, too, were embedded – but in the corporate culture. "The great panic of the 2008 crisis is the equivalent for business press of what the Iraq War was for the general press. I think there is a lot to that. This was the overwhelming important story of our time. In the case of Iraq the general press clearly had it wrong. For the business media, the financial crisis *is* the big one. This is the story of our generation. The parallel is there.

"You can extend the analogy a little bit further. In the case of Iraq, journalists were with the troops. In the case of the financial crisis you could tell that the business media corps were with the particular narratives that have their origins on Wall Street ... I don't think that the analogy between the Iraq story and the financial crisis story is out of whack at all."

I pressed Starkman on whether this type of coverage contributed to the criminality in the financial industry.

He thought about it, and concluded: "Essentially an entire industry became predatory ..."

"Predatory, like *criminal*?" I asked him.

"I mean we are talking about, deceptive marketing on a mass scale as a function of a corporate policy. Criminal? Yeah ... I'm just saying that the evidences at that point were overwhelming. The borrowers were subjected to deceptive marketing practices. A lot of time, I think, was spent on personality driven reporting ... not adequately explored."

Economist Max Wolff did not disagree, "I think the media gave free commercials for financial products. The media became cheerleaders instead of critics. That took out a critical voice that could have told people about this."

DANNY SCHECHTER

Who could blame them for their skepticism? After all, the U.S. was in the midst of an economic boom. After a decade of unparalleled prosperity, the dot-com bubble had burst in 2000. But then with help from the Federal Reserve lowering the interest rates, the housing market exploded, and America found itself a new bubble. Nay-sayers were dismissed.

In this period I tried to alert my media colleagues to the coming credit crisis in the pages of *Nieman Reports* (www. nieman.harvard.edu/reports.aspx), the journalism review of Harvard's Nieman Foundation. My concerns largely fell on deaf ears.

Even though I had many political disagreements with Peter Schiff, the two of us, despite coming from different places, were running into similar problems.

He told me, "I didn't see how this thing could have gone on for another decade. It seemed like the problem was so enormous, that the real-estate bubble was so huge, that the bad debts that had been accumulated by our financial institutions was just so enormous, I didn't see any way we could sweep it under the rug much longer. So I was pretty confident. And so even the fact that we made it to 2007 was an accomplishment."

CHAPTER 15

THE BEAR STEARNS "BLEED OUT"

The first major institution to fall in the financial crisis was Bear Stearns, one of the first banks to fuel the subprime mortgage crisis. Its stockholders would eventually be wiped out in what was described as the first government bailout. Some saw it as a case of karma: what went around, came around. Others suspect that the crime on the Street may have become crime in the suites with killer institutions gunning for each other. The people who had no compunctions exploiting the poor and uninformed also enjoy the "blood sport" of taking each other down.

Bear Stearns was the fifth largest U.S. investment bank. It was 85 years old. At first after announcing major liquidity problems, it received a 28-day emergency loan from the New York Federal Reserve Bank. "Investors were fearful that the firm's collapse could spark a collapse of the financial sector," noted the Council on Foreign Relations. "The bank traded at a high of $172 per share about two months earlier. Fears of its fall led to panic about the future of Wall Street."

In *Vanity Fair*, Bryan Burroughs sees the fall of Bear Stearns as a still mysterious financial scandal:

> The fall of Bear Stearns wasn't just another financial collapse. There has never been anything on Wall Street to compare to it: a "run" on a major investment bank, caused in large part not by a criminal indictment or some mammoth quarterly loss but by rumor and innuendo that, as best one can tell, had little basis in fact. Bear Stearns had endured more than

its share of self-inflicted wounds in the previous year, but there was no reason it had to die that week in March.

Much of the media missed the event that triggered the collapse: the crash of Carlyle Capital, a huge hedge fund and offshoot of the Carlyle Group, that was overleveraged with borrowed money and connected to prominent politicians and wealthy investors all over the world. It claimed to control $22 billion on a capital base of under $700 million. As Lorretta Napoleoni reported in her book, *Rogue Economics*: "The crash of Carlyle Capital, dragged Bear Stearns, its major creditor, into insolvency." Many of the superstars of the globalization elite took a big hit, but their names and positions escaped media scrutiny.

Most of the news focus was on the firm's larger than life, bridge playing CEO Jimmy Cayne because he was a mediagenic character. His personality seemed to overhang the story even though he was personally playing at a bridge competition when his good ship Bear went down.

According to William Cohan's book on Bear's rise and fall, *House of Cards*, Bear's behavior mirrored and set the standard for what was going on, on the Street:

> The leaders of Wall Street affirmatively made decisions year after year that made their firms extraordinarily highly leveraged and risky enterprises. They created a 24/7 production line that manufactured and sold hundreds of billions of dollars worth of mortgage-backed, and other asset-backed, securities placing them with investors all over the globe who were seduced by their high yields and their phony AAA ratings. Their reward was huge eight-figure bonuses year after year. What a great business! Over time, as the market choked on what they were selling, firms like Bear Stearns, Lehman, Mer-

rill Lynch and Citigroup, had to lard more and more of these securities on their exploding balance sheets, all supported by an increasingly smaller and smaller slice of equity.

What brought the whole proverbial house of cards to its present calamitous state was the further decision these firms made to use the risky securities on their balance sheets as collateral to obtain overnight loans through "repurchase agreements" in the so-called repo markets.

Their ridiculously high-leverage and over-investment in junk mortgage-backed securities, played a role in the loss of confidence Bear Stearns encountered. Others blame the public for taking out mortgages they couldn't afford.

There was more to the story. There were forces at work here that suggest illegal activities on a number of levels. The firm has always pictured itself as small and feisty, and in earlier Wall Street crises it pissed off competitors by not doing what others felt was its duty. *Reason* magazine explained why some on the Street hoped for its fall. According to this theory:

Bear was selected for punishment by the Wall Street colleagues it had snubbed 10 years earlier (among them future Treasury Secretary Henry Paulson, who was then working at Goldman Sachs) by declining to join a team assembled by the Federal Reserve to bail out the broken LTCM hedge fund.

The company was presented in macho terms by an anonymous executive:

On Wall Street, like on the playground when you're a kid, reputation is everything. You've got to fight to earn it, but once you earn it, it's yours to keep. We'd been around for 85 years and we'd been through our battles. We'd gotten beaten up, we'd grown tough, and we'd survived. We weren't the biggest kid on the block, but we weren't getting kicked around by the playground bully, either.

Their final crisis began when two Bear Stearns hedge-fund managers were arrested for fraud – the FBI found emails in which they admitted selling worthless securities to the public while at the same time dumping their own shares.

The two, Ralph Cioffi and Matthew Tannin, amazingly became, as of October 2009, the only major criminal prosecution in the financial crisis. One issue in the trial was the admissability of their emails, one of which expressed the fear that their fund could "blow up."

Business Insider (www.businessinsider.com) noted, "prosecutors are trying to admit evidence at trial that":

- Cioffi and Tannin effectively committed bank fraud.

- Cioffi tried to obtain documents in Florida that were the subject of a government subpoena.

- Tannin's tablet PC, which he used as an electronic notebook, and a handwritten trading notebook used by Cioffi between January 2007 and June 2007 – which includes the period of the alleged fraud – are missing.

Then there's the Gmail issue. As the *Wall Steet Journal's Law Blog* noted:

Tannin allegedly shut down his personal Google email account in March 2008, several months before he was charged, after he was aware the government had interest in the account and after it ordered that all emails and documents relevant to the hedge funds be preserved.

The Gmail account is critical because it's where Tannin may have written damning emails — privately saying that the funds were in serious trouble while publicly crowing about their success. Defense lawyers say the firm told Tannin to shut down the account and besides, there's no legal obligation to turn over the emails.

All of this shows the difficulties of prosecuting these cases on narrow issues. Their lawyers, of course, sought to keep the emails out of the case. The prosecution of the first and so far the only major case to emerge from the financial crisis may not succeed.

But there was something else going on — even the suggestion that Bear was targeted and deliberately brought down. I learned that when I spoke at length with Bill Bamber, a former Bear managing director and the co-author of *Bear Trap*.

We met in his Upper East Side apartment where he was working on the Bloomberg, a sophisticated computer created by former bond trader turned New York mayor, Michael Bloomberg. It is the type of pricey machine found in all the investment banks. I asked what it felt like for him to watch the value of his firm disappear.

His response, "You can't make this shit up? It was so surreal that basically my colleagues and I would say this to one another because it was beyond the realm of what one could normally ascribe to what was happening, and we were left with, you just can't make this shit up."

I responded, "In terms of the shit that you can't make up, there seemed to be this weird thing happening. Here is a company, 85 years old, it had a lot of money 'in the bank,' so to speak, billions and billions of dollars, claimed it had no liquidity crisis, and yet you kept reading that this firm was teetering on the brink?"

Bamber told me what happened in the week that his firm imploded, and the many questions that remain about whether it was targeted in a fraudulent way. This chronology appears in my film, *Plunder*, discussing how the price of Bear Stearns' stock fell day by day as unknown parties – so-called naked short sellers bet that the firm's share price would collapse. They would make $250 million on an investment of $1.5 million.

Matt Taibbi also investigated this mystery for *Rolling Stone*:

On Tuesday, March 11, 2008, somebody – nobody knows who – made one of the craziest bets Wall Street has ever seen. The mystery figure spent $1.7 million on a series of options, gambling that shares in the venerable investment bank Bear Stearns would lose more than half their value in nine days or less. It was madness – "like buying 1.7 million lottery tickets," according to one financial analyst.

But what's even crazier is that the bet paid.

... That this was a brazen case of insider manipulation was so obvious that even Sen. Chris Dodd, chairman of the pillow-soft-touch Senate Banking Committee, couldn't help but remark on it a few weeks later, when questioning Christopher Cox, the then-chief of the Securities and Exchange Commission. "I would hope that you're looking at this," Dodd said. "This kind of spike must have triggered some sort of bells and whistles at the SEC. This goes beyond rumors."

Cox nodded sternly and promised, yes, he would look into it. What actually happened is another matter. Although the SEC issued more than 50 subpoenas to Wall Street firms, it has yet to identify the mysterious trader who somehow seemed to know in advance that one of the five largest investment banks in America was going to completely tank in a matter of days. "I've seen the SEC send agents overseas in a simple insider-trading case to investigate profits of maybe $2,000," says Brent Baker, a former senior counsel for the commission. "But they did nothing to stop this."

Added the *Power Elite* blog (www.thepowerelite.blogspot. com), "I've been arguing for over a year now that when the forensics were done on this Great Recession, white-collar crime would be the source of it. And while much of what was done on Wall Street that ended up wrecking the economy was 'technically legal,' much of the overt illegal behavior has never been pursued or prosecuted."

Here's part of what happened pieced together, day by day, from a conversation I had with Bamber:

MONDAY, MARCH 10 – BEAR SHARE PRICE $69

BILL BAMBER: The final week as I experienced it on the trading desk was when I walked in and started to hear the first reports on Bloomberg for example. There were liquidity rumors about Bear Stearns.

DANNY SCHECHTER: Around 11 a.m. they watch their stocks begin a sharp fall. Suddenly unsourced rumors of liquidity problem were everywhere.

BAMBER: At that time, Bear Stearns was adequately capitalized … The story of Governor Spitzer broke regarding the prostitution ring … we heard: "Glad to be knocked off of the number-one news spot at the time."

TUESDAY, MARCH 11 – BEAR SHARE PRICE: $63

SCHECHTER: It was on Tuesday things really got strange.

BAMBER: We did start to notice some deep abnormal trading patterns going on with regard to deep put-money options on Bear Stearns stocks.

SCHECHTER: Someone made a $1.7 million wager that Bear Stearns value would drop more than a half in only seven business days.

BAMBER: It wouldn't take a massive drop in the share prices for those puts to go from 1% up to 2% and double your money in matter of days.

SCHECHTER: But the odds were terrible. For these so-called puts to pay out, Bear Stearns would have to fall harder in a shorter amount of time than any other Fortune 500 company in history. It was so foolish that such puts were not even sold at the time. There had to be special orders. The first time I heard of puts was after 9/11.

BAMBER: Someone knew how to profit from that event. A similar scenario played out with Bear.

WEDNESDAY, MARCH 12 – BEAR SHARE PRICE: $64

BAMBER: By Wednesday, our CEO [Alan Schwartz] went on CNBC to dispel the rumors. It's a Catch-22 situation, generally you do not want to comment on the situation. Because if you do, people think this might be true whether there is smoke or fire.

THURSDAY, MARCH 13 – BEAR SHARE PRICE: $62

BAMBER: On Thursday that is when we heard that we were bleeding out.

SCHECHTER: The questionable practice known as "naked short selling" was contributing in the steady long decline in the stock price. Obscure trading rules allow to sell a share of stock only providing the buyer with an IOU for a short period of time until so-called delivery failure can be resolved. Beginning the day the bet was placed against Bear, millions of delivery failures begin to inflate the number of shares that appear in circulation and therefore deflating the value of each share.

BAMBER: It was strange because it felt like we are being sucked into a vortex. There was very little we could do to fight it. There was a momentum that began with the rumor. That was a small force of fire that went out of control.

FRIDAY, MARCH 14 – BEAR SHARE: $58

BAMBER: Ben Bernanke announces the Fed's intervention. The shares dropped basically 50% in the opening moments. They knew it was over.

SCHECHTER: Bear Stearns employees discovered that the Federal Reserve was financing and forcing the bank sale to JPMorgan to the tune of $30 billion but only paying Bear Stearns investors $2 a share.

SATURDAY, MARCH 15 – BEAR SHARE PRICE: $25

DANNY SCHECHTER

BAMBER: We learned that it was a price dictated by the Treasury Department.

SCHECHTER: The employees who owned 30% of those shares were furious. Many believed that Bear was turned into a sacrificial lamb. They and their investors were wiped out.

Your book suggests that the Fed could have easily loaned money to Bear to get through the crisis.

BAMBER: Minutes after Bear made the deal with JPMorgan, they opened up the discount window for the very first time. Had Bear had access to that window, we'd have survived as an independent entity, we'd have had time to negotiate a deal, good for Bear, good for the shareholders, BS employees, etc., with a large financial institution.

Bear employees did get their share price up to $10 a share in exchange for refusing to approve the deal. Many shareholders were wiped out. Most of the government's money paid off Bear's creditors.

SUNDAY, MARCH 16 – BEAR SHARE PRICE: $2 (LATER NEGOTIATED TO $10 A SHARE.)

SCHECHTER: Deal was done. Bear Stearns was integrated into JPMorgan Chase. Bear Stearns CEO James Cayne would later call this forced "merger" a "conspiracy" and expressed hopes that the government would get the people who did it.

In the week before Bear Stearns collapsed, parties unknown bought so-called put options to drive down the company's share price. They were betting that a stock selling for $60 share would go down to $30

Bamber admitted they were concerned, "We did start to notice on the Monday, Tuesday, and Wednesday some abnormal trading patterns going on with regard to the depth of the money on put options, on Bear Stearns stock ... Anyone who owned that thirty-dollar-strike put option with an expiree in ten, nine, and eight days would be able to sell the stock at thirty dollars ..."

According to Bloomberg News, the people who owned those shares ended up making $250 million on an investment of $1.7 million in less than a week.

I asked Bamber for more detail on the put options: "The last time I heard about puts was on September 11, 2001. We learned later that people had taken out investments, or puts, in American and United Airlines before 9/11 expecting those stocks to go down. That's still a mystery."

Bamber agreed. "Well, yes," he said, "In terms of prior to 9/11 there was unusually high volume in the put options on airline stocks, American and United, as well as some of the reinsurance companies. So someone knew how to profit from that event. A similar scenario played out right here."

I put it to him, "You know we're taught that markets have their own laws, and that financiers are into due diligence, monitoring money closely and responsibly because it's in their interest to do so. But yet, when you look at the markets it feels like they are an insane asylum."

Bamber agreed laughing at the sentiment of my statement, "[Laughs] A good way to describe it, given the volatility that we're in right now."

Bamber acknowledged that there may have been an "element of fraud."

He explained, "There's obviously an element of fraud, you're hearing about a mortgage being sold more than one time into a securitization pool which is obviously fraud at the front end of the food chain so to speak. Also, what you have is also a problem at the rating agencies, the question that has started to come out of the congressional hearings is, 'What did they know, did they know they had a real model problem or not?'"

Wall Street Journal reporter Kate Kelly who wrote a book, *Street Fighters: The Last 72 Hours of Bear Stearns, the Toughest Firm on Wall Street*, also sees the story — which she details moment by moment as a mystery:

> Regulators may never know what really happened. But one thing is clear: Once confidence in a company falls away on such a grand scale, it can never recover. Bear started that week with more than $18 billion in capital, its largest cash position ever. Three days later, negative headlines, a stock drop, lender reticence and big withdrawals from client accounts had cut those capital levels in half. Eight hours later, it was nearly dead.

The rumors and the puts led to a loss of confidence in Bear on Wall Street. Confidence inside Bear turned to panic; in one week, the firm vaporized, explained Bamber:

> We were bleeding out. When the loan facility was announced by the Fed, coming by JPMorgan on the Friday morning, the shares dropped basically 50% in the opening moments that day. You knew it was over and probably there would be a deal done that weekend.
>
> It was then that we learned that JPMorgan Chase was buying Bear Stearns.

But then employees discovered that the Federal Reserve bank was forcing and financing the bank's sale to Morgan to the tune of $30 billion dollars but only paying Bear investors $2 a share.

Said Fed Chairman Ben Bernanke, "The Fed is strongly committed to employing our authority to alleviate this distress."

Bamber reveals that it was not until after the deal that more details were uncovered.

"We later learned that this was a number that was effectively dictated to JPMorgan and Bear by the Treasury Department.

"The employees who owned 30% of the shares were furious. Many believed Bear was being punished and turned into a sacrificial lamb. They and their investors were virtually wiped out." (The investor-employees raised holy hell and the share price was raised to $10.)

The head of the firm, Alan Schwartz had no answer for Bear executives like Alan Mintz, who angrily demanded to know how it happened. Kate Kelly reported in the *Wall Street Journal*:

> Two and a half months later, Mr. Schwartz still isn't quite sure. To Mr. Mintz and others, he has blamed a market tsunami he didn't see coming. He told a Senate committee last month: "I just simply have not been able to come up with anything, even with the benefit of hindsight, that would have made a difference."

> Others who lived through the crisis say Bear Stearns collapsed because it was at war – with itself.

> Even as Bear began to implode, some media cheerleaders like CNBC's Jim Cramer backed Bear on the grounds that

the bank was solvent. "Don't take our money out of Bear," he screamed. "That's silly."

He may not have been aware of the insider politicking, and that the decision to kill Bear Stearns had already been made in a forced marriage dictated by the Fed.

I asked Bamber, "Your book suggests that the Fed could have very simply and easily loaned money to Bear to get you through the crisis? Why go through this whole *sturm und drang* here? With JPMorgan, with this whole cataclysmic collision?"

Bamber replied, "Absolutely, in my mind, the real nexus point was of the Bear Stearns crisis was the Sunday night, minutes after Bear inked their deal with JPMorgan they opened up the discount window for the very first time to all the investment banks.

"Had Bear had access to that window would we have survived as an independent entity like we'd always been? Probably not, but we would have had time to negotiate a deal that was good for Bear, good for Bear shareholders, good for Bear Stearns employees, etc., with a larger financial institution."

That didn't happen. In this, the first of many bailouts to come – Bear employees saw it as a take-out, not a bail out – the Bear shareholders were in effect wiped out with the creditors taking the bulk of the money, 14,000 Bear employees would later get the axe.

JPMorgan Chase got the deal of the century.

Bamber told me how he and other employees perceived the events. "After the deal was announced, the market cap of JPMorgan went up about fifteen billion dollars; roughly speaking the market cap of Bear Stearns prior to the start of those rumors. We felt at that time it was a wealth transfer from Bear shareholders to JPMorgan shareholders."

The day Bear was sold to JPMorgan for (at the time) $2 dollars a share, Bamber and his Bear colleagues predicted that Lehman Brothers would be the next to go, as well as Merrill Lynch as an independent entity. They were right, Lehman filed for bankruptcy on September 15, 2008 and Bank of America announced its intent to buy Merrill Lynch a day earlier.

Former Bear CEO Jimmy Cayne was pissed. The *New Yorker* quoted his comment on Tim Geithner, the current Treasury Secretary then with the New York Fed, who orchestrated the deal:

> The audacity of that prick in front of the American people announcing he was deciding whether or not a firm of this stature and this whatever was good enough to get a loan. Like he was the determining factor, and it's like a flea on his back, floating down underneath the Golden Gate Bridge, getting a hard-on, saying, "Raise the bridge." This guy thinks he's got a big dick. He's got nothing, except maybe a boyfriend.

The week after Bear went down, Cayne – who reportedly spent 10 of 21 workdays playing golf and competing in bridge tournaments in June 2007, as two of Bear Stearns hedge funds were melting down – cashed out at Bear where he had one time owned stock work $1 billion.

He was left with just $61 million. He then closed on an apartment at the New York Plaza at a reported all-cash cost of $26 million. He needed no mortgage.

Many of the mysteries of what happened to Bear are still popping up, as this question posed to former Treasury Secretary Henry S. Paulson in the *New York Times' DealBook* column suggests:

You famously encouraged JPMorgan to offer only $2 a share for Bear Stearns in the name of moral hazard, so as to punish the Bear Stearns shareholders. Similarly, your actions with JPMorgan appeared to reflect a desire for shareholders to bear the costs of any "bailout." Can you explain why shareholders were the focus of your efforts, rather than management, who actually made the decisions that set the stage for the crisis?

That is just one of many good questions awaiting good answers. But, again the media focus was on money, not the impact of Bear's collapse on the larger economy. They cared more about the fate of investors and shareholders then the American public who were unaware at the time of the chain reaction that was coming.

Part of the reason was the coverage of financial channels like CNBC where expert hosts like Jim Cramer was still telling viewers not to sell Bear shares because the company was solid even as it began its descent. Usually, TV hosts are never held accountable for their predictions and reports. But *The Daily Show*'s Jon Stewart was on the case, challenging Cramer in one of the few televised exchanges that revealed how financial journalism operates. This transcript below appears in former *New York Times* reporter Chris Hedges excellent book, *Empire of Illusion*, and a video of the interview is available online (www.thedailyshow.com):

STEWART: This thing was ten years in the making ... The idea that you could have on the guys from Bear Stearns and Merrill Lynch and guys that had leveraged 35 to 1 and then blame mortgage holders, that's insane ...

CRAMER: I always wished that people would come in and

swear themselves in before they come on the show. I had a lot of CEOs lie to me on the show. It's very painful. I don't have subpoena power ...

STEWART: You knew what the banks were doing and were touting it for months and months. The entire network was.

CRAMER: But Dick Fuld, who ran Lehman Brothers, called me in — he called me in when the stock was at forty — because he was saying: "Look, I thought the stock was wrong, thought it was in the wrong place" — he brings me in and lies to me, lies to me, lies to me.

STEWART: [Feigning Shock] The CEO of a company lied to you?

CRAMER: Shocking.

STEWART: But isn't that financial reporting? What do you think is the role of CNBC? ...

CRAMER: I didn't think that Bear Stearns would evaporate overnight. I knew the people who ran it. I thought they were honest. That was my mistake. I really did. I thought they were honest.

CHAPTER 16

THE LEHMAN LIQUIDATION

"[Lehman Brothers] not only maintained its overall market presence, but also led the charge into the preferred space by ... developing new products and tailoring transactions to fit borrowers' needs ... Lehman Brothers is the most innovative in the preferred space, just doing things you won't see elsewhere,"
– International Financing Review (IFR) Annual Awards, one of the industry's most prestigious, December 17, 2005

Before his final public performance, he was known for cocky self-confidence as a squash player of international stature. But Americans saw a nervous and dissembling Dick Fuld, then the head and longest running CEO of Lehman Brothers, stumble for the right words to explain how his mighty bank could have tumbled so badly in testimony before Congress.

At that point, he seemed to be in shock, unclear about what had happened:

> I wake up every single night thinking, "What could I have done differently? What could I have said? What should I have done?" ... I made those decisions with the information that I had. Having said all that, I can look right at you and say this is a pain that will stay with me for the rest of my life.

His pain, however, was not as great as that of others. Many believe that the bank's demise, due largely to the unwillingness of then Treasury Secretary Hank Paulson to assist Lehman, caused a financial calamity. It was widely reported that Paulson and Fuld were enemies, not just competitors.

Without government help, Lehman went down. Many feel this was a turning point in the deepening of the crisis brought about by Fuld's arrogance and the government's mistake.

Economist Michael Hudson blamed Fuld:

Lehman brothers essentially committed suicide. Its head, Mr Fuld, had many offers from Korea and from investment banks in the U.S. to take it over. He tried to bluff them. He tried to say, "Crisis? What crisis? Our loans are perfectly good. We haven't lost a penny. We want you to pay at the book value of what we say our loans are worth."

Nobody was crazy enough to believe Mr. Fuld's bluff. These are guys who like to wipe out their partners, like to wipe out people they are doing business with. He fucked the whole firm and wiped out the shareholders. He wiped out the firm saying, "We're too big to fail." He tried to bluff. Nobody believed it.

In contrast, economist Max Wolff argues that Fuld's personality should not have been the determining factor:

Lehman Brothers, I think, will go down in history as one of the largest regulatory mistakes made in American history. In other words it was too big, it had too many counterparties, or people doing business with it in order to be structurally neutral when it went down ...

Wolff's view was echoed by many, including one incredulous investor, George Soros, who wrote in the *Financial Times*:

How could Lehman have been left to go under? The responsibility lies squarely with the financial authorities, notably the
Treasury and the Federal Reserve. The claim that they lacked
the necessary legal powers is a lame excuse. In an emergency they could and should have done whatever was necessary to prevent the system from collapsing. That is what they
have done on other occasions. The fact is, they allowed it to
happen. On a deeper level, too, credit default swaps played a
critical role in Lehman's demise.

Alan Blinder, a former Federal Reserve Bank vice chairman,
was also furious, calling it "a colossal error." He added, "Coming just six months after Bear's rescue, the Lehman decision tossed the presumed rulebook out the window. If Bear
[Stearns] was too big to fail, how could Lehman, at twice its
size, not be? If Bear was too entangled to fail, why was Lehman not? After Lehman went over the cliff, no financial institution seemed safe. So lending froze, and the economy sank
like a stone."

This quote appears in the book, *In Fed We Trust*, by David
Wessel, a *Wall Street Journal* editor, on Chairman Ben Bernan-
ke's role as the crisis manager-in-chief. His findings provoked
New York Times book reviewer Michiko Kakutani to wonder:

Although an enormous amount of recent attention has been
understandably focused on why the government let Lehman Brothers go under, an equal amount of attention might
understandably be focused on why Lehman – and other firms
like Bear Stearns and AIG – were ever allowed to engage in
the sort of reckless, illogical, self-destructive gambling that
turned them from Wall Street behemoths into combustible
houses of cards in the first place?

And one might also ask, why Bernanke, who knew how the devastation caused by fraudulent subprime mortgage lending was tearing up so many lives, did not stop it when he could have? (He issued tough regulations, but much later, well after the fact.) Does that not make him, the Fed and the government complicit in this crime?

Wessel's book also reveals that neither Ben Bernanke or Tim Geithner had any idea of the consequences of Lehman's collapse. They expected to be sending one message about moral hazard, but sent another, suggesting that big banks would be bailed out. Today, after billions were lost, their naïveté seems shocking:

> ... On a conference call the previous week, Paulson, Bernanke, Securities and Exchange Commission Chairman Christopher Cox, and senior staff members from those agencies had agreed that companies and investors who did business with Lehman had learned from Bear Stearns and would have acted to protect themselves from a Lehman failure.

Another book on Lehman's fall, *A Colossal Failure of Common Sense*, by bank insider Lawrence G. McDonald reveals that the bank's leaders had been warned repeatedly that an iceberg was in their path:

> Each and every one of them laid it out, from way back in 2005, that the real-estate market was living on borrowed time and that Lehman Brothers was headed directly for the biggest subprime iceberg ever seen, and with the wrong men on the bridge.

According to the *New York Times* review, McDonald indicts a failure of common sense skirting the issue of criminality. He blamed his bosses willingness to take on:

> … risk, more risk, and if necessary bigger risks in pursuit of short-term profits, willing to borrow more and more money (on the way to leveraging the firm to "44 times our value") in order to buy commercial and residential real estate at the top of the market, even though one of his lieutenants had warned in 2005 that the housing market was on steroids and headed for serious trouble.

Again, we see no realization in the executive suite of how these decisions, fueled by a desire to enrich themselves and other firms, would affect others. There is no sense that a crime to the world economy was underway because of the vast number of victims who would be created and then suffer enormous losses. This consideration seems conspicuous by its absence in much of the writing about the crisis. As the *Independent* said in their review of McDonald's book:

> They didn't do their homework. People were talking about the failure of Lehman Brothers from the moment of the failure of Bear Stearns in March, or before, and they didn't do a thing. If they knew there was systemic risk, why didn't they do anything about it?

To his credit, Matt Taibbi in *Rolling Stone* put these developments in a deeper context than most of the rest of the media:

> What really happened to Bear and Lehman is that an economic drought temporarily left the hyenas without any more middle-class victims – and so they started eating each other,

188

using the exact same schemes they had been using for years to fleece the rest of the country.

And in the forensic footprint left by those kills, we can see for the first time exactly how the scam worked – and how completely even the government regulators who are supposed to protect us have given up trying to stop it.

This was a brokered bloodletting, one in which the power of the state was used to help effect a monstrous consolidation of financial and political power. Heading into 2008, there were five major investment banks in the United States: Bear, Lehman, Merrill Lynch, Morgan Stanley and Goldman Sachs. Today only Morgan Stanley and Goldman survive as independent firms, perched atop a restructured Wall Street hierarchy. And while the rest of the civilized world responded to last year's catastrophes with sweeping measures to rein in the corruption in their financial sectors, the United States invited the wolves into the government, with the popular new president, Barack Obama – elected amid promises to clean up the mess – filling his administration with Bear's and Lehman's conquerors, bestowing his papal blessing on a new era of robbery.

The consequences of Lehman's collapse were catastrophic for many doing business with the over-leveraged institution. Peter Siris commented in the *Daily News*:

Lehman, like Bear, Fannie and Freddie, had too much leverage. Think of a homeowner with a 96% mortgage and credit card bills. If the value of the house declines only 5%, the homeowner is wiped out. The total leverage of companies like Lehman is difficult to calculate, but it is not unlike that of a highly over-leveraged homeowner. Small declines in the value of its assets jeopardize its solvency.

Further, it is likely that Lehman and other financial institutions did not take a hard enough look at the value of its assets when they reported quarterly results and paid handsome bonuses in previous years. Many of these assets were too complicated to value, but management always has an incentive to paint a rosy picture. Just as people deluded themselves with the value of their homes, financial institutions like Lehman deluded themselves with the value of their assets.

Could all this pressure on Lehman have been orchestrated by still unknown shadowy players? *Web of Debt* author Ellen Brown, who writes about the economy, said so on the *Huffington Post*:

> According to Representative Paul Kanjorski, speaking on C-SPAN in January 2009, the collapse of Lehman Brothers precipitated a $550-billion run on the money market funds on Thursday, September 18. This was the dire news that Treasury Secretary Henry Paulson presented to Congress behind closed doors, prompting congressional approval of Paulson's $700-billion bank bailout despite deep misgivings. It was the sort of "shock therapy" discussed by Naomi Klein in her book, *The Shock Doctrine*, in which a major crisis prompts hasty emergency action involving the relinquishment of rights or funds that would otherwise be difficult to pry loose from the citizenry.

> Like the "bombing" of Lehman stock on September 11, the $550-billion-money-market run was suspicious. The stock market had plunged when Lehman filed for bankruptcy on

September 15, but it actually went up on September 16. Why did the money market wait until September 18 to collapse? A report by the Joint Economic Committee pointed to the fact that the $62-billion Reserve Primary Fund had "broken the buck" (fallen below a stable $1 per share) due to its Lehman investments; but that had occurred on September 15, and the fund had suspended redemptions for the following week.

What dire reversal happened on September 17? According to the SEC, it was another record day for illegal naked short selling. Failed trades climbed to 49.7 million – 23% of Lehman trades.

This is another financial crisis mystery suggesting that most media accounts missed what else was going on. The *Independent* of London reported that the reasons for Washington's decision not to step in is still not clear, "It's unconscionable what they did – or more accurately what they didn't do," said Joseph Stiglitz, Nobel prize-winning economist and professor at Columbia University. "They didn't do their homework. People were talking about the failure of Lehman Brothers from the moment of the failure of Bear Stearns in March, or before, and they didn't do a thing. If they knew there was systemic risk, why didn't they do anything about it?"

With Lehman, as with mortgage-lending giants Fannie Mae, Freddie Mac and others, the meltdown hit the common stockholders hardest, while debt holders escaped largely unscathed.

Many in the industry were "astonished" reported the *Dr. Housing Bubble* blog (www.doctorhousingbubble.com):

This astonishing news comes during a weekend when most of the market on Friday was expecting that someone would surely come to the table to help the firm. Whether it was a private purchase or a government sponsored bailout like what occurred with Bear Stearns and JPMorgan, bankruptcy was not expected by many. Early talks indicated that Bank of America and Barclays were in close talks to take over the troubled investment bank.

The Federal Reserve which aided in helping the Bear Stearns deal and the U.S. Treasury which just last weekend entered into the biggest bailout known to humankind by aiding Fannie Mae and Freddie Mac both seemed unwilling to come to the aid of Lehman Brothers.

I am sure as time goes on more and more details will emerge as to why this occurred … It is unprecedented that in only six months, 3 of the top 5 investment houses on Wall Street are no longer in their previous form.

Few in the media could agree on what led to Lehman's liquidation. In *Newsweek*, Liaquat Ahamed ended up blaming politicians:

It has become conventional wisdom: the signal event of the current crisis, the transformative moment when things truly really began to spin out of control, was the government's decision to let Lehman Brothers fail. But when one looks closely at what happened in the weeks after the bank's fall – by any measure the most turbulent and dramatic period in the last 75 years of financial history – Lehman's collapse was not in fact to blame for pushing global markets and the economy over the edge. Sure, it was a shock. But the Fed's response was sufficiently imaginative, far-reaching and aggressive to mitigate most of the knock-on effects. Instead it was the political battle in Congress, which ensued over the bank bailout package, that really caused the meltdown.

Yet at the same time, this reality was not the focus of most of the media attention. According to Dr. *Housing Bubble*, Lehman Brothers was heavily invested in fraudulent subprime paper:

> Lehman could not resist the subprime markets. In August of 2007 Lehman closed its subprime lender BNC Mortgage, which left 1,200 positions gone. This clearly was only the beginning for Lehman and their mortgage and credit problems. In 2008 Lehman was posting unprecedented losses. For the most part their problems arose from holding onto lower grade tranches and holding on too long to subprime mortgages. It is up in the air whether they held onto to these assets because of a foolish investment move or whether there simply wasn't a market for these assets. For the 2nd quarter the firm had $2.8 billion in losses and was forced to liquidate $6 billion in assets. It is simply stunning to see the stock movement for the firm …

> It is easy to lose perspective of what really is going on. You need to remember that debt is at the center of all this.

Debt may have been at the center, but real people lived in the homes the firm borrowed against. What happened to them seemed to be of little concern to the bankers and the media.

Paulson opposed a bailout publicly on the grounds of "moral hazard," arguing that Lehman should not be rewarded for its mistakes.

But as the crisis accelerated, and more firms were put at risk of insolvency, that argument disappeared. Max Wolff put it this way in our conversation:

On September 15th, we were told some heavily ideological story about letting some companies fall, letting the market do its thing, not bailing everybody out. And Lehman was allowed with its 23,000 employees to collapse which sent cataclysm and shock waves through the global markets, and began the giant September to October sell-off which was apocalyptical and makes this the second worst year in the history of stock markets.

But then, the very next morning we got $85 billion of the eventual 150 billion dollars for the bailout of AIG. So they weren't even able to run their "no-moral hazard, we let the failure fall story" for even 24 full hours before they went to the rescue of another firm.

And this creates anger and hostility for years with people thinking that government regulators are picking winners and losers, and they have a "catch-as-catch-can" patch-work response which leaves some people protected and others free to fall to their deaths. And it was very bad for confidence, very bad for the markets and very bad for any notion of fairness and equity in the market.

Over, the next ten days, the insurance titan AIG was not allowed to fail, bailed out by the Federal Reserve to the tune of $85 billion. (AIG paid off claims by Goldman Sachs at 100% on the dollar to the tune of $50 billion.)

The FDIC then seized America's largest S & L institution, Washington Mutual, and sold its assets to JPMorgan Chase.

THE CRIME OF OUR TIME

The two major Wall Street firms left standing voluntarily changed their status from investment banks to bank holding companies.

There was a bittersweet reaction on Wall Street according to Bloomberg News:

> Fuld's defense of the 158-year-old firm ended when Barclays Plc. and Bank of America Corp. walked away from buyout talks, forcing the company to file for bankruptcy.

> Over 14 years, Fuld, 62, turned a money-losing, bond-trading shop into a full-service investment bank. He won acclaim from Wall Street leaders such as Lazard Ltd. Chief Bruce Wasserstein, who on June 4 called him "very able." Fuld joined the circle of CEOs sought after by boards, such as the New York Federal Reserve's. Fuld ultimately gambled almost four times the firm's shareholder equity last year on mortgage securities that he insisted were "hedged by other bets."

> "It makes me rather sad to see this organization brought to its knees as the result of what I'll call a lack of control, poor management of internal risk and ultimate self-interest," said Walter Gerasimowicz, who worked at Lehman as an investment strategist and now heads Meditron Asset Management in New York. His firm manages $1 billion and doesn't own any Lehman shares.

> Lehman had tried to escape from its subprime obsession. In August 2007 it fired 1200 employees working in their subprime bond department. At the same time, it was still trying to profit from it. A bank official told CNN then "that turmoil in the subprime mortgage business is likely to persist but that could open up some opportunities for the firm."

DANNY SCHECHTER

Lehman had been no stranger to controversy and lawsuits. The City of Chicago accused Lehman of violating a local ordinance prohibiting the city from doing business with companies that had financed the slave trade. Lehman was forced to apologize. There were investigations and lawsuits growing out of Lehman's involvement with Enron. There were suits alleging fraud according to the *White Collar Crime* blog (www.whitecollar-crimeblog.com) monitoring securities fraud suggesting "that the bankers' relationship with Enron enabled the commission of Lehman Brothers stock fraud, since Lehman Brothers had inside knowledge of the partnerships and internal financial issues at Enron."

The *New York Times* said that its residential real-estate business was also flawed: "Many factors, of course, contributed to Lehman's demise. Near the end, it carried $25 billion in toxic residential mortgages. It was wildly over leveraged. And the federal government made the fateful decision not to rescue Lehman from its mistakes."

New Jersey's Attorney General Anne Milgram accused former Lehman execs of "defrauding the state's pension funds by misrepresenting Lehman's real-estate exposure." New lawsuits have been filed in connection with the firms lending and real-estate practices.

The hardly poor Mr. Fuld became a laughing stock and worse. The Business and Media institute (www.businessand-media.org) reported:

> While former Lehman CEO Richard Fuld was testifying before the House Oversight Committee on Oct. 6th, CNBC reported he had been punched in the face at the Lehman Brothers gym after it was announced the firm was going bankrupt.

> From two very senior sources – one incredibly senior source
> – that he went to the gym after … Lehman was announced
> as going under. He was on a treadmill with a heart moni-
> tor on. Someone was in the corner, pumping iron and he
> walked over and he knocked him out cold. And frankly after
> having watched this, I'd have done the same too.

Lehman filed for bankruptcy in September 2008. Its assets were later snatched up for a relative song by the British bank Barclays for $1.35 billion, which included Lehman's Midtown Manhattan office tower supposedly worth $960 million. The firm only paid a third of that when they acquired the building from American Express Shearson.

Later, in a move to limit his personal liability by transferring ownership of a home, Fuld "sold" a multi-million-dollar mansion in Florida to his own wife for just $10.

Fuld's leadership and Lehman's bankruptcy has led to a flood of lawsuits. *Wealth Daily* reported a few weeks later:

> Just in the last few weeks, the San Mateo County [Califor-
> nia] Investment Pool formally filed suit against Fuld, Callah-
> an and other top Lehman execs, seeking reimbursement for
> financial losses after Lehman's fall to bankruptcy. The San
> Mateo lawsuit is among the first in the country to go after
> Lehman's top brass … and the $1-billion-plus in bonuses
> they were able to siphon off before the firm tanked.

According to the lawsuit, the Lehman case "represents the worst example of fraud committed by modern-day robber barons of Wall Street, who targeted public entities to finance their risky practices and then paid themselves hundreds of millions of dollars in compensation while their companies deteriorated."

DANNY SCHECHTER

In the aftermath of his company's collapse, *New York* magazine reported:

> Lest we forget, it's not just "masters of the universe" who suffered when Lehman went down last week. *DealBreaker* has informed us that Bella, the Lehman Brothers guard dog, is also now out of a job – and a home. Would the Fed have let Lehman fail if they knew that there was a puppy at stake? Would they? We think not, because everyone loves dogs more than people.

A year after Lehman's fall, Dick Fuld, once known as the "Gorilla of Wall Street" was still not willing to answer questions from the press. London's *Telegraph* reported his hard-line response to the issues that were raised:

> You know what, people are saying all sorts of crap and it's a shame that they don't know the truth, but they're not going to get it from me … I've been pummelled, I've been dumped on, and it's all going to happen again. I can handle it. You know what, let them line up … You know what, my mother loves me. And you know what, my family loves me and I've got a few close friends who understand what happened and that's all I need.

CHAPTER 17

ARE OUR MARKETS MANIPULATED?

"People of the same trade seldom meet together, even for merriment and diversion, but the conversation ends in a conspiracy against the public, or in some contrivance to raise prices. It is impossible indeed to prevent such meetings, by any law which either could be executed, or would be consistent with liberty and justice. But though the law cannot hinder people of the same trade from sometimes assembling together, it ought to do nothing to facilitate such assemblies; much less to render them necessary."
– Adam Smith, *The Wealth of Nations*, Book I, Chapter X

This subject may be above my pay grade, and beyond my own experience, but it can't be ignored. Are the markets themselves being manipulated, not just by the erratic and often seemingly irrational "market psychology" – what has been called "animal spirits" – but by schemes to influence their ups and downs?

In making my film, *Plunder*, I spoke with Mo Sacirbey, a former VP of Standard and Poor's, who went on to become a UN Ambassador. We met on Wall Street. I knew him as a rational analyst of current affairs, an experienced professional. He brought the discussion around to market manipulation.

"I think we had a transition from what truly was a free-market system to something now that is out of control and probably what I would define as a predatory system, where we are not so much dealing anymore about the notion of fair prices, and the notion of markets that – that work transparently. In fact, frequently markets are manipulated for the end of maybe a few out there, a few investors, mega-investors. Even that's very difficult to tell."

Once again, I heard the whole system being described as "predatory" which smacks of criminality. He explained: "And these market movements may not necessarily be reflective of the underlying value of that real asset whether it be a commodity or whether it be in equity. What I mean by that is frequently you see prices wildly fluctuating. As an example: How could oil be at $147 in July of 2008 and all of a sudden fall to below $40 a barrel at the end of that same year? We all knew that in fact the whole economic system was in trouble over a year ago. But the price of oil kept rising sharply. The price of food kept rising sharply."

When I asked him whether he thought this was an example of market manipulation, he replied: "I think it was manipulated. There is a lot of debate whether it's about speculation or manipulation, but there is an old expression among traders, which is, 'The trend is your friend.' What that means is that, in fact a few people can use significant resources, financial resources, freely as a weapon."

Manipulated markets used as a weapon? These are strong words – but he's not sure if it's illegal or not.

On July 28, 2009, the *Wall Street Journal*'s lead story was headlined: "Traders Blamed For Oil Spike." The story reported that the Commodity Futures Trading Commission had reviewed an earlier finding during the Bush era that blamed wild swings in oil prices on supply and demand and concluded that the data had been "flawed" and that speculators played a key role by betting on the direction prices were taking for financial gain. These bets, tied to indexes, it said, led oil-market volatility and higher prices for consumers.

For years, the world's stock markets were pictured as models of democratic capitalism, where anyone could invest and profit. Many times in college when I was told about how many ordinary Americans were "in the market." I later learned that I was being fed a deceptive story because most working people may have had money in retirement funds but were hardly active market players and made no decisions. I learned that you often only need a small percentage of shares to control companies. What I also didn't know was reported by *Science* magazine – that the financial markets are actually controlled by a small number of people and firms. The *Inside Science News Service* (www.insidescience.org) also reported:

A pair of physicists at the Swiss Federal Institute of Technology in Zurich did a physics-based analysis of the world economy as it looked in early 2007. Stefano Battiston and James Glattfelder extracted the information from the tangled yarn that links 24,877 stocks and 106,141 shareholding entities in 48 countries, revealing what they called the "backbone" of each country's financial market. These backbones represented the owners of 80 percent of a country's market capital, yet consisted of remarkably few shareholders.

Financial power, they said, is now highly concentrated. With so few dominant players, manipulation is more likely because of fewer checks and balances

I soon realized I was not alone in puzzling over how markets could be manipulated. I began looking into an official government agency known as the "Plunge Protection Team."

I often thought about the alphabet of the financial crisis: a lexicon of terms like "pricing," "panic" and "plunge." I think of this last word spelled this way: *plungeeeeeee*, as in falling off a cliff. As the *Encarta* dictionary states:

plunge *(verb)*

- *Jump or dive quickly and energetically*: Our daughters whooped as they *plunged* into the sea.

- *Fall suddenly and uncontrollably*: A car swerved to avoid a bus and *plunged* into a ravine.

- *Embark impetuously on a speech or course of action*: Overconfident researchers who *plunge* ahead.

- *Suffer a rapid decrease in value*: Their fourth-quarter operating profit *plunged* 25%.

There are many experts who see this happening today as the markets plunge in value with banks going down and very little going up except prices, foreclosures and unemployment.

The government has machinery in place to deal with plunges. It was put in place during the heady days of "Mourning" in America – the Reagan administration. It was back in 1987, when the former movie star signed on to this executive order drafted for him. The "working group" it set up was quickly labeled the Plunge Protection Team (PPT).

As the government in effect takes over mortgage giants and wrestles over what to do about the collapse of huge investment banks like Lehman Brothers – they are on alert 24/7 – scrambling to put more fingers in the dike.

This is the mechanism in place to avoid this type of crisis. In theory! Here are their overt marching orders; the covert mission is still shadowy.

Executive Order 12631 – Working Group on Financial Markets

Section 1. *Establishment.*

(a) There is hereby established a Working Group on Financial Markets (Working Group). The Working Group shall
be composed of:

    (1) the Secretary of the Treasury, or his designee;

    (2) the Chairman of the Board of Governors of the
Federal Reserve System, or his designee;

    (3) the Chairman of the Securities and Exchange
Commission, or his designee; and

    (4) the Chairman of the Commodity Futures Trading
Commission, or her designee.

(b) The Secretary of the Treasury, or his designee, shall be
the Chairman of the Working Group.

Section 2. *Purposes and Functions.*

(a) Recognizing the goals of enhancing the integrity, efficiency, orderliness, and competitiveness of our Nation's
financial markets and maintaining investor confidence,
the Working Group shall identify and consider:

    (1) the major issues raised by the numerous studies
on the events in the financial markets surrounding
October 19, 1987, and any of those recommendations that have the potential to achieve the goals
noted above; and

    (2) the actions, including governmental actions under
existing laws and regulations (such as policy
coordination and contingency planning), that are
appropriate to carry out these recommendations.

(b) The Working Group shall consult, as appropriate, with
representatives of the various exchanges, clearinghous-
es, self-regulatory bodies, and with major market par-

DANNY SCHECHTER

ticipants to determine private sector solutions wherever possible.

(c) The Working Group shall report to the President initially within 60 days (and periodically thereafter) on its progress and, if appropriate, its views on any recommended legislative changes.

Section 3. *Administration.*
(a) The heads of Executive departments, agencies, and independent instrumentalities shall, to the extent permitted by law, provide the Working Group such information as it may require for the purpose of carrying out this Order.

(b) Members of the Working Group shall serve without additional compensation for their work on the Working Group.

(c) To the extent permitted by law and subject to the availability of funds therefore, the Department of the Treasury shall provide the Working Group with such administrative and support services as may be necessary for the performance of its functions.

In actual fact, this secret branch of government has a sophisticated war room, using state-of-the-art technology to monitor markets worldwide. It has emergency powers. It doesn't keep minutes. There is no freedom of information access to its deliberations. There are 147,000 entries in Google on this powerful body, but I could only access ten.

The reports on it are sketchy, including one from the *Washington Post*:

These quiet meetings of the Working Group are the financial world's equivalent of the war room. The officials gather regularly to discuss options and review crisis scenarios because they know that the government's reaction to a crumbling stock market would have a critical impact on investor confidence around the world.

Recall how many politicians you've heard claim to worship an unregulated free market, and yet, here is the government bigfooting the market.

Noted the *Capital Observer* (www.capitalobserver.blogspot. com), an investor's blog, "I alluded to the fact that the government might be intervening in the market privately as well as publicly." It also reported on September 11th that the *Telegraph* – a newspaper in London, not Washington – called it a "black arts unit":

On Friday, Mr. Bush convened the so-called Plunge Protection Team for its first known meeting in the Oval Office. The black arts unit – officially the president's Working Group on Financial Markets – was created after the 1987 crash.

It appears to have powers to support the markets in a crisis with a host of instruments, mostly through buying futures contracts on the stock indexes (DOW, S & P 500, NASDAQ and Russell) and key credit levers. And it has the means to fry "short" traders in the hottest of oils.

As the economy continues its decline, as the markets are rocked by more failures and loss of confidence, as scandals including a sex-for-oil affair in the Interior Department surfaced, shouldn't we know more about these "plunge people" (sounds like "pod people") who may be doing to the economy what other branches of our government did so incompetently to Iraq.

For example, political operative Jim Wilkinson, who managed the media for the Coalition Press Information Center during Operation Iraqi Freedom in 2003, was also for a time the key *Bushevik* commissar at the Working Group. Politically connected at the highest levels of the administration, he first became Henry Paulson's PR man, and then his chief of staff. Wilkinson, now a PR man representing banks opposing a proposed new consumer protection agency, was also an organizer of the rowdy group of congressional aides who stopped the presidential recount in Miami-Dade County during the 2000 election. He was a leader of what was later called the "Brooks Brothers Riot."

New York magazine suggested there might be a conspiratorial explanation:

> Of course, the squishy "consult" language has long had conspiracy theorists speculating that it's just a backroom market-rigging cabal for the Establishment. Or, you could think of it as the Wall Street Superfriends, equipped with X-ray vision to see deep into our financial malaise, and magic lassos to jury-rig the markets back together.

It seemed difficult to find out what these people really do. But then I found a website, *Gaming the Market* (www.gamingthemarket.com), that offers more insight. One of its reports asked:

> Ever notice how official speeches to prop up the U.S. capital markets are timed right before a massive sell off? How about those last hour rallies when the market looks really bad? Let's explore just what the Plunge Protection Team can do. For

starters, the White House came out with the trumpets to kick off the open of 2008. The Dow then peeled off 600 points making it the worst January open the stock market has ever seen – ever. Not bad for a "strong and solid" market! On Jan. 4th President Bush said the following:

"I had quite a fascinating and productive meeting with the president's Working Group on Financial Markets, chaired by Secretary Paulson. I want to thank the members for working diligently to monitor our capital-market system, our financial system. And while there is some uncertainty, the report is, that the financial markets are strong and solid. And I want to thank you for being diligent. This economy of ours is on a solid foundation …"

The officials gather regularly to discuss options and review crisis scenarios because they know that the government's reaction to a crumbling stock market would have a critical impact on investor confidence around the world.

Some journalists were monitoring this unit, although most ignored it. Ambrose Evans-Pritchard of the *Telegraph* reported that Treasury Secretary Hank Paulson had called for the PPT to meet with greater frequency and set up:

… a command center at the U.S. Treasury that will track global markets and serve as an operations base in the next crisis. The top brass will meet every six weeks, combining the heads of Treasury, Federal Reserve, Securities and Exchange Commission (SEC), and key exchanges …

"The government has a real role to play to make a 1987-style sudden market break less likely. That is an issue we all spent a lot of time thinking about and planning for," said a former government official who attended Working Group meetings. "You go through lots of fire drills and scenarios. You make sure you have thought ahead of time of what kind of information you will need and what you have the legal authority to do."

In the event of a financial crisis, each federal agency with a seat at the table of the Working Group has a confidential plan. At the SEC, for example, the plan is called the "red book" because of the color of its cover. It is officially known as the Executive Directory for Market Contingencies. The major U.S. stock markets have copies of the commission's plan as well as the U.S. Commodity Futures Trading Commission (CFTC).

"We all have everybody's home and weekend numbers," said a former Working Group staff member. The Working Group's main goal, officials explained, would be to keep the markets operating in the event of a sudden, stomach-churning plunge in stock prices – and to prevent a panicky run on banks, brokerage firms and mutual funds. Officials worry that if investors all tried to head for the exit at the same time, there wouldn't be enough room – or in financial terms, liquidity – for them all to get through. In that event, the smoothly running global financial machine would begin to lock up.

The officials said this sort of liquidity crisis could imperil even healthy financial institutions that are temporarily short of cash or tradable assets such as U.S. Treasury securities.

John Crudele, of the *New York Post*, reported a former member of the Federal Reserve Board, Robert Heller, revealed this Plunge Protection Team's modus operandi. Heller said that disasters could be mitigated by "buying market averages in the futures market, thus stabilizing the market as a whole."

I know I am in over my head here since the dynamics of markets, much less market manipulation, is like a foreign country I have never visited. There are criticisms of this suggestion of government manipulation – namely it would be too expensive, and if it became known, it would undermine the credibility of the market system. While this was debated by financial bloggers and their readers, the theories keep coming.

Robert McHugh, MBA, Ph.D., has provided a description of how it works which seems consistent with the comments of Robert Heller. McHugh lays it out like this:

> The PPT decides markets need intervention, a decline needs to be stopped, or the risks associated with political events that could be perceived by markets as highly negative and cause a decline; need to be prevented by a rally already in flight.

> To get that rally, the PPT's key component – the Fed – lends money to surrogates who will take that fresh electronically printed cash and buy markets through some large unknown buyer's account. That buying comes out of the blue at a time when short interest is high. The unexpected rally strikes blood, and fear overcomes those who were betting the market would drop. These shorts need to cover, need to buy the very stocks they had agreed to sell (without owning them) at today's prices in anticipation they could buy them in the future at much lower prices and pocket the difference.

> Seeing those stocks rally above their committed selling price, the shorts are forced to buy – and buy they do. Thus, those most pessimistic about the equity market end up buying equities like mad, fueling the rally that the PPT

started. Bingo, a huge turnaround rally is well underway, and sidelines money from hedge funds, mutual funds and individuals rush in to join in the buying madness for several days and weeks as the rally gathers a life of its own.

I would leave it at that except for this one development that became public in July 2009. Bloomberg News reported:

> Sergey Aleynikov, an ex-Goldman Sachs computer pro-grammer, was arrested July 3 after arriving at Liberty International Airport in Newark, New Jersey, U.S. officials said. Aleynikov, 39, who has dual American and Russian citizenship, is charged in a criminal complaint with stealing the trading software. At a court appearance July 4 in Manhattan, Assistant U.S. Attorney Joseph Facciponti told a federal judge that Aleynikov's alleged theft poses a risk to U.S. markets. Aleynikov transferred the code, which is worth millions of dollars, to a computer server in Germany, and others may have had access to it, Facciponti said, adding that New York-based Goldman Sachs may be harmed if the software is disseminated.

The next sentence is particularly significant:

> "The bank has raised the possibility that there is a danger that somebody who knew how to use this program could use it to manipulate markets in unfair ways," Facciponti said.

The *New York Times* said the so-called proprietary "black box" software programs were of "incalculable" value because of their use in "making lucrative rapid-fire trades in the financial markets." It was part of "multi-million-dollar technology that is increasingly employed by the world's biggest banks to gain an edge in financial markets." (One would have to assume that governments with massive intelligence capacities employ, or should we say, "deploy" similar technologies.)

J. S. Kim who runs an independent investment research and wealth consultancy firm commented on this development on the financial site, *Seeking Alpha*:

> It's curious to note that Goldman Sachs has admitted that it has developed trading software that could be used to, in their own words, "manipulate markets in unfair ways," yet nobody in the mainstream media has questioned whether Goldman Sachs was, and is, using its proprietary trading platform to manipulate markets in unfair ways. Only extremely naïve investors with zero understanding of how global stock markets operate would deny that there has been continual and excessive intervention into U.S. stock markets to prop them up over the past several months.

Curious to note? Oh really? This seems another open secret in financial circles where trading is a form of warfare with more than a hint of criminality. Two weeks after this story appeared, a front page report in the *New York Times* reported how stock traders were using "high-frequency" trading computers that are suddenly the "most talked about and mysterious forces in the markets."

Critics quoted in the article suggested these computers are being used to "manipulate prices." William H. Donaldson, a former New York Stock Exchange chairman and CEO, said, "This is where all the money is being made." Investors without access to this technology have a decided disadvantage.

At the same time, despite a profit surge in some banks, many remain insolvent with fraud, a not insignificant element in their decline, according to the widely read financial blog *Jesse's American Café*, (www.jessescrossroadscafe.blogspot.com):

> … mismanagement and losses will continue to deepen, and the government (public) will own the acid core of thirty years of white-collar crime, burning a hole in the fabric of the national economy and monetary system.
>
> It will be a financial Vietnam, with Larry Summers playing Robert McNamara and Obama as LBJ. It will be a cascade of corruption and deception and will tear the country apart.
>
> At the other end of the nationalization spectrum, the government will "take over" the bad banks as they did in the S & L crisis, and restructure them.
>
> There are between five to ten banks in the country that are hopelessly insolvent through mismanagement bordering on fraud. At the moment they are sucking up capital at a ferocious rate through bailouts, and crowding out constructive uses of capital.

Do the American people know or even suspect this? Do we have an accurate accounting of the nation's money supply? Is all the information we need to make a judgment publicly available? This is why members of Congress and some in the news media are demanding full financial disclosure by the Federal Reserve Bank, a demand the bank has rejected arguing bank secrecy is essential.

House Financial Services Committee Chairman Barney Frank has joined those calling for an audit of the Fed. A federal judge has also ordered the bank to make a full disclosure of its funding practices. This issue is unlikely to be resolved.

Democratic Congresswoman Marci Kaptur of Ohio compares the Federal Reserve to counterfeiters bankrupting the system. Republican Judge Andrew Napolitano, a Fox News legal correspondent, has argued that Ben Bernanke and Henry Paulson, as well as several bank presidents, should be arrested.

I tend not to be a conspiracy theorist because the incompetence and "fuck-up" theory of history often offers better explanations for why events occur even as it is clear that there have been criminal conspiracies at play in this crisis. Could there be more to this?

John Mack, then head of Morgan Stanley, compared the financial crisis to an "economic 9/11" according to Andrew Ross Sorkin's book, *Too Big Too Fail*. He paints a picture of "an entire economy on the verge of collapsing," a good reason for the financial panic that gripped Wall Street.

Just as so much of the financial system was literally re-engineered including the derivatives markets and exotic investment products, is it possible that the collapse itself was in some way engineered?

Len Bracken explores this theory in an extensive article for the *Wayne Madsen Report* (www.waynemadsenreport.com):

With the lesson of 9/11 in mind – what was purported to be an intelligence failure was in fact a brilliant success – one must ask whether the same is the case for the current financial crisis. So far the central bank and U.S. government have committed $12.8 trillion dollars to the financial rescue effort, a sum that nears last year's gross domestic product of $14.2 trillion. The bailout will likely surpass the GDP once Treasury Secretary Geithner's "public to private" investment program goes into full swing, providing hedge funds 14 to 1 leverage with taxpayer money and no downside risk to buying toxic assets. Would this vast sum have been spent, lent or otherwise extended to financial institutions in the absence of a crisis? No. Was the crisis engineered? Quite possibly.

We know that on May 5, 2006, the same day that Porter Goss resigned as the director of the CIA, President Bush gave his intelligence czar, John Negroponte, the authority to excuse publicly traded companies from their accounting and securities disclosure obligations. This was the first time this authority has been delegated to someone outside of the Oval Office, giving Negroponte the "function of president" under the law in question. It was also in early 2006 that Wall Street's major firms agreed to standardize credit default swaps on collateralized debt obligations, enabling speculators to pay relatively small fees for what would prove to be huge rewards when these bonds began defaulting.

Greed motivated the general sequence of financial maneuvers at the epicenter of the crisis. Banks and the shadow banking system, including hedge funds, would issue commercial paper (short-term loans) often provided by money market funds. Instead of investing directly in real estate or other assets, firms would invest in securities based on pools of those assets, commonly mortgages, in the form of collateralized mortgage obligations or CMOs. The financial engineers on Wall Street, notably Goldman Sachs, created these structured products with their many tranches, including the notorious super-senior tranches that would supposedly never default, not just out of mortgages but virtually any form of debt-student loans, car loans, credit card debt-packaging them into collateralized loan obligations or collateralized debt obligations.

And so here we have yet another avenue for a deeper investigation into a system that was rigged by Wall Street with complicity by government agencies before unraveling. Economist Simon Johnson told Bill Moyers that he doesn't expect the government will make the changes that need to be made: "Rahm Emanuel, the president's chief of staff, is widely known for saying, 'Never let a good crisis go to waste.' Well, the crisis is over. The crisis in the financial sector, not for people who own homes, but the crisis for the big banks is substantially over, and it was completely wasted. The administration refused to break the power of the big banks when they had the opportunity earlier this year, and the regulatory reforms they are now pursuing will – in my opinion and I do follow this day to day – turn out to be essentially meaningless."

Rage and rhetoric continued and continues today to escalate on the Ron Paul Right and the Dennis Kucinich Left. In response, Chairman Bernanke left Washington to speak at events to defend his role, first campaigning for reappointment to his job and later expanding his portfolio to include consumer protection. (President Obama did reappoint him.)

He has mostly defended what he has done in terms of what he claims he prevented – a collapse of the economy into a new depression. He insists his interventions and manipulations were needed. "I was not going to be the Federal Reserve chairman who presided over the second Great Depression," Bernanke said.

"When you're in a situation like this, a perfect storm, sometimes you have to do things that are a little unorthodox, out of the box."

Bernanke skillfully ingratiated himself with the media, politicians and his own staffers. He was known for eating with the workers at the Fed cafeteria and being approachable in ways his predecessor was not. (Many of his executives spent weeks sleeping in their offices when the crisis was most intense.) He was, however, taken aback by all the loud criticism in Congress by elected representatives he believed did not understand the Fed's role as a "lender of last resort," or as an agency that paid money back into the Treasury under the Federal Reserve Act. He probably did more than any official to unify activists on the left and right in their opposition to what they saw as the agency's unchecked power. He was known as "Helicopter Ben" for all the money he printed and then dropped all over the financial landscape.

Financier Peter Schiff, whom I interviewed for my film, *Plunder*, blasted Bernanke from the libertarian Right:

"Bernanke is being praised for avoiding a collapse in the financial system. While he has forestalled some short-term pain, he has in turn forsaken long-term gain. The 'green shoots' that set the pundits alight are nothing more than the direct effects of massive monetary expansion. What we have is nominal growth in the unproductive service and consumption sectors ...

"Bernanke's re-nomination [was] a politically safe decision for President Obama, and at least Bernanke is a devil we know. However, this lack of a 'change' for the better should squash any 'hope' for a genuine recovery. If the Bush years were as bad as the Democrats claim, then it is curious that they are mimicking and magnifying the same mistakes. No one has been held accountable for a financial crisis that the professors, pundits, and politicians told us would not come. All the same players are running the game, always changing the rules so they stay on top."

Eliot Spitzer, the former Democratic governor of New York who is considered an expert on Wall Street crime, was fiercely critical of Bernanke and the Fed on MSNBC. He calls it a "Ponzi scheme." I will quote him at length since his views have gained mainstream acceptance:

The Federal Reserve has benefited for decades from the notion that it is quasi-autonomous, it's supposed to be independent. Let me tell you a dirty secret: The Fed has done an absolutely disastrous job since [former Fed Chairman] Paul Volcker left.

The reality is the Fed has blown it. Time and time again, they blew it. Bubble after bubble, they failed to understand what they were doing to the economy.

The most poignant example for me is the AIG bailout, where they gave tens of billions of dollars that went right through – conduit payments – to the investment banks that are now solvent. We [the taxpayers] didn't get stock in those banks, they didn't ask what was going on – this begs and cries out for hard, tough examination.

You look at the governing structure of the New York [Federal Reserve], it was run by the very banks that got the money. This is a Ponzi scheme, an inside job. It is outrageous, it is time for Congress to say enough of this. And to give them more power now is crazy.

The Fed needs to be examined carefully.

So even as manipulation occurs, as it creates a new class of technology-armed winners, it still doesn't seem able to stem the tide of the deeper structural crisis.

DANNY SCHECHTER

CHAPTER 18

THE TESTOSTERONE FACTOR

Would the Wall Street crime-wave have been checked earlier if political leaders like Eliot Spitzer, once considered the "Sheriff of the Street," had still been a prosecutor as he was as attorney general of New York State?

He was known then as a terror to many in the finance industry, who cheered when he got caught up in a sex scandal that led to his resignation as governor.

Just two days before his exposure as "Client Number 9" of a high-priced call-girl ring, he had been testifying in Congress and writing an op-ed in the *Washington Post* arguing that the Bush administration was a "partner-in-crime" with predatory lenders:

> Several years ago, state attorneys general and others involved in consumer protection began to notice a marked increase in a range of predatory lending practices by mortgage lenders.
>
> Not only did the Bush administration do nothing to protect consumers, it embarked on an aggressive and unprecedented campaign to prevent states from protecting their residents from the very problems to which the federal government was turning a blind eye.

The thrust and reality of his charges were buried and then forgotten in the storm of sensation that followed the "Gotcha" coverage of his affair with a prostitute in a Washington hotel.

It was later revealed that he had been a regular patron, spending thousands of dollars in the pursuit of discrete pleasure.

This personal morality play displaced the political morality confrontation that he was trying to ignite when he wrote this denunciation in the *Washington Post*:

> When history tells the story of the subprime lending crisis and recounts its devastating effects on the lives of so many innocent homeowners, the Bush administration will not be judged favorably. The tale is still unfolding, but when the dust settles, it will be judged as a willing accomplice to the lenders who went to any lengths in their quest for profits.

Only a few journalists went after the media's hypocrisy. Greg Palast wrote on his website (www.gregpalast.com):

> While New York Governor Eliot Spitzer was paying an "escort" $4,300 in a hotel room in Washington, just down the road, George Bush's new Federal Reserve Board chairman, Ben Bernanke, was secretly handing over $200 billion in a tryst with mortgage bank industry speculators. Both acts were wanton, wicked and lewd. But there's a *big* difference. The governor was using his own checkbook. Bush's man Bernanke was using ours.

Was Spitzer set up by a government agency or parties unknown? In the same way that Spitzer was able to go after Wall Street because he had been part of that world, working in a corporate law firm as well as a local prosecutor's office and knew it well, his sexual appetites may have been an extension of that very same high-stress culture. Illegal sex and Wall Street has long been linked, wrote Heidi Moore:

This is all a reminder that the financial district hasn't always been gleaming skyscrapers and Starbucks. Consider this passage from *City of Eros: New York City, Prostitution, and the Commercialization of Sex, 1790–1920*: "Adjacent to the Wall Street business district, prostitutes worked in saloons along Greenwich Street, taking men upstairs. In addition, immediately south of Wall Street was the Battery Tenderloin, on Whitehall Street. The Water Street area, however, remained the most significant and poorest waterfront zone of prostitution. Amid the rookeries, rat pits and dance halls, prostitutes exposed in each window to the public view plied their trade."

In the modern era, many of the Street's most macho traders are, according to David Russell who worked in the industry for two decades, known as "swinging dicks." It is well known that the big money in Wall Street has kept a vibrant, upscale sex industry alive and well. Just as the Japanese Army had "comfort women," so did Wall Street. Tokyo forced women to submit, Wall Street could afford to pay them.

There has been one scandal after another. Here are a few cases cited by Moore before Spitzer's demise:

- BP Chief Executive John Browne left both his post at the oil company and his directorship at Goldman Sachs Group last year after it was revealed that Lord Browne had lied to a court about his young male lover, whom he had met through an escort-service website.

- A group of six women sued Dresdner Kleinwort in 2006 for $1.4 billion on allegations that male executives entertained clients at strip clubs and even brought prostitutes back to the office. The case was settled out of court in 2007.

THE CRIME OF OUR TIME

- Canadian hedge fund-manager Paul Eustace in 2007, by his own admission in a deposition filed in court, lied to investors and cheated on his wife with a stripper.

- In 1987, Peter Detwiler, vice chairman of E. F. Hutton & Co., was, according to court testimony, instructed by his client, Tesoro Petroleum Corp. Chairman Robert V. West, to hire a blonde prostitute for the finance minister of Trinidad & Tobago, which had been supporting a tax issue that would have hurt Tesoro's profits.

- A woman claiming to have been Bernard Madoff's mistress published a book about their secret liaisons. [Madoff's] secretary said he had a fondness for massages in an article in *Vanity Fair.*

Wall Street's fall is said to have brought down the sex industry almost as if it had been a fully owned subsidary, if not an extension, of the financial services business.

One sex blog (www.thefrisky.com) noted, "It's been a world of pain for the sex workers who have been complaining about the recession. While prostitutes are reporting record business and lay people are doing it like bunnies, the niche market has been beaten down." *Time* reported a steep drop off in global sex tourism, as well.

At the same time in other parts of the world, economic crisis-driven joblessness can lead to more sex workers, not fewer. *Short News* (www.shortnews.com) reported:

> Due to the global financial crisis, sex workers in Cambodia are getting fewer customers with less money, causing them to do things that puts them at a higher risk. 60,000 factory workers lost their jobs causing a rise in the number of sex workers.

DANNY SCHECHTER

Controversial human trafficking legislation that was passed in February 2008 criminalized sex work and led to months of brothel busts which resulted in the sex workers taking to the streets, night clubs, and karaoke parlors.

Ly Pisey, from Woman's Agenda for Change, said that sex workers who work independently of brothels are more likely to be affected by the economic downturn, because they are less protected and often more desperate for money.

I doubt that this issue raises much concern on Wall Street.

There are other ways in which the high-pressure world of Wall Street and the sex business are interconnected, if not interdependent, and this may have more to do with the risky behavior in trades and investments.

To find out more, I spoke to Jonathan Albert, a psychologist practicing in mid-Manhattan.

He told me, "I see a lot of clients in NYC who are impacted by the economic crisis. People deal with stress in many different ways. Some people exercise, some people over-eat, some use drugs and alcohol, some even sexualize those feelings."

"Sexualize?" I asked him, how do they sexualize these feelings?

His response, "I've seen a lot of Wall Streeters who sexualize feelings of anxiety and stress and depression. So for example they might rely on adult sexual services to deal with those feelings."

Author Loretta Napoleoni, who worked on Wall Street for several years, offers a provocative thesis for how the need for paid sex "on the wild side" became part of its culture of irresponsibility.

"I can tell you that this is absolutely true because being a woman, having worked in finance 20 years ago, I could tell you that even at that time – when the market was not going up so much – these guys, all they talk is sex."

She complemented her personal experience by citing a study by researchers from Oxford University.

"The study discovered, that an excessive production of testosterone, in a period of fantastic financial exuberance, creates a sort of confusion. It is what people in sports call 'being in the zone,' which means you get in a certain situation where you feel that you will always win. That you are infallible."

I asked Dr. Albert if that finding may have indeed had relevance to Spitzer or be endemic in the industry. His reply, "I do see this a lot in the finance industry, yes. People in positions of power often feel as if they can perhaps get away with it. There is sometimes a sense of entitlement."

"They feel entitled to take part in risky behavior?" I pressed.

"High-risk behavior. It's similar to what they do on a daily basis. They invest millions and millions of dollars and there is a great risk involved with that. The same is true with using the services of a prostitute. Obviously there are great health risks; their relationship is in great danger if they are using the services of a prostitute.

"A lot of people skate on the excitement, on that euphoric rush."

The culture of risk on Wall Street was intoxicating to many in the same way that gamblers become addicted or report a rush when they are winning. They might be compared to bungee jumpers or race car drivers. Years earlier, the writer Graham Greene wrote about a link between suicidal risk and sex in a discussion of the motives some had for playing Russian roulette.

I remember the extraordinary sense of jubilation, as if carnival lights had been switched on in a dark drab street. My heart knocked in its cage, and life contained an infinite number of possibilities. It was like a young man's first successful experience of sex.

The euphoria of life in the fast lane often implodes when one's luck runs out leading to depression and family breakups. One remedy is going to self-help groups like this one I found:

The "Wall Street Wives Club" was formed to empower and serve the needs of wives and girlfriends whose husbands or significant others work in the stressful and volatile brokerage community. The pressure filled aspect of jobs within the financial sector often lead men to feel depressed, weak, incompetent, isolated, anxious and emotionally exhausted. Long work hours often impair the communication between partners in a relationship. Often it is as if the couple has become "two ships passing in the night." Men are often uncomfortable expressing their feelings.

Some of Dr. Albert's clients coped with the pressure on them to perform in kinkier ways.

"… they just want to let loose, relax and take a very passive role in their sexual practice. So they may seek out the services of a dominatrix, where they are at the mercy of this sex worker. I've had clients who seek out services where they get whipped, cuffed, put on a leash like a dog."

In my own research, I came across an article in *Dealmaker* magazine about an event in which young male traders attended sex parties for wealthy older women for a fee; others or who took clients to sex clubs, a practice that women on the Street objected to because it was both sexist and discriminatory. Some even sued. There was another case of traders funding a sex club in the Hamptons.

So now we can add to the lack of regulation and the greed that fueled criminal practices, a cultural pathology that is far more personal and self-destructive. I am not being moralistic here, but a climate of narcissism and living secret lives often desensitizes its practitioners leaving them little time to think of how their actions may affect others.

CHAPTER 19

THE ROLE OF REGULATORS AND POLITICIANS

M ost of the blame for the crimes detailed in these pages rests with those who benefited or profited most directly, especially the executives and key shareholders who banked the outsized dividends, salaries and bonuses.

Yet they did not act alone, nor could they.

A complicated restructuring of the financial system did not occur overnight, nor was it engineered by the finance and banking system alone. To create an enabling environment for a culture of crime, and what the Wall Street world calls "extraction," you need a legal system that will permit it and a regulatory framework that will not interfere.

The financialization of our financial system did not just happen; it was engineered, projected as socially beneficial "modernization" and "innovation."

Who could be against that?

Back in 1850, Frederic Bastiat, the French free market philosopher, understood that clearly and saw it as a precondition for plunder, writing in *The Law*: "When plunder becomes a way of life for a group of men, they create for themselves in the course of time a legal system that authorizes it and a moral code that glorifies it."

Key to the new system was: dismantling old regulation, rewriting laws and allowing industries to "capture" regulatory agencies, in the sense that their values and priorities came to shape their priorities.

A former Treasury Department official, Catherine Austin

Fitts, said this strategy was advanced by a major strategic lobbying effort. Campaign contributions and plans developed by non-governmental think tanks resulted in what she calls a "financial coup d'etat" that:

- Engineered a fraudulent housing and debt bubble.

- Illegally shifted vast amounts of capital out of the U.S.

- Used "privatization" as a form of piracy – a pretext to move government assets to private investors at below-market prices and then shift private liabilities back to government at no cost to the private liability holder.

Many members of Congress come from the world of business or law firms servicing businesses. Many have a corporate orientation, investments in the market, and even have the right to engage in insider trading on information they obtain in the course of their legislative work. Congressional reformers like Public Citizen are campaigning to end this practice, which they explained this way:

Members of Congress, high-ranking appointees in the executive branch, and other federal employees who have access to non-public information about publicly traded companies can use that information to buy or sell securities or commodities for personal gain.

Lobbyists – and "political intelligence consultants" paid specifically to haunt the halls of Congress for insider tips – can also get away with this crooked and potentially corrupt practice.

This kind of insider trading is already illegal for corporate executives, Wall Street brokers, and ordinary citizens. This kind of insider trading should be illegal for people who work in and around the government, too.

Paul Kane reported in the *Washington Post* that many on the oversight committees have invested in the companies they supposedly regulate:

> On the Senate banking committee, at least a half-dozen senators had significant investments in companies that benefited from the $700-billion-bailout legislation that the panel helped draft last fall. Sen. Charles E. Schumer (D-NY) reported $18,000 to $95,000 in investments in Freddie Mac and Fannie Mae bonds, and also that he sold at least $15,000 in Fannie "step-up" bonds at the end of last year. The committee's ranking Republican, Sen. Richard C. Shelby (Miss.), reported holding $260,000 to $850,000 in money market and retirement accounts with Countrywide, Citigroup and Wachovia.

For years, the committees charged with regulating were actually in the deregulation business. Deregulation was the free market mantra promoted by many politicians and business leaders. When they were successful, there were fewer cops on the beat as economist Loretta Napoleoni explained in her book, *Rogue Economics*. She told me:

> What has happened is that the Chinese walls which were then dividing the barrier between one branch and the other branch of the same bank in order to prevent insider trading, in reality, did not work as they should have. And the reason why it didn't work is because it is a sort of self-regulating procedure. Soon, the government was no longer controlling what was happening inside the bank.

And that, she said led to an upsurge in corporate crime:

> The reason why the line between what is criminal and what
> is not criminal has disappeared is because of deregulation.
> When you remove all the restrictions, all the controls, then of
> course, there is a blurring of what is legal and what is illegal.

The Center for Responsive Politics released a stunning
report in March 2009, detailing how Wall Street got its way
with our government:

> The financial sector invested more than $5 billion in political
> influence purchasing in Washington over the past decade,
> with as many as 3,000 lobbyists winning deregulation and oth-
> er policy decisions that led directly to the current financial col-
> lapse, according to a 231-page report issued today by Essen-
> tial Information and the Consumer Education Foundation.

> The report, "Sold Out: How Wall Street and Washington
> Betrayed America," shows that, from 1998–2008, Wall Street
> investment firms, commercial banks, hedge funds, real-estate
> companies and insurance conglomerates made $1.725 bil-
> lion in political contributions and spent another $3.4 billion
> on lobbyists, a financial juggernaut aimed at undercutting
> federal regulation.

> Nearly 3,000 officially registered federal lobbyists worked for
> the industry in 2007 alone.

> The report documents a dozen distinct deregulatory moves
> that, together, led to the financial meltdown. These include
> prohibitions on regulating financial derivatives; the repeal of
> regulatory barriers between commercial banks and invest-

ment banks; a voluntary regulation scheme for big investment banks; and federal refusal to act to stop predatory subprime lending.

"The report details, step-by-step, how Washington systematically sold out to Wall Street," said Harvey Rosenfield, president of the Consumer Education Foundation, a California-
based non-profit organization. "Depression-era programs that
would have prevented the financial meltdown that began last
year were dismantled, and the warnings of those who foresaw
disaster were drowned in an ocean of political money. Americans were betrayed, and we are paying a high price – trillions
of dollars – for that betrayal."

"Congress and the executive branch," said Robert Weiss-
man of *Essential Information* (www.essential.org) and the lead
author of the report, "responded to the legal bribes from the
financial sector, rolling back common-sense standards, barring
honest regulators from issuing rules to address emerging problems and trashing enforcement efforts. The progressive erosion
of regulatory restraining walls led to a flood of bad loans, and
a tsunami of bad bets based on those bad loans. Now, there is
wreckage across the financial landscape." Some stats:

Total official lobbyists for the financial sector in 2007: **2,996**
[Astonishing!]

Covered official lobbyists for 20 profiled firms, decade-long
total (1998–2008): **142**

You can read the details in the full report online at *Wall Street
Watch* (www.wallstreetwatch.org/reports/sold_out.pdf).

The money came from banks and security firms, investment
houses and accountants. In my film, *In Debt We Trust*, I report-

ed on the $151 million that was used to change bankruptcy laws in the name of "reform."

It's important to note that this occurred on a bipartisan basis, with both Democrat and Republican hands out and willingly complicit. Noted the Center's report:

> The betrayal was bipartisan: about 55 percent of the political donations went to Republicans and 45 percent to Democrats, primarily reflecting the balance of power over the decade. Democrats took just more than half of the financial sector's 2008 election cycle contributions.

> The financial sector buttressed its political strength by placing Wall Street expatriates in top regulatory positions, including the post of Treasury Secretary held by two former Goldman Sachs chairs, Robert Rubin and Henry Paulson.

For the record, this transformation happened in steps and stages. According to their impeccable research there were twelve steps. (When you think of 12 step programs, you rarely think of this type of strategy.)

1. In 1999, Congress repealed the Glass-Steagall Act, which had prohibited the merger of commercial banking and investment banking.

2. Regulatory rules permitted off-balance sheet accounting – tricks that enabled banks to hide their liabilities.

3. The Clinton administration blocked the Commodity Futures Trading Commission from regulating financial derivatives – which became the basis for massive speculation.

4. Congress in 2000 prohibited regulation of financial derivatives when it passed the Commodity Futures Modernization Act.

5. The Securities and Exchange Commission in 2004 adopted a voluntary regulation scheme for investment banks that enabled them to incur much higher levels of debt.

6. Rules adopted by global regulators at the behest of the financial industry would enable commercial banks to determine their own capital reserve requirements, based on their internal "risk-assessment models."

7. Federal regulators refused to block widespread predatory lending practices in the early '00s, failing to either issue appropriate regulations or even enforce existing ones.

8. Federal bank regulators claimed the power to supersede state consumer protection laws that could have diminished predatory lending and other abusive practices.

9. Federal rules prevented victims of abusive loans from suing firms that bought their loans from the banks that issued the original loan.

10. Fannie Mae and Freddie Mac expanded beyond their traditional scope of business and entered the subprime market, ultimately costing taxpayers hundreds of billions of dollars.

11. The abandonment of antitrust and related regulatory principles enabled the creation of too-big-to-fail megabanks, which engaged in much riskier practices than smaller banks.

12. Beset by conflicts of interest, private credit rating compa-
    nies incorrectly assessed the quality of mortgage-backed
    securities; a 2006 law handcuffed the SEC from properly
    regulating the firms.

That pretty much sums it up. There is more of course, including new rules that motivated agencies to seek financial settlements to avoid prosecutions in practices deemed harmful to
consumers or investors.

This leads us to the current moment where the Obama
administration is caught up in the contradictions of the financial crisis – colluding with many of the institutions and individuals responsible for it, and at the same time committed to
financial reforms and economic recovery. The reform rhetoric is
often in collision with the power of an industry that wants to
control what changes, if any, are to be made. There is another
danger, that fraudsters may target the bailout and stimulus
programs like TARP. That's the expectation of the "top cop" on
this beat, as the *Los Angeles Times* reported:

> The TARP itself may be the biggest fraud of all, but Inspector
> General Neil Barofsky said today that he's already examining
> 20 potential cases of criminal fraud having to do with the
> program.

> Barofsky said the complex nature of the bailout program
> makes it "inherently vulnerable to fraud, waste and abuse,
> including significant issues relating to conflicts of interest
> facing fund managers, collusion between participants, and
> vulnerabilities to money laundering."

The AP explained:

The report said little about who is under investigation and how the fraudulent schemes work, but investigators are already on alert for a long list of potential scams. Such schemes could include obtaining bailout money under false pretenses, bilking the government with phony mortgage modifications, and cheating on taxes with fraudulent filings.

"You don't need an entirely corrupt institution to pull one of these schemes off," Barofsky said. "You only need a few corrupt managers whose compensation may be tied to the performance of these assets in order to effectively pull off a collusion or a kickback scheme ..."

By July 2009, there had been no full accounting with the usage of the TARP monies. The *Washington Post* reported, "Many of the banks that got federal aid to support increased lending have instead used some of the money to make investments, repay debts or buy other banks." The *Daily Beast* broke it down, "Of the 360 banks that got money through the end of January, 110 had invested at least some of it, 52 repaid debts, and 15 bought other banks."

Others had invested millions in lobbying reported the public interest news website *ProPublica* (www.propublica.org): "The banking industry hasn't stopped lobbying just because it's received billions in bailout money from the government ... The *Hill* reports that the eight large banks that first received bailout funds back in October spent a total of 'more than $12.4 million in the first half of 2009,' slightly more than they spent in the first half of 2008."

The AP provides more of the individual totals: Bank of America ($52.5 billion in aid) spent $800,000 lobbying in spring 2009, up from $660,000 spent in the first three months of that year, and Citigroup ($50 billion in aid) spent $1.7 million from April through June 2009, even more than it spent during that same period in 2008. Even the auto companies spent millions lobbying: GM ($50.4 billion in aid) spent $2.8 million. About the only bailed-out company that isn't lobbying Congress on legislation is AIG, which stopped after criticism over its lobbying last fall.

Individual politicians also benefited from their connections to lenders and received favorable rates. *Web of Deception* reported that House Speaker Nancy Pelosi's son Paul worked for Countrywide which provided a low cost mortgage to her daughter Alexandra. It also noted that Henry Paulson, 5 weeks before he became Treasury Secretary, received a Fannie Mae/Freddie Mac 30-year-fixed, below-rate mortgage for his 82-year-old mother in May 2005 for 5.37%. Hillary and Bill Clinton's daughter Chelsea Clinton went to work for a hedge fund whose CEO told us in 2007 that hedge funds were stabilizing the economy. When he graduated from college, Barack Obama worked for a Wall Street business intelligence firm, Business International. There seems to be an incestuous relationship between Wall Street and the political elite.

The AP also reported:

> Two influential Senate committee chairmen were told they were getting special VIP deals when they applied for mortgages, an official who handled their loans told Congress in closed-door testimony. Democratic Sens. Christopher Dodd and Kent Conrad had denied knowing they were getting discounts when they negotiated their loan terms.

American politics is fueled by cash from the financial services industry. We can't leave out the vast political donations made to candidates by executives in the banking and finance worlds. They see this as a business investment, not just personal philanthropy. *Politically Drunk* (www.politicallydrunk. blogspot.com) monitored the Obama campaign's use of "bundlers" to package large amounts of money from the industry. Their findings – and these are not final figures:

> In Obama's speeches across the country he has repeatedly criticized the Bush administration for allowing "evil" subprime mortgage lenders and investment banks to lead this county into our current mortgage meltdown. Obama's rhetoric on the mortgage crisis has been pointed and blunt, as stated on his own campaign website, "Obama will crack down on fraudulent brokers and lenders ... Obama has been closely monitoring the subprime mortgage situation for years, and introduced comprehensive legislation over a year ago to fight mortgage fraud and protect consumers against abusive lending practices."

> Throughout the campaign season Obama has attacked Wall Street's financial sector and run a campaign based largely upon his "good judgment." The problem with Obama's rhetoric rests in the fact that tucked away in his database of 2.5 million donors is the approximately 180,000 power brokers that have funded nearly 60% of his campaign. Included in this list are the more than 594 campaign bundlers including 15 lobbyist bundlers who have accounted for over $140 million in contributions. Included in this list are just 36 bundlers accounting for over $18 million dollars, with two bundlers raising over $1 million, and one over $2 million.

> These amounts are impressive considering that just 552 individuals have accounted for nearly 1/3 of his total campaign contributions. Of course determining the occupation can be tricky considering the Obama campaign lists nearly

100 bundlers as having unknown occupations, nearly 100 who are listed as "self-employed," and dozens of "home-makers" and "retired" individuals.

Among Obama's campaign contributors are many Lehman Brothers executives, such as CEO Richard Fuld ($2,300), President Joseph Gregory ($4,600) and dozens of other top Lehman executives ... Lehman shareholders filed suit against Fuld and Gregory for the company's exposure in the subprime market. In addition to dozens of Lehman executives are Obama's bundlers from Lehman Brothers who have raised top dollar for the campaign. Direct contributions from Lehman Brothers have exceeded $395,000 for Senator Obama.

Some members of Congress, like Florida Democrat Alan Grayson, have been crusading for accountability and full disclosure from the Federal Reserve. At the same time, it appears that he too was victimized in a Ponzi scam. The *Hill* reported: "Freshman Rep. Alan Grayson (D-Fla.) lost $3 million in a stock swindle between 2000 and 2005, a Florida television station reported."

Is it any wonder that Robert Johnson who is affiliated with the Eleanor Roosevelt Institute wrote on *New Deal 2.0* (www.newdeal20.org):

We are amidst a crisis of political legitimacy. The leaders of our complex financial firms have failed. They have failed as stewards of our nation's future. They have failed as protectors of our public Treasury. Now, with trillions guaranteed, hundreds of billions of bailouts paid, and very little in the way of investigation, firings, or prosecution of the perpetrators, we are all being asked to calm down, move on, and stop acting like populists (a pejorative term when used by elite media or financiers). In the mean time, the perpetrators of this disaster confidently pay their political soldiers for another round of lobbying and campaign-contribution money.

And now, Jamie Dimon, the CEO of JPMorgan Chase, describes his company's government lobbying as their "seventh line of business."

For his part, President Obama seems to have become more critical of Wall Street than he was when he was Candidate Obama, raising money there. He told Jim Lehrer on PBS on July 20, 2009:

> You had a Wall Street that took excessive risks, acted irresponsibly and almost dragged the entire economy into a depression. We had to intervene and did, to stabilize the financial system because if you had a complete meltdown then things would actually be far worse. Unemployment would be higher and it would be even harder for us to get out of the hole.
>
> The problem that I've seen, at least, is you don't get a sense that folks on Wall Street feel any remorse for having taken all these risks; you don't get a sense that there's been a change of culture and behavior as a consequence of what has happened … if we didn't stop the bleeding in the financial system, then it would have been even worse for everybody.

So where are we? Obama is proposing modest reforms that are unlikely to curb the practices he criticizes. In fact, as economist Michael Hudson wrote in *Counterpunch* (www.counter-

punch.org), the reforms the administration wants will do little
to curb fraud:

> Sound regulations against fraud are on the books, many of
> them from the New Deal. But as the Bubble Economy saw
> levels of financial fraud unprecedented since the 1920s,
> officials who wanted to prevent abuses found their depart-
> ments unfunded.

> Mr. Obama's proposal fails to address this problem. There are
> ... millions of Americans who signed contracts they did not
> always understand offered by lenders who did not always tell
> the truth, he acknowledged in introducing his plan on June
> 17. Mr. Obama promised enforcement will be the rule, not
> the exception. But where is the funding for the FBI's criminal
> fraud division? Where is effective consumer protection from
> insurance companies that don't pay, from crooked contrac-
> tors and mortgage companies using property appraisers,
> lawyers and collection agencies, or from stockbrokers pack-
> aging junk mortgages into junk securities?

> They've been given a fortune in recent years – and can keep
> it to set themselves up to make yet a new killing. It looks as
> if as little will be done to financial fraud as will be done to
> the Guantanamo torturers and the high-ups who condoned
> their actions.

Even worse are the signs that the sleazy securitization market
is being restarted, according to Andrew Reinbach, a veteran
finance reporter, wrote on the *Huffington Post*:

> In other words, we can expect a new wave of mortgage-
> backed bond defaults to hit the headlines any day now. And

considering the size of your typical commercial mortgage, that wave should be pretty impressive; S & P isn't the only one that rated this sort of paper. It doesn't take much to imagine what news like that will do to the stock markets.

Yet Wall Street's factories – sorry, investment banks – continue grinding out what amounts to re-named, iffy bonds like sausage, and even worse, institutions continue to buy the sausage, and rating agencies are apparently continuing to rate them AAA.

Just to aggravate matters, regulators aren't stopping it, since said regulators are on record as wanting to re-start the securitization markets. As though the securitization market wasn't the scene of the crime.

But it was. It was various sorts of securitized debt that tipped us into what's still being called a global recession; securitized debt that was salted with garbage, structured with the help of esoteric math, rated AAA by the rating agencies, and sold around the world like gilt-edged cluster bombs.

Reinbach doesn't mince any words in tying this to resurgent criminality:

Investment bankers and career criminals have something in common: When they get caught, they spend their time figuring out what they did wrong, so they can do it better next time.

Despite all the talk of recovery and stabilization, thoughtful economists like MIT's Simon Johnson say there may be a next time sooner rather than later. (Even President Obama agrees that's possible without serious regulatory reform that is moving at a snail's pace.) Johnson suggested in congressional testimony that despite what's been done by Washington, we are still at risk of systemic failure. Our government, that has been so co-opted and compromised, is unwilling to bite the hand that feeds it – and do what must be done to repair a frail system. He explained:

> The collapse of a single large bank, insurance company, or other financial intermediary can have serious negative consequences for the U.S. economy. Even worse, it can trigger further bank failures both within the United States and in other countries – and failures elsewhere in the world can quickly create further problems that impact our financial system and those of our major trading partners.

> As a result, we currently face a high degree of systemic risk, both within the United States and across the global financial system. This risk is high in historical terms for the U.S., higher than experienced in most countries previously, and probably unprecedented in its global dimensions.

> Short-term measures taken by the U.S. government since fall 2008 (and particularly under the Obama administration) have helped stabilized financial markets – primarily by providing unprecedented levels of direct and indirect support to large banks. **But these same measures have not removed the longer-run causes of systemic instability. In fact, as a result of supporting leading institutions on terms that are generous to top bank executives (few have been fired or faced other adverse consequences), systemic risk has likely been exacerbated.**

DANNY SCHECHTER

The president spoke out again on Wall Street's irresponsibility in bringing the economy down at his July 22, 2009 press conference:

> We were on the verge of a complete financial meltdown. And the reason was because Wall Street took extraordinary risks with other people's money. They were peddling loans that they knew could never be paid back.
>
> They were flipping those loans and leveraging those loans and higher and higher mountains of debt were being built on loans that were fundamentally unsound. And all of us now are paying the price.

Is economic justice even possible under circumstances riddled with so many banksters still in charge and tangled up in so many conflicts of interest? In this environment, can we look forward to any serious fraud prevention effort, much less a mass prosecution?

Transparency remains another big obstacle. When there's lots of money to be made, insiders don't like prying eyes, especially on their exotic derivatives including the ones that helped caused the crisis. Mark Mobius of the Templeton Fund told Bloomberg:

> **Banks make so much money with these things that they don't want transparency because the spreads are so generous when there's no transparency.**

> In Washington and Wall Street especially, lobbyists and hobnobbers are busy beavers these days. They're working to ensure the $592-trillion-dollar international derivatives market (10 times the GDP of all the countries in the world

combined) continues to generate staggering amounts of wealth by remaining unregulated.

Will they get away with it? What can be done? Will there be a day of reckoning?

With the political system totally compromised and paralyzed, some hope that the courts may become the conscience of last resort, punishing those who have bought up the politicians and avoided accountability. Bloomberg News, which to my eye has done the best coverage of the crisis in the U.S., reported right after Labor Day in 2009:

> The executive and legislative branches have been discussing reforms such as more regulation of hedge funds and transparency for derivatives as a response to the financial crisis that began a year ago. As that battle with a reluctant Wall Street inches forward about how to prevent another disaster, judges are taking the first steps toward the same goal, punishing executives and issuing rulings with national impact.
>
> Last week, U.S. District Judge Shira Scheindlin threw out a key free-speech defense that credit raters had used for years to thwart investors' fraud suits, knocking $1.5 billion off the market value of Moody's Investors Service Inc. and the parent of Standard & Poor's LLC.
>
> "Judges have lifetime appointments and are freer to act on their conscience than regulators," said Charles Elson, chair of the University of Delaware's corporate-governance center. Judges can act more decisively than regulators or politicians because they're "insulated from the political process," he said.

DANNY SCHECHTER

Blogger Larry Doyle agreed:

With the gap between Wall Street and Main Street never wider, the American public is left wondering who truly is looking out for their interests. The Wall Street lobbying machine is working overtime to dilute real regulatory reform. The financial regulators themselves are increasingly exposed as overmatched and incompetent, if not worse. Where can the American public turn to get some relief? Slowly but surely the courts are taking action to address the gross injustices that the American public has had to bear at the behest of Wall Street and with the protection of Washington.

If so, this is a hopeful sign.

CHAPTER 20

JUDGMENT DAY

"Call it for what it is. It has more names than Satan. Call it plundering. Call it pillaging. Call it extortion, Call it fraud. Call it racketeering. Call it the financial raping of the middle class. Call it criminal."

– John Bougearel, director of Futures and Equity Research at Structural Logic

Just as I was completing my first draft of this book on Labor Day weekend in September 2009, the financial press was buzzing with optimistic scenarios for recovery, while the mainstream media was reporting more bank failures and upticks in unemployment. Who and what can we believe? Is the crisis over, or as many fear, will the economy plunge even more?

My principal sources are not optimistic. Former Goldman managing director, Nomi Prins, for one, told me "this economic cycle is not finished going downward."

Many of the other experts I consulted for my film, *Plunder*, and this book agreed.

Economist Max Wolff, who works in a financial firm, added, "Sadly there is evidence that we're going to flush our tax dollars and our opportunity down the toilet to rebuild an unfair system that rewarded only the top at the expense of everybody and was fundamentally unsound."

As new regulations were beginning to be put into place, governments had already spent trillions on stimulus programs, which began to feel like a joke. Economists like Paul Krugman and businessmen like Warren Buffet, both Obama supporters, advocated for a new and bigger stimulus, a call

President Obama initially rejected, asking that we all give his plan "time to work."

So far, what has been done is clearly not enough. The "reforms" often pumped money into the very institutions that caused the problems. The bailouts benefited the wealthy as efforts were made, more to restore a failed system, than to build a foundation for a new one. It has become clear that the structure of the economy itself has to be transformed, as do the rules that govern it.

The administration realizes this but it may be boxed in. President Obama's own chief of staff, Rahm Emanuel, was quoted as saying in August 2009, "The [finance] industry is already back to their pre-meltdown bonuses. We need to make sure we don't slip back to risky behavior where the institutions have all the upside and the taxpayers have all the downside, which is why we need regulatory reform."

Congressional action is problematic because, if the past is any guide, the special interests that reshaped the economy permitting the plunder of the near past, will not sit idly by. They are already working to limit the scope of investigations and changes in the law that could lead to more aggressive enforcement of the way the industry functions.

White-collar criminal Sam Antar has even written to President Obama warning of massive fraud because of all the bailout monies being pumped into the economy. He believed that the disclosures of these frauds in a few years will jeopardize his re-election. The FBI seems to share his fears, estimating that as much as $50 million dollars could be at risk because of fraud, poor management and controls.

Investigative reporter Gary Weiss cautioned me against expecting that criminal practices would be ending any time soon.

"I wouldn't say that we are doomed to repeat the same

mistakes again. I'd say that we will willingly and cheerfully make the same mistakes again; because that is the way the system is set up. The system is not designed to correct or to change in a fundamental way. Nothing that's happened, so far, none of the actions taken by the Obama administration regarding the financial crisis portends change."

I asked him, "What would portend real change?"

"Well, the only way that you're not going to see a continuing plunder of resources is if there's a structural change," he said, "a structural change in the way the Street is allowed to do business."

Even as books like this one offers a critique of the corporate and institutional industry-driven crimes behind the meltdown, the right-wing smear machine is mobilizing around another picture, one that only blames Democrats (who were certainly part of the problem) and the government. Jerome Corsi, one of the creators of the "swift-boating" attacks that accused war hero John Kerry of being a liar and traitor in Vietnam during the 2004 presidential election, is at it again with a tract about the financial bubble that was promoted widely in right-wing media.

Critic Paul Rosenberg wrote about this effort on *Open Left* (www.openleft.com), to muddy the waters of all deeper critical thinking Corsi disagrees with ideologically, and substitute simplistic message points and conspiracies:

> Appearing on *Hannity* to promote his latest book, *America for Sale*, author Jerome Corsi purported to explain the causes of the mortgage bubble by advancing a litany of falsehoods and misinformation: repeating the myth that the Community Reinvestment Act [CRA] was responsible for the bubble; claiming that President Obama was tied to the housing bubble through conservative bogeyman ACORN;

and falsely suggesting that Obama lowered interest rates to "zero or close to zero."

What's wrong with this? Superficially, it's easy: the CRA was not responsible for the housing bubble – rather it was non-CRA, non-bank institutions that lead the way, ACORN fought against irresponsible lending practices, both with respect to CRA-and non-CRA-based lending, and Obama's limited tangential connections with ACORN had nothing to do with ACORN's low-income-housing advocacy.

Congressman Keith Ellison wrote about this in the *Minneapolis Star Tribune*, noting that it was not federal policy that caused the crisis but the lack of federal regulation:

> The most abusive and predatory lenders were not federally regulated. More than 50 percent of the subprime mortgage loans made in 2005 and 2006 were originated by lenders not subject to federal supervision. Mortgage brokers, finance companies and payday lenders made toxic home and consumer loans with few limits – loans with little or no documentation – commonly known as "liars' loans."

Will we see more prosecutions? Criminal law expert John Coffee said he expects so, but stresses that the rights of defendants must be assured.

Antar, who was a defendant, said the government only has the capacity to investigate and prosecute a relative handful of cases.

The courts also seem unequipped to deal with complex criminal cases, wrote Gillian Tett in the *Financial Times*:

> Some senior figures in the financial world are looking for

solutions to this. Jeffrey Golden, a prominent lawyer who helped to create the modern derivatives world, for example, thinks there is an urgent need for a specialist, cross-border financial court (in much the same way, say, that there are specialist family or trade courts.) This, he argues, could be staffed by former derivatives experts and lawyers, since these not only understand finance but also have a vested interest in ensuring that their beloved derivatives business is built credible foundations.

But there seems to be a limited chance that Golden's sensible suggestion will fly soon. Right now, in other words, the Western financial system is stuck with a legal structure that seems ill-equipped to cope.

But, even if there are more prosecutions, that may not lead to the changes we need argues Max Wolff, "I think you will see a bunch of people get some prison sentences. More importantly, and a bigger question to me is, will we see a structural change or will we go through a long, bad recession while we waste our money struggling to rebuild an unsustainable system that should have never been erected in the first place?"

I share Wolff's sense that just tossing more people in prison will not solve the problem, even if feels good to know these predators are not getting away with it. Incarceration alone is not necessarily a deterrent and is not the panacea. Perhaps we could come up with a way in which convicted white-collar criminals could be allowed to do supervised community service and assist organizations that could use their expertise to fight for economic justice.

In the aftermath of Bernard Madoff's conviction, Signe Wilkinson wrote in the *Philadelphia Daily News*:

But what about the millions of other Americans whose lives have been upended by the fraudsters who caused the global economic crisis?

Yes, we mean fraud, not innocent mistakes or incompetent miscalculations, or even weak government regulations. There's evidence that the subprime-mortgage boom, the ensuing housing bubble and the financial catastrophe that followed were built on deceit. And the perpetrators and their co-conspirators are laughing all the way to the – you should pardon the expression – banks.

Imagine if U.S. District Judge Denny Chin had told Madoff that he wants to "look forward" and focus on making sure that monstrous frauds like Madoff's don't happen again – and so would let him off with a stern lecture and no punishment. That's pretty much the Obama administration's message to Wall Street.

And speaking of looking forward, we might consider acting forward with an emerging movement that calls itself A New Way Forward (www.anewwayforward.org) to organize for financial reform. It is taking on those whom FDR called the "banksters," a term I also used earlier. Their program:

Any bank that's "too big to fail" means that it's too big for a free market to function. The financial corporations that caused this mess must be broken up and sold back to the private market with strong, new regulatory and antitrust rules in place – new banks, managed by new people. An independent regulatory body must protect consumers from predatory practices.

As Wall Street corporations grew bigger and bigger until they were "too big to fail," they also became so politically powerful that they led to distorted and unfair policies that served companies, not citizens.

It's not enough to try to patch up the current system. We demand serious reform that fixes the root problems in our political and economic system: excessive influence of banks, dangerous compensation systems, and massive consolidation. And we demand that the reform happen in an open and transparent manner.

To the surprise of many critics, calls to break up the big banks are now drawing support from insiders. The widely shared ideological consensus that the banks must be saved and enabled to prosper is cracking. When former chairmen of the Federal Reserve Bank, like Alan Greenspan and Paul Volcker, unite across party lines to call for a break-up of big banks, you know cracks in elite opinion are registering on a Richter scale.

President Obama, who engorged his campaign with the bundling of donations from the financial industry, seems to have had enough, too.

In response to the public furor over a new round of outsized bonuses and compensation from companies that are only in business because of government loans, the *New York Times* reported:

The Obama administration will order the companies that received the most aid to deeply slash the compensation to their highest paid executives. He condemned Wall Street execs earlier this week at a fundraiser for reckless speculation and deceptive practices and short sightedness and self-interestedness from a few.

DANNY SCHECHTER

This began happening against the background of what Reuters calls, "The watering down of U.S. financial regulation reform in Congress." This has left consumer advocates wondering what will be left of the Obama administration's plan once lawmakers are done compromising it to nothingness. This is leading to a new pushback from on high. The influential website *Baseline Scenario* website explained:

> Just when our biggest banks thought they were out of the woods and into the money, the official consensus in their favor begins to crack. The Obama administration's publicly stated view – from the highest level in the White House – remains that the banks cannot or should not be broken up. Their argument is that the big banks can be regulated into permanently low risk behavior.

The *Financial Times* began carrying articles arguing that Goldman should be allowed to fail too even as the bank's vice chairman told a London conference that "that inequality created by bankers' huge salaries is a price worth paying for greater prosperity."

Mervyn King, the governor of the Bank of England, lashed out at the big banks too: "Never in the field of financial endeavor has so much money been owed by so few to so many. And, one might add, so far with little real reform … The belief that appropriate regulation can ensure that speculative activities do not result in failures is a delusion."

Demands like these are always up against the forces mobilized to keep things the way they are, to save the status quo, as has often happened after crises like this according to muckraker Gary Weiss who argues:

> After every major crisis, there has been a return to busi-

ness as usual. And, criminal acts, types of fraud, practices
that are improper, which, are going to be causing problems
several years from now – they're just starting to take place
right now. I don't know what they are, but you can bet that
a whole new wave of criminal actions is just now taking,
beginning to take, in corporate, in global corporations on
Wall Street.

The economist Simon Johnson now believes that the Obama
administration itself was "captured" by the financial services
industry:

We are entering a new, more global era of state capture,
and the U.S. government (or, more precisely, its credit) was
handed over – rather meekly – during the past 12 months.

Many states have been taken over by bankers; there is no
shame in fighting and losing against what Jefferson called
the "monied aristocracy." But few governments, even the
weakest, have handed over the keys as quietly as we did.

As Lloyd Blankfein said, to an aide, on their way to the greatest sales job in the history of the republic, "You're getting
out of a Mercedes to go to the New York Federal Reserve.
You're not getting out of a Higgins boat on Omaha beach."
The winners among our financial elite are very far from the
Greatest Generation, but they are the Best Paid Generation
for a reason.

Already the big boys in the big banks want to calm and mas-
sage public opinion. JPMorgan Chase overlord Jamie Dimon
speaks for the industry in saying: "If you let them vilify us too
much, the economic recovery will be greatly delayed."

DANNY SCHECHTER

Yet, we are not talking about vilification, but structural reform and change. Simon Johnson of MIT sees the emerging conflict this way:

> The "center vs. the pitchforks" idea fundamentally misconstrues the current debate. This is not about angry Left or Right against the center. It's about centrist technocrats (close to current big finance) versus [other] centrist technocrats (suspicious of big finance: economists, lawyers, nonfinancial business, and – most interestingly – current and former finance, other than the biggest of the big, particularly people with experience in emerging markets).

When you read the comments on Johnson's own blog, you find anger steaming up from insiders, even if, like the writer of this comment, they still hide behind anonymity:

> ... until people start getting locked up for this fraud it will never change. And because I highly doubt that will ever happen the U.S. equity markets will continue to fall apart until the last bag holder, uhh I mean, shareholder says "F-this" and starts putting money in his mattress. The level of corruption is past that of a third-world dictatorship.

At the same time, a handful of banks including Chase, Citi, Bank of America, and, of course, Goldman Sachs, reported record profits and another round of lucrative bonus payouts.

Goldman was widely criticized because it received billions in bailout funds, which the bank insisted it pay back. But there was more to it, as Diane Francis, a Canadian newspaper columnist, explained in the *National Post*, an idea that merits repeating:

Goldman received an estimated three times more, or U.S. $30 billion, in an indirect bailout, which was funneled through bankrupt insurer AIG.

Washington bailed out AIG's counterparties, to whom it owed hundreds of billions; because AIG had sold to them unbacked credit default swaps (a form of insurance on bond values). Goldman was not only ahead of the queue in collecting its IOU, but is reported to have gotten 100 cents on the dollar to boot.

Goldman was made whole even though it is arguable that it was imprudent to buy these swaps which were not actuarially approved and had no capital behind them as insurance products are supposed to. Even so, Goldman and AIG's other foolish customers got backstopped for lousy business practices. (That means they were paid even as some questioned the legitimacy of those payments.)

Rolling Stone's Matt Taibbi characterizes Goldman's conduct as criminal:

Four billion in second-quarter profits, what's wrong with the company so far earmarking $11.4 billion in compensation for its employees? What's wrong is that this is not free-market earnings but an almost pure state subsidy.

When Hank Paulson told us all that the planet would explode if we didn't fork over a gazillion dollars to Wall Street immediately, the entire rationale not only for TARP but for the whole galaxy of lesser-known state crutches and safety nets quietly ushered in later on, was that Wall Street, once rescued, would pump money back into the economy, create jobs, and initiate a widespread recovery. This, we were told, was the reason we needed to pilfer massive amounts of middle-class tax revenue and hand it over to the same guys who had just blown up the financial world. We'd save their asses, they'd save ours. That was the deal.

It turned out not to happen that way.

Lloyd Blankfein, chief executive of Goldman Sachs, has now stunningly admitted that banks lost control of the exotic products they sold in the run-up to the financial crisis, and said that many of the instruments lacked social or economic value.

And a quiescent press and compromised politicians are not demanding deep reforms.

Most insiders are too jaded to speak up. There has to be a populist response too, to intensify the pressure, to make noise, and press for accountability. Economist Paul Krugman tells us that the policy wonks, most pols, and the bankers want to rebuild a corrupt system:

> Despite everything that has happened, most people in positions of power still associate fancy finance with economic progress. Can they be persuaded otherwise? Will we find the will to pursue serious financial reform? If not, the current crisis won't be a one-time event; it will be the shape of things to come.

The fact is that conservative ways of looking at the crisis are dominant among Democrats and Republicans. Most accept the same assumptions about what went wrong, and what can be done to insure it won't happen again.

Economist Brad Delong wrote on his blog (www.delong.

typepad.com) that both parties are in the grip of "conservative interventionism."

> At this stage in the worldwide fight against depression, it is useful to stop and consider just how conservative the policies implemented by the world's central banks, treasuries, and government budget offices have been. Almost everything that they have done – spending increases, tax cuts, bank recapitalization, purchases of risky assets, open-market operations, and other money-supply expansions – has followed a policy path that is nearly 200 years old, dating back to the earliest days of the Industrial Revolution, and thus to the first stirrings of the business cycle.

This conservative interventionism in domestic policy mirrors imperial interventionism abroad. It is driven by the belief that the only way to save the economy is to save Wall Street. Roger Ehrenberg wrote on his financial blog *Information Arbitrage* (www.informationarbitrage.com), that the tax payers have been looted to benefit the bankers without reform or change in the system.

> Wall Street's weakest link, it's super-leveraged capital structure and reliance on overnight funding, was laid bare in the depths of the financial crisis. If not for the wide-open purse strings of the U.S. government, institutions ranging from Citigroup to Goldman Sachs would have gone down.

> No doubt. This was the moment in history when smart minds could have gotten together and projected – really projected – what a better, safer, smarter Wall Street might look like, a Wall Street that wouldn't have collapsed like a house of cards so completely in the face of the mortgage crisis and

> credit derivatives melt-down. Rather than mindlessly shovel-
> ing liquidity in the system to prop up a broken model and
> failed institutions ...

> What we have is a return to business-as-usual. Except it's
> worse than that. The U.S. taxpayer has been systematically
> looted out of hundreds of billions of dollars ...

Former *New York Times* foreign correspondent Chris Hedges
goes further, pointing to the ideology that this orientation
produces among ordinary people. On *Common Dreams* (www.
commondreams.org), he contended:

> This flight into the collective self-delusion of corporate ide-
> ology, especially as we undergo financial collapse and the
> pillaging of the U.S. Treasury by corporations, is no more
> helpful in solving our problems than alchemy. But there are
> university departments and reams of pseudoscientific schol-
> arship to give an academic patina to the fantasy of happiness
> and success through positive thinking. The message that we
> can have everything we want if we dig deep enough inside
> ourselves, if we truly believe we are exceptional, is pumped
> out daily over the airwaves in advertisements, through the
> plot and story lines of television programs and films, and bol-
> stered by the sickeningly cheerful and upbeat banter of well-
> groomed television hosts. This is the twisted ideological lens
> through which we view the world.

What about the media? What have they learned? Not much,
said Peter Schiff, the man whose accurate predictions of the
coming collapse were laughed off the air. He was not optimistic in telling me, "A lot of the media I appeared on were kind
of captured by the industries. You know everybody that comes

on television is working for government or working for Wall Street. They all have invested interest. They are all trapped inside the bubble and so from their vantage point they don't know they are in a bubble ..."

And finally, what about the public?

Without outrage, without protest, little is likely to change, said ex-banker Nomi Prins:

> People should be angry. People should be angry with Wall Street because there was – when the money was being made, when the securities were being created – there was a lot of partying. There was a lot of backslapping. There was a lot of extraction.

And she believes there will be more to come.

Yet, this financial crisis will not be turned off like a light switch. Millions are struggling to survive, as conditions get worse. A recovery for the financial sector does not translate into a recovery for those who have been hurt the most. Experts are now floating the idea of a "jobless recovery." Critical analysis needs to be offered, heard and seen.

Movements for economic justice need our support and if we want the government to do the right thing, we're going to have to press it to do so, and not just with emails. I began this investigation of wrongdoing and crime on Wall Street with a hope that others would join. Some have, most have not.

Unfortunately the most accurate coverage has been on the "fake news" Comedy Central shows.

For starters, we need a full investigation with subpoena power like the Pecora Commission, which followed the Great Crash of 1929. We need to know who benefited from one of the most insidious crimes in history.

How did Wall Street's wizards engineer this disaster, and

who was complicit with them? Will wrongdoers ever be shamed, prosecuted or held accountable?

Even as some progress is being reported, even as these issues are finally getting visibility, experts on the financial system are saying there was "no real reform on any issue central to how the banking system operates. The financial sector lobbies appear stronger than ever."

As Paul Krugman explained, there had been a rescue without reform, and thus:

> Washington has done nothing to protect us from a new crisis, and in fact has made a new crisis likely. There have been many reports on what Wall Street firms did, and continue to do to transfer wealth to their own coffers, but little in the way of a criminal investigation as if it is all above rigorous scrutiny.
>
> The government itself has had shifting rationales for bailouts that have transferred billions in taxpayer dollars into big banks who used the money to revive their fortunes, not the credit markets or the economy.
>
> All the while, they deceived the public about their motives and logic. One example: Henry Paulson admitted to Congress seven months after he left office that he lied, too.

The *Independent* of London reported on July 16, 2008:

> The Bush administration and Congress discussed the possibility of a breakdown in law and order and the logistics of feeding U.S. citizens if commerce and banking collapsed as a result of last autumn's financial panic, it was disclosed yesterday.

THE CRIME OF OUR TIME

> Making his first appearance on Capitol Hill since leaving office, the former Treasury Secretary Hank Paulson said it was important at the time not to reveal the extent of officials' concerns, for fear it would "terrify the American people and lead to an even bigger problem."

Yet it was they who were terrified and in a state of panic fearing, they now admit, "financial havoc."

Once again, the public was deceived, kept in the dark by officials who knowingly misled them. Who can stop them? Who will stop them? Wrapping the stock exchange in yellow "crime scene" tape, as on the cover of this book, is a symbolic start to the work that remains to be done.

All the extraction should lead to a major reaction. Will an age of plunder usher in an age of major structural reforms or will we need an age of protest and pitchforks first? As Paul Krugman wrote, "If you are not angry, you are not paying attention."

And it's not just the bankers who deserve our rage but the regulators and media outlets that enabled them. They were, in the parlance of some financial outlets, captured by the game. The term for this is "deep capture" which suggests the process is not visible to most.

The urgency of such a response is not lost on many in the industry and business world. Most fear, but some like Shoshana Zuboff of the Harvard Business School are demanding it. In *Business Week*, she asked:

> Shouldn't the individuals whose actions unleashed such devastating consequences be held accountable?
>
> I believe the answer is yes. That in the crisis of 2008, the mounting evidence of fraud, conflicts of interest, indifference to suffering, repudiation of responsibility, and sys-

temic absence of individual moral judgment produced an administrative economic massacre of such proportion that it constitutes an economic crime against humanity.

So far, world leaders have not risen to the challenge, and avoid focusing on the crimes of our time, as Stefan Steinberg reported on the *World Socialist Web Site* (www.wsws.org) as the G8 meeting came to an end in July 2009:

> G8 leaders were unable to come to any firm agreement on how to combat the financial crisis. Acknowledging the dangers posed by the crisis, the summit issued a statement on Wednesday that declared, "The situation remains uncertain and significant risks remain to economic and financial stability."

> President Barack Obama spoke of a historic consensus on environmental policy and German Chancellor Angela Merkel declared that "considerable progress" had been made at the summit. In fact, most of the decisions announced over the past three days were vague and non-committal. In general, they marked a retreat from positions agreed (and not carried out) at preceding G8 summits.

This pattern continued at the G20 meeting in Pittsburgh in September 2009. Clearly, we also need a cultural shift and a deeper debate. We need more citizen activism, if only to prod governments to do more. We also need a discussion of values beyond the material; something religious leaders have been calling for over decades, if not longer.

As the G8 gathered in Italy, Pope Benedict XVI issued an encyclical, as reported by Christopher Caldwell in the *Financial Times*:

> The Pope does not think that making capitalism more moral will be a simple matter of bringing a few malefactors to account, whether this involves summoning a half dozen bankers to hearings in Westminster or Washington, or chanting slogans against Bernard Madoff in Manhattan streets.

Never mind that, there are, as this book has shown, quite a few "malefactors" behind the extraordinary crimes documented in these pages. But what Pope Benedict did say goes beyond that. He sees a need for a totally transformed and restructured new financial order:

> There is urgent need [for] a true world political authority ... that can manage the global economy, guarantee the environment is protected, ensure world peace and bring about food security for the poor. The economy needs ethics in order to function correctly, not any ethics, but an ethics which is people centered. Once profit becomes the exclusive goal, if it is produced by improper means and without the common good as its ultimate end, it risks destroying wealth and creating poverty.

Amen.

The chances of a just outcome are only possible if and when the "People," in whose name all this was done, and rationalized, rise up to demand it be undone. Jim Cramer, the much maligned cable TV "moneycaster," often a caricature to be scorned, has it right in the pages of *Lapham's Quarterly*. There, he noted, that more banks today are robbing than being robbed: "It's more of a James Steinbeck tale," he wrote, "and we are the victims, a new generation of Tom Joads, and it's the damn bankerman who broke us. No there won't be a police offer to investigate, and the government, at least this federal government won't save us … Get ready, many more dollars will vanish before you discover you've been robbed."

And you won't hear that from the chattering upper classes on CNBC. In fact by August 2009, CNBC's ratings began to slide. The *Observer* newspaper commented:

> The drop in ratings is irresistible fodder for CNBC's critics. The channel is loathed by many on the left for its shouty style and unrestrained embrace of Ayn Rand-style capitalism. It apes the machismo of the trading floor and in gaps between genuinely informative reportage, its presenters jostle to out-opinion each other. Tom Rosenstiel, director of the Pew Research Center's Project for Excellence in Journalism, said many of its shows are built around "punditry and personality" rather than any genuine attempt to report business news …

> Rosenstiel says that despite devoting its entire output to finance, the channel failed to flag up warning signs sufficiently prominently before the credit crunch began: "They missed the financial meltdown. They missed the effect of derivatives and toxic mortgages on the financial system. They missed the big stuff."

By the fall of 2009, I felt vindicated as other journalists, filmmakers and writers piled on. Michael Moore was out with a film covering some of this ground and roasting capitalism, Oliver Stone was making his sequel to *Wall Street*, subtitled *Money Never Sleeps*, and my own investigative film on the crisis as a crime story, *Plunder: The Crime Of Our Time*, was finally nearing completion.

Finally, there are more voices in the debate challenging not only the financial system but the dominant interpretation of its collapse.

"There is no doubt that class antagonism is stewing," wrote Yves Smith, the editor of the blog *Naked Captalism*. She expressed a fear of a reaction that will go way beyond flag-waving tea parties:

> ... I am concerned this behavior is setting the stage for another sort of extra-legal measure: violence. I have been amazed at the vitriol directed at the banking classes. Suggestions for punishment have included the guillotine (frequent), hanging, pitchforks, even burning at the stake. Tar and feathering appears inadequate, and stoning hasn't yet surfaced as an idea. And mind you, my readership is educated, older, typically well-off (even if less so than three years ago). The fuse has to be shorter where the suffering is more acute.

Alan Blinder, a former vice chairman of the Fed, fears that pressure for financial reform is losing steam in part because of the power of what he calls the "Mother Of All Lobbies." He wrote, "in the case of financial reform, the money at stake is mind-boggling and one financial industry after another will go to the mat to fight any provision that might hurt it."

One is reminded of the title of the movie *There Will Be Blood*. Rather than show contrition or compassion for its own victims, Wall Street is hoping to jack up its salaries and bonuses to pre-2007 levels. The men at the top are oblivious to the pain they helped cause. Every day, they come up with new schemes such as going into the death business and buying up life insurance policies to gamble with.

And so far, they've only occasionally been scolded by politicians that have mostly enabled, coddled, bankrolled, funded, rewarded, and genuflected to their power. Ditto for our get-along by going-along media.

DANNY SCHECHTER

Wall Street's behavior may be predictable but how can we account for the silence of so many organizations that should be out there organizing the outrage that is building?

Knock, knock, Obama supporters, bloggers, trade unionists, out of work workers, progressive organizations, civil rights organizations, student activists suffering under unfair loan burdens, dislocated professionals, displaced homeowners, homeless activists, human rights groups, concerned journalists, laid off educators and all fellow Americans: We are all victims.

Will we fight back against the crime of our time or roll over?

EPILOGUE

COMBATING FINANCIAL PIRANHAS

By the spring of 2010, the "crime narrative" that informs this book had begun to percolate into the debate over financial reform, even as the major media and most mandarins of economic thought were largely dismissive of it.

As outrage built in the public, especially among those whose homes and jobs had disappeared, an angry clamor for economic justice could be heard echoing in public opinion. I asked scores of workers, marching on Wall Street in April 2010 under the aegis of the AFL-CIO, if they thought there was crime behind the crisis. To a person, they responded as if the question was obvious and need not be asked. "Of course," was the unanimous response.

Reuters divined the popular nerve by reporting, "The American public wants to see bankers' heads on spikes for triggering a global financial crisis, but so far prosecutors and regulators have come up empty. Federal and state authorities are struggling to hold banks accountable, but cases have proven to be extremely complicated and hard to win, if they get brought at all."

How hard that "struggle" to make cases has been is extremely problematic; in fact, there has been little evidence of it.

Why?

Here are **ten of the well-planned but flawed factors that help explain** the procrastination and rationalization for inaction. The government is not just to blame either. Several industries working together, through their firms, associates and well-paid operatives, collaborated to financialize the economy to their own benefit. They took over the political system to guarantee their control over the economic system. It was done with foresight and malice.

First, many of those who might be charged with financial crimes and criminal fraud invested in lobbying and political donations – to insure that tough regulations and enforcement was neutered – before the housing bubble they promoted took off. They did so in the aftermath of the jailing of hundreds of bankers after the S & L crisis, to insure that could never happen again.

In effect, they deliberately "decriminalized" the industry to make sure that practices that led to high profits and low accountability would be permissible and permitted. The once illegal soon became "legal." The cops and watchdogs were taken off the beat. Anticipating and then neutering restraints, they engineered a low-risk crime scene in the way the Pentagon systematically prepares its battlefields. This permitted illicit practices, to be encouraged by CEOs in a variety of control frauds to keep profits up so that the executives could extract more revenue.

Second, the industry invented, advertised and rationalized exotic financial instruments as forward looking "innovation" and "modernization" to disguise their intent while enhancing their field of maneuver. This was part of creating a shadow banking system operating below the radar of effective monitoring and regulation. Where is the focus on controlling the out of control power of the leverage-hungry gamblers at unregulated hedge funds?

Third, the industry promulgated economic theories and ideologies that won the backing of the economics profession which largely did not see the crisis coming, making those who favored a crackdown on fraud appear unfashionable and out of date. As economist James Galbraith testified to Congress:

...the study of financial fraud received little attention. Practically no research institutes exist; collaboration between economists and criminologists is rare; in the leading departments there are few specialists and very few students. Economists have soft-pedaled the role of fraud in every crisis they examined, including the Savings & Loan debacle, the Russian transition, the Asian meltdown and the dot-com bubble. They continue to do so now. At a conference sponsored by the Levy Economics Institute in New York on April 17, the closest a former Under Secretary of the Treasury, Peter Fisher, got to this question was to use the word "naughtiness." This was on the day that the SEC charged Goldman Sachs with fraud.

Fourth, prominent members of the financial services industry were appointed to top positions in the government agencies that should have cracked down on financial crime, but instead looked the other way. The foxes were indeed guarding the chicken coop guiding institutions that tolerated if not enabled an environment of criminality. Alan Greenspan and Ben Bernanke were repeatedly warned by underlings at the Federal Reserve Bank about pervasive predatory practices in the mortgage and subprime markets and they chose to do nothing. Now Greenspan acknowledges pervasive fraud but decries the lack of enforcement while Bernanke wants to run a consumer protection agency after ignoring consumer complaints for years. Even as the FBI denounced "an epidemic of mortgage fraud" in 2004, their white-collar crime units were downsized.

Fifth, the media was complicit, seduced, bought off and compromised. The housing bubble mushroomed in the very period that the media was forced to downsize. Dodgy lenders and credit card companies pumped billions into advertising in radio, television and the internet almost insuring that there would be no undue investigations. Financial journalists increasingly embedded themselves in the culture and narrative of Wall Street, hyping stocks and CEOs. The Bernard Madoff $65-billion-dollar Ponzi scheme went on for a decade as the SEC and the media fell down on the job. It only became public after Madoff went public for reasons that are still not fully understood.

The "guests" routinely chosen by media outlets to explain the crisis were often part of it, said Jim Hightower:

> Many of the "experts" whom I read or see on TV seem clueless, full of hot air. Many of their predictions turn out wrong even when they seem so self-assured and well-informed in making them.

> Don't be deterred by the finance industry's jargon, which is intended to numb your brain and keep regular folks from even trying to figure out what's going on.

Sixth, politicians and corporate lawyers preferred settlements of abuses that were exposed rather than prosecutions. This led to practices such as the deliberate engineering of mortgages to fail to be "settled" as a cost of doing business. Financial executives were often rewarded with bonuses and huge compensation for profits that skirted or crossed the line of criminality. Intentional violations of the spirit and letter of laws were justified because "everyone does it" by high-priced legal firms that often doubled as lobbyists. Conflicts of interest were sneered at.

Seventh, as the economy changed and industries that were once separated began working together, laws were not changed. In a FIRE economy, Finance works closely with Insurance companies and Real-Estate firms. Financial crime is still seen almost entirely under the framework of securities laws that are designed to protect investors, not workers or home-owners who suffered far more in the collapse. Cases are framed against individuals with a high standard of proving intent, not under RICO laws used to prosecute organized crime and conspiracies. Their standard of proof is actually lower.

By defining crimes narrowly, prosecutions are few and far between, reported Reuters:

> Cases against Wall Street executives can be difficult to prove to the satisfaction of a jury because of the mind-numbing volume of emails, prospectuses, and memos involved in documenting a case.

> "It's not like a shooting on the street," said Siegal, the former federal prosecutor, who is now an attorney with Haynes and Boone. "It's an enormous and potentially overwhelming task. Typically what you need is a whistle blower."

> The complexity of the cases means that they take a long time to put together. Other high-profile cases in the Enron collapse and the Galleon insider trading case have taken years of investigation but ultimately did end with criminal charges being filed.

Convicted financial criminal Sam Antar, who appears in my film, *Plunder*, is contemptuous of how the government tends to proceed in these cases, in part because they don't seem to understand how calculated these crimes and their cover-ups are. He told me:

> Our laws – innocent until proven guilty, the codes of ethics that journalists like you abide by, limit your behavior and give

the white-collar criminal freedom to commit their crimes, and also to cover up their crimes.

We have no respect for the laws. We consider your codes of ethics, your laws, weaknesses to be exploited in the execution of our crimes. So the prosecutors, hopefully most prosecutors, are honest if they're playing by the set of the rules; they're hampered by the illegal constraints. The white-collared criminal has no legal constraints. You subpoena documents, we destroy documents; you subpoena witnesses, we lie. So you are at a disadvantage when it comes to the white-collared criminal. In effect, we're economic predators. We're serial economic predators; we impose a collective harm on society.

These are complicated white-collar crimes, of which the government does not have the resources to thoroughly prosecute. And the white-collared criminals know it; so they set it up, not as a single transaction that's a crime, but a series of transaction, that once it's all put together, makes it a crime.

White-collar crime by its nature takes about three to seven years to investigate. It requires enormous resources, interdisciplinary resources, forensic accountants, even sociologists to understand what the criminals are doing.

Most prosecutors are inherently lazy: so it makes it very easy for us. We know that people, our victims, are eventually gonna run out of steam. And time is always on our side, not on, not on the side of justice, unfortunately.

Eighth, even as the economy globalized, and U.S. financial firms spread their footprint worldwide, there was no interna-

272

tionalization of financial rules and regulations. Today, as the French and the Germans propose such rules, Washington still opposes a tough global regime of codes of conduct.

Overseas, in Greece and England, and other parts of Europe, there's been an indictment of American corporate predators, especially Goldman Sachs. They are being denounced as "financial terrorists" and discussed in terms of their links to various elite business formations like the Bilderberg Group. While unions say workers are being targeted in an economic war, the Left also sees a counterrevolution underway against democracy'with power moving firmly into the hands of bond traders and markets demanding austerity and dictating their demands to parliaments and elected politicians. European leaders say they are at war, too, against "speculators."

In Iceland, the first European economy to collapse in the great recession, thanks to international financial machinations, a government commission produced a more than 2,000-page report suggesting that fraud was present. In May 2010, bankers began going to jail.

Ninth, with the exception of a few industries and polite inquiries by a financial-crisis inquiry commission, there has been no intensive investigations in the United States even like the tepid 9/11 Commission.

While Senator Levin of Michigan did spend a day aggressively grilling Goldman Sachs on one deceptive practice, their defense was more telling about the real nature of the problem: "Everyone did it."

Few politicians have even denounced financial crimes. Eliot Spitzer, the disgraced former governor of New York, once dubbed the "Sheriff of Wall Street" called predatory lending "criminal" but a sex scandal quickly silenced him. Today, Senator Ted Kauffman of Delaware is among the few arguing that fraud caused the crisis.

Former bank regulator William Black, who helped send 1,000 bankers to jail after the S & L crisis, makes the same argument. Some state attorneys general are mounting localized investigations and subpoenaing documents.

Billionaire investor Jim Chanos asked in a financial conference I attended, "So, where are the perp walks? How long does it take before we see any investigations? It boggles the mind that $150 billion is vaporized. There haven't been any arrests, any indictments, nor any convictions at any major bank or at any of the government-owned financial institutions Fannie, Freddie and AIG."

The case for criminality has still not achieved critical mass to become a dominant explanation for why the economy collapsed. In fact, it is still being sneered at or ignored. Reported Reuters:

> "A financial meltdown is not a crime," said David Siegal, a former federal prosecutor in New York.

> Nor is being stupid or greedy ...

> "It's politics in the broadest sense," said Ed Grebeck, the chief executive of Tempus Advisors and an instructor at New York University. "We know that Congress and the regulators who missed the structured finance credit crunch are trying to make a name for themselves acting like they are going to take the next step to stop this from happening again."

"Trying," but not too hard.

Reuters also spoke with Janet Tavakoli, president of Tavakoli Structured Finance Inc in Chicago and author of a book on synthetic CDOs. She called the activity of big banks "malicious mischief" and said regulators' efforts to bring accountability have amounted to "publicity stunts that aim to miss":

> "It distracts the public from the real issue of the damage done to the U.S. economy for which the taxpayer ended up being on the hook to bail out banks," Tavakoli said.

Finally, **tenth**, a big problem in my countdown, are the progressive critics of the crisis who also largely ignore criminality as a key factor and possible focus for an organizing effort.

They treat the crisis as if they are at a financial seminar at Harvard, focusing on the complexities of derivatives, credit default swaps and structured financial products in language that ordinary people rarely can penetrate. They argue that banks should be "not too big to fail" but not "too big to fail." Few of the progressive activist groups invoke morality, much less criminality. There is little solidarity with the newly homeless or jobless. Where is the active empathy, compassion and the caring for the victims?

The focus on complexity fosters that MEGO (My Eyes Glaze Over) complex in TV viewers. Some critics care more about showing off how smart they are than translating the crimes that have been committed into right and wrong, not just Right and Left. Rather than adopt the crime narrative, and push for economic justice they get lost in a muddle or empiricism and academic discourse.

To my surprise, I found the right-wing organization Accuracy in Media (www.aim.org) more on target:

> Consider that the business publication *Barron's* has an article headlined on its cover, "A Savvy Hedge-Fund Manager Reveals How to Make Money on Old World's Woes." A better headline would have been "How to Exploit Human Suffering." At a time when people are dying in Greece because of riots

in response to economic problems, what kind of publication would openly advertise how to make money at the expense of others and profit from their misery?

But this is how the hedge-fund short sellers and their apologists work.

No wonder the popular response to the crisis has been so muted. There is little pressure from below on the administration and Justice Department – which has now created a financial crimes task force – to take action. It is as if this "crime crisis" within the economic crisis does not exist.

Even after the markets melted down, even after bonus scandals and bailout disgraces, Wall Street has hardly been humbled. It is still spending a fortune on PR and political gun slinging with 25 lobbyists shadowing every member of Congress to scuttle real reform. Its arrogance is evident in an email the *Financial Times* reported was "pinging around" trading desks. It reads in part:

> We are Wall Street. It's our job to make money. Whether it's a commodity, stock, bond, or some hypothetical piece of fake paper, it doesn't matter. We would trade baseball cards if it were profitable ... Go ahead and continue to take us down, but you're only going to hurt yourselves. What's going to happen when we can't find jobs on the Street anymore? Guess what: We're going to take yours.
>
> ... We aren't dinosaurs. We are smarter and more vicious than that, and we are going to survive.

When will we call a crime a crime? When will we demand a jailout, not just more bailouts. Unless we do, and until we do, the people who created the worst crisis in our time will, in effect, get away with the biggest rip-off in history. It is no means assured either that a collapsed economy will come back. There is the danger of a new "double-dip" recession in which inflation rises, or something worse. A jobless recovery is not a real recovery.

Jailing the offenders will not solve the structural and system problems in our economy – the deep and growing divisions of wealth and power – but they will strike a blow for economic justice and restore faith where there is today only cynicism and despair.

Can this situation be changed? That's the hope motivating this book and my film, *Plunder The Crime Of Our Time*. Hopefully, my obsession with these issues will become your challenge to do something about it.

DANNY SCHECHTER

ABOUT THE AUTHOR

DANNY SCHECHTER
NEWS DISSECTOR / INVESTIGATIVE
JOURNALIST / PRODUCER / DIRECTOR

Danny Schechter is a television producer and independent filmmaker who often writes and speaks about
media issues. He is the executive editor and blogger-
in-chief of *Media Channel* (www.mediachannel.org),
the world's largest online media issues network. His *News Dissector* blog won blog of the year from Hunter College's James
Aronson Award for Social Justice In Media in 2009. He hosts the
weekly *News Dissector* radio show on Progressive Radio Network and is frequently interviewed in print, and on radio and
television.

Schechter is co-founder and executive producer of Globalvision, a New York-based television and film production company now in its 20th year, where he co-produced 156 editions
of the award-winning series *South Africa Now* and *Rights &
Wrongs: Human Rights Television*. In 1998, a human rights special, *Globalization and Human Rights*, was co-produced with
Rory O'Connor and shown nationally on PBS.

A Cornell University graduate, he received his master's
degree from the London School of Economics, and has an
honorary doctorate from Fitchburg College. He was a Nieman
Fellow in Journalism at Harvard University, where he has also
taught.

Earler, he was a full-time civil rights worker and then communications director of the Northern Student Movement;
he worked as a community organizer in a Saul Alinsky-style

War on Poverty program, and, moving from the streets to the suites, served as an assistant to the mayor of Detroit in 1966 on a Ford Foundation grant. (Dick Cheney was also a "fellow" in the same program!)

Schechter's professional broadcasting career began in 1970, when he was named news director, principal newscaster, and "News Dissector" at WBCN-FM in Boston, where he was hailed as a radio innovator and won many industry honors, including two Major Armstrong Awards.

His television-producing career was launched as an on-air reporter at WGBH and then as a producer with the syndicated *The Joe Oteri Show*, which won the New England Emmy and a NATPE IRIS award in 1979. In 1980, he created and produced the nation's first live late-night, entertainment-oriented TV show, *Five All Night, Live All Night* at WCVB in Boston.

Schechter left Boston to join the staff at CNN as a producer based in Atlanta. He then moved to ABC News as a producer for *20/20*, where during eight years he won two National News Emmys (and two nominations), two regional Emmys, a National Headliner award, and later the Society for Professional Journalists award for an investigative documentary. Amnesty International has honored him for his human rights television work.

Schechter has reported from 63 countries and lectured at many schools and universities. He was an adjunct professor at the Graduate School of Journalism at Columbia University. Schechter's writing has appeared in leading newspapers and magazines including the *Nation*, *Newsday*, *Boston Globe*, *Columbia Journalism Review*, *Media Studies Journal*, *Detroit Free Press*, *Village Voice*, *Tikkun*, *Z*, and many other newspapers, magazines and websites, including the *Huffington Post*, *Buzzflash*, *Alternet*, *ZNet*, *Global Research* and others. His books have been translated into Korean and Chinese.

DANNY SCHECHTER

OTHER WORKS BY THE AUTHOR

BOOKS

2008   *Plunder: Investigating Our Economic Calamity*

2007   *Squeezed: America As The Bubble Bursts*

2006   *When News Lies: Media Complicity and the*
        Iraq War

2005   *The Death of Media (and The Fight for*
        Democracy)

2003   *Embedded: Weapons of Mass Deception:*
        How the Media Failed to Cover the War on Iraq

2003   *Media Wars: News at a Time of Terror*

2001   *News Dissector: Passions, Pieces and Polemics*

2000   *Hail to the Thief: How the Media "Stole" the 2000*
        Election (Edited with Roland Schatz)

2000   *Falun Gong's Challenge to China*

1997   *The More You Watch, the Less You Know*

FILMS AND TV DOCUMENTARIES

2010   *Plunder: The Crime Of Our Time*

2009   *Barack Obama, People's President*

2008   *Viva Madiba: Nelson Mandela at 90* (Contributing
        Director)

2007   *Boob Tube*

2007   *A Work In Progress: Putting the Me Back in Media*

2006   *In Debt We Trust*

2004   *Weapons of Mass Deception*

2002   *Counting On Democracy* (Narrated by Ossie
        Davis and Ruby Dee)

2001   *We are Family (A 9/11 film)*

2000   *Falun Gong's Challenge to China*

2000   *Nkosi: Saving Africa's AIDS Orphans*

1999   *A Hero for All: Nelson Mandela's Farewell*

1998	*Beyond Life: Timothy Leary Lives*
1996	*Sowing Seeds/Reaping Peace: The World of Seeds of Peace*
1995	*Prisoners of Hope:* (Co-directed by Barbara Kopple)
1994	*Countdown to Freedom: Ten Days that Changed South Africa* (Narrated by James Earl Jones and Alfre Woodard)
1993	*Sarajevo Ground Zero*
1992	*The Living Canvas* (Narrated by Billy Dee Williams)
1992	*Beyond JFK: The Question of Conspiracy* (Co-directed with Barbara Kopple and Mark Levin)
1991	*Give Peace a Chance*
1990	*Mandela in America*
1989	*Globalization and Human Rights* (Produced with Rory O'Connor)
1987	*The Making of Sun City*
1968	*Student Power*

TV

1998–1991	*South Africa Now* (Executive Producer)
1993–1997	*Rights & Wrongs* (Co-produced with Rory O'Connor)
2002	Editorial Producer, *The Tina Brown Show* (CNBC)
1986	Broadcast Producer, *The Last Word* (ABC)
1981–1988	Producer, *20/20* (ABC News)
1980	Producer, *Sandi Freeman Show* (CNN)
1980	Producer, *Five All Night, Live All Night* (WVCB-Boston)
1979	Producer, *The Joe Oteri Show* (WLVI, Boston)
1978	Reporter, *The Ten O'Clock News* (WGBH, Boston)

EARLIER MEDIA WORK

1970–1977 News Director/News Dissector, WBCN-FM,
           Boston
1966–1969 Contributing Editor, *Ramparts* Magazine
1964–1965 Editor, *Freedom North* (Northern Student
           Movement)
1961–1964 Editor, *Dialogue Magazine* (Cornell University)
1960   Editor-in-Chief, *Clinton News* (DeWitt Clinton
           High School)

MORE INFORMATION AND CONTACT INFO

For continuing coverage and updates on the issues discussed in this book, visit Danny Schechter's **News Dissector** *blog*: **www.newsdissector.com/blog**.

For more on the issues covered in this book, see: **www.plunderthecrimeofourtime.com**.

For more on Danny Schechter's history, see: **www.newsdissector.org/dissectorville**.

Feedback welcome: **dissector@mediachannel.org**.

GET THIS BOOK'S COMPANION DVD

Investigative journalist Danny Schechter looks into how the recent financial crisis developed, from the mysterious collapse of Bear Stearns to the shadowy world of trillion-dollar hedge funds. Insiders who work in the industry and know it well, tell the real stories behind the headlines. This film shows how hastily arranged government bailouts did not revive the economy and lost billions.

Documentary: Current Affairs / Economics • 100 Mins + Bonus Footage
• $19.98 (U.S.) • UPC: 826262006198 • ISBN: 978-1-934708-53-8